OK
BOOMER, LET'S TALK

Also by Jill Filipovic
The H-Spot: The Feminist Pursuit of Happiness

OK
BOOMER,
LET'S TALK

How My Generation Got Left Behind

Jill Filipovic

**ONE SIGNAL
PUBLISHERS**

ATRIA

New York · London · Toronto · Sydney · New Delhi

ONE SIGNAL
PUBLISHERS

ATRIA

An Imprint of Simon & Schuster, Inc.
1230 Avenue of the Americas
New York, NY 10020

First One Signal Publishers/Atria Paperback edition August 2020

ONE SIGNAL PUBLISHERS / ATRIA PAPERBACK and colophon
are trademarks of Simon & Schuster, Inc.

For information about special discounts for bulk purchases,
please contact Simon & Schuster Special Sales at 1-866-506-1949
or business@simonandschuster.com.

The Simon & Schuster Speakers Bureau can bring authors to your live
event. For more information or to book an event, contact the Simon
& Schuster Speakers Bureau at 1-866-248-3049 or visit our website at
www.simonspeakers.com.

Interior design by Debbie Berne

Manufactured in the United States of America

1 3 5 7 9 10 8 6 4 2

Library of Congress Cataloging-in-Publication Data is available.

ISBN 978-1-9821-5376-2
ISBN 978-1-9821-5377-9 (ebook)

For my favorite Boomers, Mom and Dad,
who are pretty okay.

Old man, look at my life
I'm a lot like you were
—Neil Young

CONTENTS

Introduction

A conservative radio host called it "the n-word of ageism." A Supreme Court justice asked if saying it while deciding whether or not to hire someone might qualify as age discrimination. The novelist and critic Francine Prose suggested it was evidence of bigotry against the elderly.

OK Boomer.

No, it's not nice. But a petty insult isn't what started the generation wars. It was merely the first return fire to really sting Boomers, in a battle nearly as old as the millennium.

Can you blame us for firing back? The Millennial stereotype of an indulged, immature, hypersensitive narcissist is a convenient mask for the ugly realities that make our lives emotionally and economically precarious—realities set in motion by Baby Boomers. "OK Boomer" is more than just an imperious insult; it's frustrated Millennial shorthand for the ways the same people who created so many of our problems now pin the blame on us. It's us realizing we're never going to win inane arguments over our own purported ineptitude, and so best to just short-circuit the debate.

Older Americans have been maligning Millennials since the oldest of our generation graduated high school, and "Millennial" continues to be used interchangeably with "young." But Millennials were born between 1980 and 1996, which means the youngest Millennials are in their midtwenties, while the oldest are pushing forty. We are widely chastised but poorly understood. Conservative news outlets still dedicate entire segments to lampooning easily triggered Millennial college students—even though most college students are Gen Zers. In a press briefing in March 2020, White House officials suggested that Millennials bore disproportionate responsibility for America's COVID-19 outbreak. "Hey, millennials, this isn't spring break. It's a pandemic," the *Philadelphia Daily News* tweeted. Early in the outbreak, a *New York Times* article asserted that Millennials, many of whom entered the workforce into the 2008 recession, "are now facing their first economic crisis."

The tropes are almost passé at this point: Millennials want participation trophies for everything. We're delicate special snowflakes demanding safe spaces and trigger warnings. We're obsessed with identity politics and sneer "Check your privilege" instead of debating in good faith. We're socialism-curious at best, America-hating communists at worst. We expect to be rewarded and promoted and head-patted and hand-held. We're at once too self-involved and too concerned with the feelings of everyone else. We want immediate gratification and crave the affirmation of "likes" and retweets. We're self-indulgent perpetual adolescents who refuse to grow up. We live in Mom's basement, don't have a job, don't have babies, don't even pay rent. We gorge on avocado toast instead of buying homes. The cartoon image of the Millennial, the writer Jia Tolentino put it in *The New Yorker*, is "a twitchy and phone-addicted pest who eats away at beloved American institutions the way boll weevils feed on crops." An abridged list of the beloved institutions we've killed: America, American cheese, the American dream, banks, bar soap, beer, business wear, cable television, canned tuna, cars, casual dining restaurants, cereal, college football, credit, cruises, dairy, democracy, department stores, diamonds, dinner dates, doorbells, dress codes, the European Union, fabric softener, golf, gyms, Home Depot, hotels, light yogurt, lottery tickets, marriage, mayonnaise, McMansions, motherhood, motorcycles, napkins, razors, sex in parks, and wine corks. We are, as one book's title put it, "The Dumbest Generation."

The first big outpouring of "OK Boomer" was on TikTok, in response to a video of an older man proclaiming that "Millennials and Generation Z have the Peter Pan syndrome: they don't ever want to grow up; they think that the utopian ideals that they have in their youth are somehow going to translate into adulthood. And that somehow they're going to create this utopian society in which everything is equal." "OK Boomer," came the irreverent Gen Z reply. The meme exploded into the mainstream when the journalist Taylor Lorenz wrote about it in the *New York Times*. Off of TikTok and into the pages of the Gray Lady, "OK Boomer" suddenly had Boomers' attention.

Tired of being lectured and scorned by the older folks who torched their futures, teenagers and twentysomethings struck back, and "OK Boomer" was their revenge. Now it's emblazoned on t-shirts and tote bags. It's the go-to dismissal of a bad tweet or a parental command. Fox even filed to secure a trademark on it (they failed).

Meanwhile, Millennials picked up the meme and ran with it.

One irony in the story of this generation war is the close personal ties between Boomers and Millennials. Boomers were the original parent-friends, developing relationships with their children that put authority aside in favor of genuine respect and mutual connection. In the process of writing this book, I heard from hundreds of Millennials via both survey and in individual interviews. Most of the Millennials I talked to were critical of Boomers as a generation—"selfish" was the most common descriptor—but said that their own Boomer parents were great. "OK Boomer" doesn't mean *my* Boomer; I'm talking about Boomers out in the wild.

Many of these same Millennials were quick to note that our Boomer parents gave us a nurturing base from which to grow. They encouraged us to do what we love, pursue our passions, and never settle. They allowed us the room to explore creative fields and seek meaningful work. They modeled good parenting, and, for many Millennials with kids, Boomer parents fill the holes in our thin safety net by helping out with childcare. For all of this, many of us are individually grateful.

But much of what individual Boomers did for the benefit of their own kids their generation didn't do for society at large. Instead, they hoarded resources for themselves. They redirected tax dollars toward their own entitlements and away from investments in younger generations, enjoying the security of Medicare and Social Security while we struggle to get decent health care and look forward to empty federal coffers when we retire. They

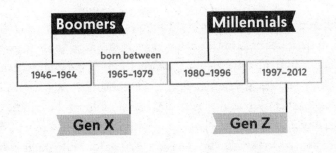

The generations at a glance.

refused to adequately combat the threat of climate change. They walked back earlier progress toward racial equality, which left our more diverse generation broke and struggling. They allowed the gap between the wealthiest few and the poorest many to expand into a vast gulf. So yes, we're a little resentful. And when Boomers then berate us for a litany of perceived flaws? We get angry.

A quick note on terminology here: I'm using "Baby Boomer" to mean people who were born between 1946 and 1964 and "Millennial" to mean people who were born between 1980 and 1996 (there's also Gen X, born between 1965 and 1979, and Gen Z, born between 1997 and 2012). The edges of all of these cohorts are fuzzy, and given that the Boomer and Millennial generations span nearly two decades apiece, there are experiences and cultural markers particular to older Boomers versus younger ones, and ditto older versus younger Millennials. Generalizing about any age group is tricky, since virtually nothing, apart from being born within a particular a set of years, is true of *all* Boomers or *all*

Millennials. No statement in this book about Boomers generally, or statistic about Boomers on average, is meant to apply to every Boomer individually. It's particularly dicey to generalize about Boomer politics, given that Boomers are the most politically polarized generation in America, cleaved right down the middle of the liberal/conservative divide, and with more or less equal numbers hewing to the left and the right. Not so for Millennials, who are, as a whole, significantly more liberal.

But American Boomers and Millennials alike grew up against particular political and social backdrops. Both generations are unique, and their collective experiences are distinct. And so while generational groupings are imperfect, they are nonetheless important if we want to understand the arc of history, and what we collectively inherit.

I'm an "older Millennial," a child of Boomer parents. One September day in my first month as a college student, I was stirred awake by a low rumble I first thought was a garbage truck; it was an airplane headed for the Twin Towers, just two miles from my dorm. The first day of my first full-time job as a lawyer just out of school was September 15, 2008: the day Lehman Brothers filed for bankruptcy, still the largest in American history, and sent the entire economy tumbling down.

The 2008 financial collapse was spectacular. Older Millennials were just entering the workforce and suffered some of the downturn's hardest blows. Many of us lost our jobs; many others couldn't get jobs to begin with. Our health suffered. Our student loan debt accrued. We took earnings losses from which we still have not recovered. We might never fully come back.

For many Millennials, there is a feeling of failure as we compare the leaps we saw our parents make to our own lives, which feel like the equivalent of trying to walk up the down escalator.

When my parents were my age, they were married and raising two children and a golden retriever in a home they owned. My father paid his way through law school by working in the Chicago steel mills and living at home. My mother got a nursing degree without carrying a dime of student loan debt. Together, they supported a family in middle-class comfort on the salaries of a nurse and a public defender. We were far from rich, but we had a house in a neighborhood with good schools, two cars, annual vacations to places like Disneyland and the Grand Canyon, the ability to pay for sports uniforms and music lessons, and a college fund on top of that.

That is not what my life looks like.

I have a law degree like my dad, but it came with six-figure debt. I got married at thirty-four, before most of my close friends, and live with my husband and two cats in an apartment that costs close to half of each of our monthly take-home pay. (My husband and I own a condo in another city, the down payment for which I would have never been able to afford on my own.) I have very little saved for retirement, and largely live freelance paycheck to freelance paycheck. We don't have kids. That's partly because we don't know if we want them, partly because we aren't sure it's ethical to bring them into a world increasingly devastated by climate change, and partly because we couldn't afford them without radically changing our lives.

But it's not all bleak. I'm exceptionally lucky to have what I consider a great life, and as a white Millennial raised in the middle class, I'm a lot more fortunate than much of my generation. My parents sought to give my sister and me opportunities they never had, and we have taken them. The differences between our lives and our parents' are partly about economics, policy, and opportunity, and partly about values—not in the values we hold, which are similar, but in the values we live.

But it seems unlikely that I will ever do "better" than my parents—just as it seems unlikely I'll be able to rely on programs like Social Security and Medicare as I age into retirement. Millions of Millennials are in the same boat. And while we don't blame our individual parents—not my Boomer!—we do blame their cohort. In one 2018 poll, more than half of Millennials said that Baby Boomers made things worse for our generation; only 13 percent of us said Boomers made things better.

Nor do things seem to be *getting* better. Already on shaky ground, younger Millennials were at the dawn of their working lives and older Millennials were entering our prime earning years when we were slammed again, this time by a pandemic that plunged the economy into a recession that many fear could rival the Great Depression. As I make final edits on this book, close to 40 million Americans have lost their jobs and applied for unemployment benefits; economists predict that 47 million could be furloughed or laid off, and close to one in three working-age Americans could end up out of a job, before this book hits the shelves. Many Millennial women with kids are suddenly in charge of full-time childcare and homeschooling in addition to work for pay, while their supposedly egalitarian male partners put their own paid work first. When this crisis ends, those same mothers will inevitably be seen as less dedicated and less productive, which, especially in a downturn, puts their continued employment at risk. Women's earnings also typically begin to level off when we're in our midthirties and peak earlier than men's, all of which means that Millennial women may get pummeled particularly hard in the coronavirus's economic aftershocks.

There's already some evidence that Millennials, and particularly black and Hispanic Millennials, will bear the brunt of the 2020 economic crisis. A *Washington Post* analysis found that in March and April 2020, Millennial employment decreased by 16 percent, while Gen X and Baby Boomer employment dropped by 12 and 13 percent, respectively. In 2019, Millennials had surpassed Gen Xers as the largest segment of the full-time workforce. But Millennials' 2020 job losses have been so extreme that those gains are projected to reverse. An April 2020 survey from Data for Progress showed that more than half of voters under forty-five—a group that is majority Millennial—said they had already lost their job, been put on leave, or seen their hours scaled back, and black Americans were worse off than whites. Older voters—those over the age of forty-five, so mostly Boomers and Gen Xers—are faring better: Only about a quarter of them said they've seen their jobs impacted. Three-quarters of them said nothing has changed and they don't expect it to.

There is no way to fully comprehend the insecurity of Millennial life without putting race at the center of the story.

Millennials are the most racially diverse adult generation in American history, and Gen Zers—some of them still children—are more diverse still. But centuries of racist policies, laws, and norms have cut black and brown people out of the American dream. As Millennials hit adulthood, the numbers bear out all the ways in which long-fermenting racial injustices have exploded into generation-wide devastation, leaving our cohort poor, insecurely housed, physically ill, and underemployed, despite the fact that we are also the most educated adults in American history. Millennials' financial lives have been stymied by the slowest economic growth any American generation has ever seen, while opportunities for Millennials of color have been further constrained by widespread incarceration, the methodical thwarting of generational wealth-building, and systemic discrimination in hiring and pay. Even though our generation is less white, the racial wealth gap has grown wider—there are proportionately fewer white people, but they hold proportionately more wealth. We are the grandchildren of the civil rights movement, and yet money and power remain concentrated in white hands.

When George Floyd, an unarmed black man in Minneapolis, Minnesota, and Breonna Taylor, a black emergency medical technician in Louisville, Kentucky, were killed by police in the spring of 2020, rage and righteousness boiled over. Millions of people took to the streets in the midst of a pandemic, to protest police abuses and murders of black men and women. The police reacted by rampaging: walloping protesters with billy clubs, firing tear gas and rubber bullets into peaceful crowds, and attacking and arresting journalists. The protests were first and foremost about ending police violence against African Americans. But a closer look at the crowds in any of hundreds of American cities and towns revealed a movement dominated by young people. The demands of many of the protesters, moreover, reflected generational as well as racial neglect. "Defund the police," came one rallying cry, so that governments can instead invest in communities of color: redirecting public dollars to schools, health care, job opportunities, safe and secure housing, and neighborhoods cleaned of pollutants and toxins. "Ultimately," Boomer president Barack Obama wrote in the midst of the demonstrations, "it's going to be up to a new generation of activists to shape strategies that best fit the times."

The question is whether that new generation will be able to wrest power from the old one. As we plunge into a second recession, Boomers are, on the whole, better-off than those of us under forty. They're also the ones designing the recovery packages and bailout plans. As young people march for racial justice and community investment, it's Boomers, who fill a majority of the seats in Congress, on the Supreme Court, and in state legislatures, who maintain disproportionate power in determining the political response. Millennials and Gen Zers are watching this all unfold and realizing that, again, our futures may be mortgaged so that the wealthiest Baby Boomers can continue to live large.

I'm not exactly the voice of my generation, even if I am part of a Millennial demographic (white, heterosexual, highly credentialed, city-dwelling) that is over-represented in media and entertainment. But I am a journalist (and a person with eyes and ears). What I see around me, even from a privileged perch, and what I've heard again and again in reporting this book, is that Millennials have faced unique hardships that set our generation apart. We're only now starting to grasp the degree to which we have gotten screwed. And we're responding with desperation and sometimes anger. That's where "OK Boomer" comes from: it's a final, frustrated dismissal from people suffering years of political and economic neglect.

Generational warfare is nothing new. When today's Boomers were college-aged hippies, they were warning each other not to trust anyone over thirty. Part of Millennial-Boomer tension is simply the usual cycle of change, with the young resenting their elders and the elders complaining about kids these days. The kids were beatniks before they were hippies before they were snowflakes. Soon enough, Millennials will be shaking our fists at the youngsters, demanding they get off our environmentally friendly succulent-speckled rock lawns.

What's different now, though, is that there is a moneyed system interested in sowing generational discord and stoking fear. Call it the Boomer Anxiety Industrial Complex. It's a largely right-wing machine targeted at older Americans, encouraging a nearly manic obsession with the alleged wrongdoings of younger, more liberal people. Shocking stories about college students encroaching on free speech are a staple. So are more pedestrian narratives about college students being too sensitive, too emotional, or too "politically correct." This didn't start with Millennials; the seeds of the anti-PC/"college students versus free speech" propaganda were planted in the nineties, part of a backlash against Bill Clinton, the first Boomer president.

Today, Fox News is the primary anti-Millennial television outlet, but there's also generationally tailored content on websites like Breitbart and Townhall, and hackneyed memes that circulate among the over-fifty set on Facebook and Twitter. Boomers are more likely to watch Fox News than almost any other network, and close to half of them told Pew that in the previous week, they'd gotten political news from Fox.

That's bad news. Researchers and media scholars alike have pointed out that Fox has long been profoundly and intentionally biased in favor of conservative causes. As part of this right-wing political project, the higher-ups at Fox have also learned that nothing fires up their Boomer audience like fear: fear of immigrants, fear of Islamic extremism, fear of a changing world, and even fear of mainstream media sources. As one character in the movie *Bombshell* put it, "You have to adopt the mentality of an Irish street cop. The world is a bad place. People are lazy morons. Minorities are criminals. Sex is sick but interesting. Ask yourself, 'What would scare my grandmother, or piss off my grandfather?' And that's a Fox story."

This is odd, because Boomers also lay claim to everything from the civil rights movement to second-wave feminism to antiwar activism to some of the best music America has ever produced. And it's not just aging lefties who say Boomers were the OG activists, protesters, and social justice warriors; even the conservatives of Fox claim to be anti-racist and celebrate Martin Luther King Jr. (whose legacy they have distorted beyond recognition, casting the civil rights icon as apolitical, and Donald Trump as his ideological heir). Boomers on the left and the right cast their early adult years as a period of idealism and progress. They think of themselves as having improved the world.

A few Boomers certainly did, but overall, the Boomer generation brought us a rapid national shift away from the ideals of gender equality, racial justice, and pacifism. Perhaps this generation-wide self-delusion helps explain why Boomers have such a casual relationship with the truth. In a study of "prevalence and predictors of fake news dissemination on Facebook," researchers from New York University and Princeton found that Americans over sixty-five share false or misleading content at seven times the rate of younger ones, regardless of ideology.

Boomers, in other words, take credit for twentieth-century social progress while binge-watching Fox News and disseminating conspiracy theories on Facebook (where algorithms feed them more and more of the same). According to a Nielsen publication aimed at media advertisers, "The aging brain likes repetitions—and will believe information that is familiar to be true." This is Fox's persuasion strategy: repeated themes that, because of said repetition, begin to feel spot-on.

Here's a smattering of what Fox News viewers and readers of FoxNews.com have heard from anchors, contributors, and guests: "Millennials are abandoning religion for good"; "Millennials clean their bathrooms less frequently than other age groups"; "Most Americans think Millennials are selfish and entitled"; "Most Millennials are intimidated by plants"; "The Millennial generation is going to be the first generation that doesn't do anything"; "Millennials are lazy, they have a lack of drive";

Millennials are "Easily offended cocoon-dwellers"; "Millennials, yes, they are officially the most narcissistic generation"; "Are Millennials to blame for all of the world's problems?" "Are Millennials going godless?"; "Halloween is ruined and it's all thanks to Millennials"; "In 2017, the average terrorist is a Millennial"; Millennials are "psychotic"; and "They're the most pampered, ignorant—biggest crybabies I've ever seen."

The message: Millennials are a threat to the American way of life.

The target: Boomers. Keeping them aggrieved, annoyed, and afraid is good for business.

The result: a ginned-up generation war.

This doesn't just help keep conservatives in power; it enables Boomers to avoid taking responsibility for the world they're leaving their children. A true reckoning with the consequences of Boomer policies and decisions casts a harsh light on the children of the Greatest Generation. It reveals how few of the Boomers' own ideals they managed to live up to. And, hopefully, it will inspire the many well-meaning Boomers to do something before it's too late.

This book is that reckoning. It is also a peace offering to those Boomers who are worried about the world they're leaving their children. But peace deals aren't brokered with platitudes. We won't reconcile this generational divide or move beyond it if we don't take a hard and sometimes uncomfortable look at what caused it. OK, Boomer—are you ready to talk?

Millennials are projected to make up 75% of the global workforce by 2025.

Millennials are the generation most affected by mass incarceration.

The gender wage gap has stagnated over the past several decades—that is, women still don't make as much as men, and it's not improving anytime soon. The racial wage gap isn't any better, and the racial wealth gap is worse.

17% of black Millennials work in the gig economy, and nearly a third have a side hustle to make extra cash.

Many more jobs require a college degree now than did when Boomers were coming of age. But they don't pay nearly as well as degree-required jobs did then.

JOBS

A favorite trope of the last decade has been how unreasonable Millennial expectations are in the workplace: we want to move up the ladder too quickly, we job-hop with no sense of loyalty, we're overly sensitive to criticism and under-receptive to feedback. But the reality is essentially the opposite: we are working exceptionally hard just to tread water. We just work differently than previous generations. That's partly out of choice. But it's mostly because of the double whammy of two financial crises.

Boomers were the last generation to enter a job market offering living-wage blue-collar work. In Rust Belt towns, even in the mid-1960s, you could graduate high school straight into a factory job that would keep a nuclear family afloat. A college degree was far from a universal job requirement, but if you did have one, it was a big advantage: it meant higher compensation, status, and social mobility. Boomers also grew up in a different cultural landscape, where men were still expected to be the primary breadwinners for nuclear families, but women were entering the workforce in record numbers. A job meant not just a paycheck but a whole package of benefits, including vacation, sick time, and retirement.

For Millennials, it's a different world. Our colossally expensive college degrees are more important than ever, often mandatory for jobs that would have required only a high school education a few decades ago. But getting those degrees costs more, leaving many Millennials in debt before they receive their first paycheck. That higher price of entry doesn't come with higher real wages, though, and these high-credential jobs are clustered in high-priced cities with ever-rising rents. Women in the workforce are now the norm, but women with advanced degrees don't advance as far as their male peers—despite graduating in larger numbers from law school than men, women make up less than a quarter of law firm partners, for example—and are more likely to step back when they have children. Millennial women without college degrees are funneled into "pink-collar" jobs (home health care, domestic work, retail) that come with lower pay and fewer benefits than the traditional blue-collar work that allowed Boomer men to support entire families. Meanwhile, as factories continue to shutter and mines close down, eliminating America's last well-paying blue-collar jobs, Millennial men are hesitant to move to "women's work" like eldercare and nursing, even as female-dominated industries like health care grow.

The global economic downturn caused by the coronavirus has already hurt Millennials more than any other generation, and that's on top of the damage done by the 2008–2009 Great

Recession. Add to all of this the fact that so many members of our cohort, and especially the men of color, have been incarcerated at astronomical rates (further denting their income and job prospects), and it's easy to see why it's hard out there for a Millennial.

Less Money, More Problems

There are two big stories about Millennials and work. The first lies in the numbers; the second is about our priorities.

As a result of the financial collapse and the Great Recession of 2008–2009, many Millennials graduated college into the worst economic landscape in nearly a century. That made it harder for older Millennials to get their first jobs and more likely that they would be let go from any position they managed to pin down. Younger Millennials had a brighter path—until COVID-19 hit in 2020. The markets tanked, and millions of Americans, disproportionately Millennials, lost their jobs. "This is a jobs crisis of the young, the diverse, and the contingent, meaning disproportionately of the Millennials," Annie Lowrey, a journalist at the *Atlantic* and one of the most astute and prescient thinkers on Millennials and economics, wrote in the early days of the pandemic. "They make up a majority of bartenders, half of restaurant workers, and a large share of retail workers. They are also heavily dependent on gig and contract work, which is evaporating as the consumer economy grinds to a halt. It's a cruel economic version of that old Catskill resort joke: These are terrible jobs, and now all the young people holding them are getting fired."

The ensuing economic fallout will reshape America as we know it. And for Millennials, the economic outlook is especially grim. Whether we are just beginning our careers or are reaching our prime working years, Millennials will experience income losses in this recession (or depression) that will dog us for the rest of our lives. That's because if you start off being underpaid, even with standard raises, you're going to continue making less than someone who was paid more from the get-go (this is one reason why gender and racial wage gaps tend to get more extreme with age).

That's not a maybe; we've already seen it happen. Since 1980, when the first Millennials were born, US GDP has increased by a whopping 79 percent. But we haven't seen the benefits of that increased output: we make an average of $2,000 less, adjusted for inflation, than our parents did the year our generation came into existence.

A Millennial male head of household, a Federal Reserve report found, earned over 10 percent less in 2014 than a Boomer head of household did in 1978, even though 2014 America was significantly wealthier. And even though Millennial women are more likely than Boomer women to both work outside the home and have college and advanced degrees, Millennial female heads of household still make only marginally more than Boomer female heads of household did when they were young. When you

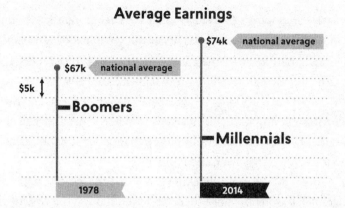

Average Earnings

$74k national average

$67k national average

$5k

Boomers

Millennials

1978

2014

Boomers' household earnings were just $10,000 behind the nationwide average when they were young. Millennials make closer to $25,000 less.

look at median income, Millennial female heads of household make *less* than their young Boomer counterparts did.

One of the most jarring comparisons is what Boomers made when they were young versus what Millennials make today—and the now massive gap between what a young family earns and what the average American family makes. Adjusted to 2016 dollars, the average young Boomer household led by a male breadwinner made $56,100 in 1978; in 2014, Millennial households at the same age brought in just $49,500. Even worse: While young Boomers were catching up to their elders, Millennials are not. Boomers' household earnings were just $10,000 behind the nationwide average when they were young. Millennials make closer to $25,000 less.

The stats aren't any better when you jump ahead a decade and look at Boomers in 1989, when the youngest were twenty-five and the oldest in their early forties. In a 2017 report the youth advocacy group Young Invincibles found that Millennials make about $10,000 less per year than Baby Boomers did when they were young adults in 1989—a 20 percent decline. Our net wealth and our total assets amount to half of what Boomers had amassed when they were about our age.

This is all the more shocking given that the average national income has gone up since then. And even though the American economy has nearly doubled in size since the late seventies, the average income for a young household has gone down. Now with the 2020 crash, Millennials stand to lose even more.

To be fair, American wages have stagnated across the board. But that stagnation does the most harm to the folks who made the least to begin with and who are entering their prime working years with the most to gain. Gen Xers were pummeled by the wave of the 2008 recession, too, and they were actually the hardest hit by the initial tsunami. They were mostly in their thirties—roughly the same age older Millennials are now, as we get slammed for a second time—and as young workers and homeowners, they lost more wealth than both their Boomer elders and their Millennial juniors. A Pew Research Center analysis of Federal Reserve data found that in 2007, on the eve of the Great Recession, the average Gen X household was worth $63,400 and had $66,000 in home equity. When the economy went over the cliff, Gen X incomes and home values went with it: in 2010, the average Gen X household was worth just $39,200 and had $37,600 in home equity.

But here's the thing: As the economy righted itself and began to grow again, Gen Xers fully recovered. Boomers, who were doing better than Gen Xers to begin with, also steadied themselves.

Millennials didn't.

That means that as we enter the second major recession of our young lives, we're in a worse position than Gen Xers were as they stood on the precipice of the 2008 crash. A much worse position, in fact. Far from the $63,400 that the mostly thirtysomething Gen X households were worth in 2007, twenty- and thirtysomething Millennial households were worth a paltry $12,300 in 2016. Americans under thirty-five are worth 40 percent less today than that same age group was in 2004. But in the same period in which young Americans saw our resources decline, Boomer fortunes grew: the net worth of Americans sixty-five-plus grew by 9 percent.

While Millennials were the most likely group to lose a job in the 2008 recession, we did end up with the most significant employment recovery, with more of us returning to work by 2017 than older adults. But a return to work does not necessarily mean a return to normalcy. The shock of unemployment translated into a 7 percent loss of earnings for Baby Boomers. Millennials lost nearly double that amount. And Boomers saw significant recovery afterward. By 2010, their losses had already shrunk by 65 percent. Millennials didn't see a comparable bounce back.

With limited employment histories, little or no savings, and a vanishing social safety net, we didn't really stand a chance. And now we're gearing up for round two.

The hangover from the 2008 recession means that today's young workers face high rates of unemployment and under-employment: working less than they'd like or at jobs they're overqualified to do—for example, bartending when they have a college diploma, as Millennial congresswoman Alexandria Ocasio-Cortez did after she graduated from Boston University. A study by the consulting firm McKinsey & Company found that nearly half of recent college grads are working at jobs that don't require a college degree. A 2019 New America analysis was even more dire: only about half of Millennials, by now adults in our twenties and thirties, were employed full-time. And unemployment is especially pronounced for young workers of color. A 2017 analysis by Elise Gould at the Economic Policy Institute found that young black workers, those aged sixteen to twenty-four, are unemployed at more than twice the rate of their white counter-parts, and four times the rate of all workers aged twenty-five to fifty-four.

The pandemic-fueled 2020 recession only widened these ra-cial disparities. Shelter-in-place orders meant that certain em-ployees could work from home, while others were simply out of work. This worked out especially badly for black and Hispanic workers: Bureau of Labor Statistics data shows that while close to 30 percent of white employees have jobs that can be done via telework, the same is true of just 20 percent of black employees, and 16 percent of Hispanic ones. And the best-paid employees are six times as likely to be able to work from home as the lowest-paid ones.

The 2008 recession, coupled with demands to cut costs by squeezing employees, also meant that basic benefits were slashed, and it's Millennials making do with the tatters. In 1980, half of workers had access to a retirement plan through their employer; by 2015, the Pew Research Center found, that share had slipped to 45 percent. But even that proportion doesn't tell the whole story. While nearly 70 percent of working Boomers had access to employer-sponsored retirement plans in 2012, a Pew analysis of Census Bureau survey data found, more than 40 percent of working Millennials aren't even eligible to participate in retirement plans—because their company doesn't offer one, because they work too few hours to qualify, or because they haven't been employed long enough. And the youngest Millennials were the worst off: by 2015, Pew found that only 30 percent of workers aged sixteen to twenty-four had access to a retirement plan, compared to more than half of fifty-five- to sixty-four-year-olds. And when Millennials do get the chance to contribute to a sponsored plan, it raises the question: With what money? Extra cash goes to paying back student loans, paying for childcare, or making rent, not investing in the future. Millennials are, in fact, saving more for retirement than our Gen X predecessors did at our age, a small bright spot in a blighted financial landscape. But still, according to the National Institute on Retirement Security, two-thirds of us don't have any retirement savings.

So what do Millennials get out of these lower-wage jobs that demand higher credentials and offer fewer benefits? It's not less work, that's for sure. Not only do Americans work more than we did in 1980, but we work nearly an extra *month* every year.

What a raw deal.

The Head and the Heart

The numbers are stark. But there's something else going on here, too, that has less to do with wages and more to do with values. Millennials grew up hearing that we could be anything we wanted to be. We were raised with creativity and ambition. Boomers were the original helicopter parents, and Millennials were the first generation to be so intensively parented—raised with strict rules around television-watching and bedtime, helped with our homework, encouraged to forgo drugs and delay sex so that we could realize our dreams. Millennials, and especially but not only the more privileged among us, grew up being micromanaged and overscheduled; our lives from toddlerhood through college were extremely structured.

The crankiest folks now complain that Millennials all think we're special snowflakes. We have *too many* interests outside of work. We're *too* idealistic. "Millennials who have grown up on a steady diet of participation trophies and self-esteem boosting seem uniquely unable to adapt when the feedback and coaching

Not only do Americans work more than we did in 1980,
but we work nearly an extra month every year.

comes in forms they don't like," griped Nebraska senator (and, despite his Boomer energy, technically Gen Xer) Ben Sasse in his book *The Vanishing American Adult*. "The generation's shared sense of entitlement in the workplace seems to reflect a reduced sense of toughness, grit, and resilience compared to that of their ancestors."

But guys: Who do you think made us that way? Our Boomer (and Gen X) parents buckled us into the car seats they never had; they worried that we'd end up on a milk carton. We absorbed that greater scrutiny of our safety and well-being, and the perhaps inflated sense of our own importance. We didn't buy those participation trophies for ourselves.

So what does this have to do with jobs? For more than a decade, Millennials have been begrudged for our individualism, our idealism, and our alleged sensitivities. But these values actually make for a generation of relatively decent people. You can cast our values as naïve—we want to change the world, we all think we're so damn special—or you can open the frame a little wider and see us for who we are: in general, people who want to be good, do good, and make things better for those around us. Yes, that means we are more open to, say, using pronouns that reflect a person's gender identity. It also means that we want to do work that promotes our values, or at least be in workplaces that are somewhat aligned with what we value. Add this to the fact that we have never been able to count on either the government or the market to take good care of us, and that we know we may never financially thrive, and well, you can see why we conclude that if we're not going to be rich, we might as well be happy.

This is certainly true for Justin Pinn. Born to a teenage mother in rural Ohio, he heard again and again that college would be his "Willy Wonka Golden Ticket": the promise of a good life. He was the first in his family to go to college, and after Georgetown, he could have gone to law or medical school, like many of his peers, or taken any number of handsomely paid jobs on offer to graduates of elite schools. Instead, he gravitated toward work that felt more personally meaningful: teaching. Justin, now twenty-nine, joined Teach For America, which brought him to Miami, Florida.

"I realized that I was making forty thousand dollars a year," Justin says. "And that is the largest amount anyone in my family had ever made—legally, that is."

Even so, $40,000 isn't much when you're renting an apartment in Miami, let alone supporting family back home and trying to pay down credit card debt you racked up when you were a broke student. "People like me still want to contribute to service in powerful ways, and finances shouldn't fully deter us when it's just basic necessities like housing—it's not like I want to drive a Lamborghini," Justin says. "I think you're going to see a hemorrhaging of talent, especially of first-generation students of color, because financially it's not possible," he says. What he means is that the near impossibility of working in mission-driven jobs and still making rent will force talented Millennials out of the work they love.

For now, Justin is putting off the rest of an adult life. A house and kids? He would love that, but even though he's nearing thirty, it doesn't seem possible anytime soon. "When I was younger, I was like, oh, maybe later in my twenties, that's when I'll think about it," he says of owning a home, getting married, and having children. "And now it's like, okay, maybe in my thirties. It's kind of like we're kids. And it's because of money."

Yes, privileging a specific city and career over a house and children is a choice, and one some Boomers (and Gen Xers, let's be real) may deride. After all, Justin doesn't have to live in a big, expensive city. He didn't have to teach in an underserved school, or teach at all, or move into his current role as a director at Teach For America. He could relocate to a cheaper city where he could afford more even on a relatively low salary, or take a higher-paying job. But for Millennials like Justin, happiness and purpose are just as important as, if not more important than, wealth and security—perhaps because they have seen how easily the latter two things can be yanked away.

"I love Miami. Miami has taken me in," Justin says. "I think about the rising cost of housing and all the challenges that come with it, and in my head I think, hmm, I love the service work I do, but what if I went and worked in the Midwest and went to corporate America and made some money and then could come back to the work I love? But that wouldn't make me happy and it's not mission-aligned."

"A defining characteristic of Millennials is that we are the first generation that is not going to be better-off than our parents."

Of course Justin could choose one—the corporate life, say, or the job in the Midwest—but he doesn't want to compromise. And Millennials understand better than just about any other generation that even well-paying jobs aren't guaranteed to last. That's a very shaky promise of success, and just isn't enough of a guarantee to cede one's happiness.

Matt Dubin, a thirty-one-year-old Los Angeles native, holds a PhD in organizational psychology and leads a consulting practice focused on developing company culture and bridging generational divides in the workplace. He draws a straight line from the financial challenges Millennials have faced to the kind of values-based career decisions that Millennials like Justin make. "The recession was a rude awakening," Matt says. "Millennials growing up were told that they can be and do anything they want. Follow your passion. And as a result of the recession, a lot of Millennials couldn't even find a job, let alone follow a passion or do whatever you set your mind to do." That in turn disabused

Millennials of the notion that hard work would mean a good job and a stable life, a prescription that many of our parents had conveyed as a promise.

"In an instant the economy can crash and we can't even find jobs. It totally altered the mentality that Millennials have toward work and what they look for out of a workplace," Matt says. "A lot of the cultures that are more interesting or innovative and provide flexibility, almost everything we see out of a modern workplace, is somewhat a result of the recession. What was promised to us, that's not happening, so we have to carve our own path and work a different way. We're not going to be able to climb up the corporate ladder the way our parents were."

And if we're not climbing the ladder, then what are we focused on achieving instead?

"A defining characteristic of Millennials is that we are the first generation that is not going to be better-off than our parents," Matt says. "So there's a big push to decide, okay, I might not be able to buy as nice of a house as my parents had, or send my kids to the same types of schools, so how can I make life just as meaningful? How can I set goals to be happy? A defining characteristic of our generation is that work is more than a paycheck—I want to find something that is interesting to me, that I enjoy going to every day, that is a source of meaning."

Millennials obviously did not invent the desire for meaning in life. But we do seem to be distinct from Boomers in that we want our workplaces to be as reflective of our values as our families or homes are. That doesn't mean we're all working at nonprofits. But it does mean we may prefer to work for, say, Netflix instead of Fox, or Sweetgreen instead of Chick-fil-A. Nearly nine in ten Millennials say they would consider a pay cut to work at a company if they believed in its mission and shared its values (barely one in ten Boomers said the same). And even if our job or our company isn't an extension of our values, we want our workplace to be open-minded and fair. We want to feel heard and respected.

So is that why we change jobs so often? Not exactly.

"I think the stereotype of Millennials as job-hoppers stems from an idea of Millennials as snowflakes, as self-centered in some way that somehow Boomers weren't," says Gray Kimbrough, an economist at American University (and, according to his Twitter bio and a *Washington Post* reporter, a "serial millennial myth debunker"). "But they're not job-hopping. They're actually switching jobs less than people used to at the same age. So it's just a complaint about young people."

Boomers also changed employers frequently in their early years in the workforce, but eventually settled into jobs with clear trajectories, often staying at the same company for years or even decades, incentivized to put down roots. Millennials don't have that luxury. Many of our jobs were casualties of the recession, or never came to be because of that downturn. That may make us *more* likely to stay put in the early years of our careers. But we know that when companies downsize and cut jobs and benefits, we're often first on the chopping block. So we stay nimble—even as Boomers forget their own job-hopping and see ours as disloyal.

There is also "a huge conflict around paying your dues versus being entitled," Matt says. Boomers were raised on hierarchy, and the workplaces they built tend to be hierarchical. But they didn't raise Millennial children with the same rules. "Boomers say, 'I've been in this company for twenty or thirty years, I had to pay my dues, I didn't get my first promotion until I was thirty-three, and then these Millennials come in and they want to be CEO right away.'"

Matt points to how Millennials are dinged for wanting "instant gratification." Our generation, he says, doesn't understand the point of waiting seven or eight years to rise to the top, particularly because there is another model out there—new companies, with younger CEOs, where their friends rise fast. "There used to be a mentality of, your boss tells you to do something and you just do it," Matt says. "Millennials have a different view of authority now. Their parents were often their friends, coaches were friends, teachers were friends. They don't see the boss as an end-all be-all authority figure. They have to understand the why behind the what, and how their work is contributing to the company and the team."

Millennials also prioritize efficiency and a logical and collaborative (rather than traditional and hierarchical) way of doing things. This means that there are communication breakdowns between generations: I don't understand why my boss doesn't respond to my emails and insists on wasting time talking things out; she thinks Millennials can't make eye contact, are always staring at their phones, and expect instant personal and professional gratification. (To that, Matt says: "With Google and all these apps and instant communication, instant gratification and reinforcement is what they've grown up with. You can't get mad at someone for having life be a certain way for them and having that be what they expect at work.")

That emphasis on efficiency also has a lot of us wondering why we spend forty-five minutes or an hour commuting each way to work, just to sit in an office surrounded by our coworkers, each of us wearing noise-canceling headphones. There are of course some jobs that have to be done in person—you can't be a remote food-service worker, ambulance driver, or plumber—but for many jobs in the growing information and creative sectors, sitting in an office all day (not to mention getting to and from an office) feels pointless, which is why so many of us have long clamored for remote work. That our desire for more flexible workplaces abruptly became reality thanks to the coronavirus wasn't exactly how we wanted this to go. But Millennials have long been pushing for the kind of work-from-home ability—not to mention economic security—that we're now seeing as more valuable than ever.

This was certainly the case for Rhiannon Cook, who began her career in Pittsburgh, Pennsylvania, at a legacy advertising firm. "Advertising is a Boomer's game," she says. "Things are done a certain way based on tradition. My office was in Pittsburgh and my client was in Atlanta. I would fly down probably once a month for a meeting in person. The client had mostly Millennials on their marketing team, and sometimes they were able to work from home. Because Atlanta's traffic is so terrible,

I would fly down for their meetings, get to the meeting on time, and end up having a video conference with a client in Atlanta because they couldn't get there."

This clearly was a ridiculous system. But in a traditional vertical workplace, it didn't matter. "No matter how bad of an idea something was, we had to do it if it came from someone higher up," Rhiannon says. "Business operated a lot on ego. I cannot count the number of times I said, 'This is a horrible idea that's not going to work,' and everyone was like, 'I know, but it's Bob's idea, so we have to make it work.'"

I talked to Rhiannon, thirty-one, via video chat from her current home on a coffee farm in Manizales, Colombia. She's not flying to Atlanta anymore to meet with clients who conference in from a few miles down the road. Instead, she's working at a coffee subscription start-up, founded and run by Millennials, with no central office and a workforce that is 100 percent remote.

"The larger theme of a lot of my career and life has been built around 2009, when the economy tanked," she says. "It's not unique to me, it's the story of a lot of Millennials, the idea that I did everything I was supposed to do, I followed all the rules, I did all the internships and the externships, the teaching roles, the study abroad, all of it, and 2009 hit and nobody wanted to give me a job. That made me think differently about what we're told we have to do and how we do it, because there are no guarantees." After a few years in the first corporate job she landed at after the recession, she began to wonder, Why am I working in a way that works for other people but doesn't work for me?

Rhiannon's mother had raised her with the view that it's okay to make your own way and do your own thing. "She lived a very nontraditional life, raising a biracial child as a single parent in rural northeast Ohio in the nineteen-eighties, before having children a different race from you was trendy," Rhiannon says. And she felt pushed, she says, by "learning so much about American history and the history of people of color everywhere, knowing that so many people don't have any opportunities, and I had the opportunity to do this. And it feels like, not an imperative, but you feel the blessing of being able to live this way. Culturally so many people who look like me and come from where I come from are just trying to get free. And I look at one definition of freedom—getting a job—and it's a lovely life, there's nothing wrong with the traditional American way of doing things. But it didn't look like my brand of freedom. I didn't feel free."

So when she got a job that let her work anywhere, she flew south. And while the digital nomad life is temporary—she will likely end up back in the United States at some point—this way of working is not.

"Right now, the thing I most value and what I know would be hard to give up is freedom," Rhiannon says. "Freedom in the sense that my time is my own. I can choose where I want to be. No one can tell me anymore that I have to be on a flight to Atlanta at eight a.m. on Monday morning for a twelve p.m. meeting. No one can tell me I can't spend time with my grandmother. Nobody can tell me that you have to be creative and productive between nine a.m. and five p.m. because that's when the world is creative and productive ... I'm a better person. I'm healthier. I get more exercise. I get to make my own schedule. I produce way better work for my employer because I'm not forcing myself to be creative or productive. It's flowing out of me much more naturally."

This, Matt Dubin says, is typical, and challenges the stereotype of the lazy Millennial. "Millennials are willing to work really hard," he says. "It's a misconception that they don't want to work as hard and just want crazy work-life balance. But they do want flexibility. They're willing to work their butts off, and they're willing to work at night and on the weekends, but having the flexibility of 'I want to work from home today' or 'I want to come in late today' or 'I need to go to an appointment on this day.' They don't want their workplaces to be rigid. They wonder, Why do I have to sit in this chair and get all my work done from nine to six?"

Maybe to Boomers this all sounds indulgent. To Millennials, it just seems smart.

Rise 'n' Grind

And yet.

There is a downside to this new work culture. A flexible and always connected workplace also means an always-on workplace. And a desire for meaning and personal betterment combined with an economy that has already proved capricious and tenuous leads to a whole lot of young workers who feel like they can never take a break—and that they need to keep racking up the professional and personal accomplishments to stay relevant. The #hustle is real, and it's Millennials who shoulder the demands of the new always-on lifestyle. We feel all the exhaustion, anxiety, and burnout that comes with it.

Takeru Nagayoshi is twenty-eight and a teacher in an underserved school. He works in New Bedford, Massachusetts, and lives in Providence, Rhode Island. The son of Japanese immigrants, he grew up doing well in school, graduated from Brown, and chose to work in a field where he felt like he was living out his principles. That choice didn't come without sacrifice— Takeru lives in a house with five roommates (all fellow public school teachers) so that he can afford to live in Providence, an exciting and culturally rich city, on a teacher's salary. But doing good matters more to him than making bank.

Doing good as a teacher, though, means doing a lot more than it used to.

"A lot of us Millennials are so conscious about branding ourselves that every single part of what we do, be it work or hobby, becomes an extension of that self," he says. "Teaching is a profession that requires you to stay constant from seven a.m. to three p.m., but also has a lot of gigs and outside work that you can take on. A lot of the work I do is cultivating this teacher-educator brand, and I feel like that's such a Millennial mindset that my colleagues from other generations don't understand."

For Takeru, who goes by "TK" in professional settings

("because most people don't bother to remember a foreign name," he says), building a brand, bettering himself as a professional, and being a Millennial all go hand in hand. "I do think there's something Millennial about this desire to constantly work, constantly brand yourself, hustle and grind," he says. He is on Teacher Twitter (he skips the also popular Teacher Instagram). Both are loose networks of educators who exchange ideas, and some barbs, via social media. He is in three different fellowship programs that focus on projects as diverse as recruiting and retaining teachers of color and aligning third-party curriculums with state standards. Every week he's at three or four different networking engagements: maybe he's speaking on a panel, or attending the Teachers Union's LGBT committee meeting, or going to a professional development event. He writes the occasional op-ed. Oh, and he also teaches five classes a day, five days a week. Recognized for his dedication—Takeru was named the 2020 Massachusetts Teacher of the Year—he loves his work.

The #hustle is real, and it's Millennials who shoulder the demands of the new always-on lifestyle.

But he's exhausted.

"No one tells me I have to join all these fellowships and do these projects and offer consulting services," Takeru says. "And yet I feel this need to. I feel like that toxic pressure is such a Millennial trait."

Hard work has long been part of the American ethos. But the idea that work should be all-encompassing and central to one's identity is newer. The shift toward the workplace-as-everything perhaps began in Silicon Valley, where tech companies like Google and Facebook began offering perks that encouraged employees to stay at or around the office all day long: lavish cafeterias, fancy gyms, even massages and dry cleaning. The idea was to make things easy for employees, sure, but it was primarily about efficiency: the less time employees spend dropping off their own dry cleaning or going out for sushi, the more time they can spend at their desks. For employees, that kind of efficiency and the productivity it allowed was supposed to pay off in higher wages and more leisure time.

Instead, Millennials are getting paid less and working more. Even our "leisure time" is spent on activities that aren't leisurely at all: networking, brandbuilding, essentially *performing*.

The exhausting Millennial hustle became a topic of broad conversation when *BuzzFeed* writer Anne Helen Petersen published "How Millennials Became the Burnout Generation," an essay that quickly went viral in January 2019. Petersen detailed all of the ways in which Millennials were raised to be production machines, having been promised that hard work and efficiency would pay dividends. "Yet the more work we do, the more efficient we've proven ourselves to be, the *worse* our jobs become: lower pay, worse benefits, less job security," she wrote. "Our efficiency hasn't bucked wage stagnation; our steadfastness hasn't made us more valuable. If anything, our commitment to work, no matter how exploitative, has simply encouraged and facilitated our exploitation. We put up with companies treating us poorly because we don't see another option. We don't quit. We internalize that we're not striving hard enough. And we get a second gig."

The hustle may feel especially acute for the many Millennials trying to jump into the middle class. Prita Piekara grew up in a challenging family situation, dropped out of high school as a sophomore, and ended up moving from California to Washington, DC, with her sixteen-year-old sister, whom she then raised, despite barely being an adult herself. She worked all day, took Georgetown classes at night, and then switched to an online university. Many of the jobs she's held since graduating came through recommendations from coworkers, contacts, and former bosses. When it comes to the hustle, "I feel like I had to," Prita says. "In DC I feel like jobs are gotten by who you know, and who can lift your resume out of a stack of papers." Her husband, Evan, agrees. "Millennials get knocked for being lazy and entitled, but from what I've seen there are a lot of people in our generation who are hustling," he says. "They're part of the gig economy, they have side things, they're networking and joining meetups."

The two talk about retiring eventually—Evan's parents, Boomers in their sixties, are both stepping back from work, and that has Prita and Evan considering their own futures—but "we don't think we will retire, or at least not fully," Prita says. "We can't imagine, 'Oh, we're just done and we're not doing that anymore.'" The hustle culture, she says, is too built into their habits and identities. And the hustle doesn't stop for anything. "I'm on maternity leave right now and I'm still calling into team meetings when they'll let me," Prita says. "I'm still trying to do networking things even though I'm on leave and can unplug, but I don't think either of us know how to do that fully. It's ingrained in us: there is no completely offline."

It's easy to say that no one is forcing us to work until we drop. But Millennials aren't wrong that the demands of the modern workplace (and world) are more extreme than ever before. Since 1980, the Pew Research Center found, the number of jobs that require social, analytical, communication, computer, and critical thinking skills has increased by about 80 percent. More than twice as many people now work in jobs that require social, analytical, and communication skills than work in jobs requiring higher-level physical skills like carpentry or dry cleaning. And jobs that require these social and communication abilities are clustered in the fastest-growing sectors of the economy. In short, they are the jobs of the future. Workers know this, which is perhaps why 85 percent of them say that computer skills are either very or extremely important to succeed in today's economy; more than a third say the same about social media skills. Nearly all of us are anxious about what automation will mean for our jobs.

The jobs of today also require more preparation, whether that's formal education, training programs, certificates, or licensing requirements. That's econ-speak for: people who want these jobs have to hustle, spending more money and time to get the credentials they need. Workers know this, too: according to a

2016 Pew report, almost half say they took an extra class or training program in the past year.

People today are more likely to be working as contractors or freelancers—something that researchers call "contingent" or "alternative" work arrangements, and which the Bureau of Labor Statistics didn't even start tracking until 1995. Gig economy jobs like driving for Uber or running errands as a TaskRabbit remain a tiny slice of overall employment, and demographics can be hard to obtain, but most research indicates that Millennials are disproportionately represented in them. Estimates of how many Millennials work in the gig economy range from as low as 10 percent to as high as nearly 50 percent. And gig economy Millennial workers are disproportionately people of color: some 17 percent of black Millennials have held gig economy jobs, and even more—31 percent of employed black Millennials—have taken on second jobs and supplemental contract work, according to researchers at New America. That's also true of 20 percent of Latinos, 18 percent of whites, and 11 percent of Asian-Americans. Worldwide, half of Millennials say they would consider ditching their traditional jobs for full-time gig work; 61 percent say they would supplement their existing jobs with gig assignments. Close to half of Millennials have taken on freelance work.

The number-one reason Millennials say the gig economy appeals to them? Money. Side hustles are an economic necessity in a nation where wages have stagnated, and where the federally mandated minimum wage is so low that a parent can work a full-time minimum-wage job and still live below the poverty level.

"There is not a single day, a single moment that passes that I don't think about money," says Constance C. Luo, a twenty-seven-year-old community organizer in Houston. She pinches pennies and lives in an affordable apartment, but worries about her student loan debt keep her up at night, and she often finds herself browsing "how to make money" self-help articles at two or three in the morning. "Sometimes I feel like I'm being gaslit by the media, gaslit by older folks—some of whom are people that I look up to in the workplace and my own family," she says. "On one hand I'm told that I'm entitled, lazy, unambitious, spending money on all the wrong things, and generally worthless, and on the other hand, coming from my end, I think about money all the time."

Estimates of how many Millennials work in the gig economy range from as low as 10 percent to as high as nearly 50 percent.

Millennials also realize that we are not staring up at the same career ladders that our parents climbed. If we want to be successful, there's a sense that we can only count on ourselves. Intellectually, we understand that's not true. We know that you can hustle your whole life and still die at the bottom, if there's no broader social mechanism to enable you to climb the ladder. We know that employers rely on gig workers to cut their costs, not to help employees thrive or live better lives. We know gig jobs are not the solution to our financial insecurity; we've already seen them collapse during the COVID-19 pandemic. Overwhelmingly, Millennials say we would prefer a long career at a single company to cobbling together gigs and freelance projects. But as Constance puts it, "To me what defines being a Millennial is this daily constant struggle of staying in the game, staying employed, staying in your home, and trying to balance it all without losing your mind." What other choice do we have?

More Diversity, Less Security

As demanding as our new work culture is, it's particularly challenging for Millennial women, who are still paid less than their brothers and husbands, and still doing more on the home front. We think of Millennials as "young," but in reality, we're adults, and many of us are parents. To be sure, compared to their fathers, Millennial men have stepped up in taking on home labor, but Millennial women still do most of the work at home. We're hustling, grinding, *and* raising babies. Meanwhile, expectations for work, womanhood, and parenting seem to have no ceiling.

There are a couple of positive economic stories for Millennial women. The first is that we're working outside of the home more often than women of previous generations, and for women, work outside of the home is correlated with a slew of positive outcomes for ourselves and those around us: better mental health, a more stable financial life, and a greater ability to leave an abusive partner or an unhappy relationship. Our husbands treat their female coworkers and subordinates more fairly, our daughters do better in school, and our sons are more egalitarian and do more in their own homes once they grow up. For much of this, we have Boomer women to thank. They entered the workforce in unprecedented numbers, at a time when the workplace was obscenely hostile to female employees (it's still far from perfect, but things have improved). To be clear, low-income women and women of color have long worked outside the home. But women en masse began to enter the workforce as the Boomers were coming of age.

Right away, wage disparities were a problem. Feminists began drawing attention to the gender wage gap in the 1960s and '70s, and slowly, through the 1970s and '80s, the gap started getting smaller.

And then it stagnated.

While the pay gap gets a *tiny* bit better every few years, it's not decreasing nearly as quickly as, say, women are entering the workforce or doing the same jobs as men. Public policy think tank Third Way found that the pay gap actually widens as women progress in their careers: women start out at a deficit, only making about 90 percent of what men earn, and that gap grows to 82 percent by the time women are in their late thirties and early forties. The numbers are especially bad for black and Hispanic women. The Washington Center for Equitable Growth found that the average black woman makes just 64 cents to a white man's dollar, and the gap is even larger when you look at yearly earnings: a black woman earns, on average, 61 percent of what a white man earns in a year. Part of that has to do with the kinds of jobs black women are funneled into as compared with the jobs white men have access to. But even when you control for those variables—job, industry, education, age, and family structure—more than half of the gap remains unaccounted for. A black woman of the same age and education level working the same job in the same industry is still only making 80 cents to a white man's dollar. Those missing 20 cents are a straight-up identity tax.

Socioeconomic factors affect the wage gap as well. High-income women face wage disparities, but they have seen their wage gap narrow pretty significantly as their wages have increased. Poor women, though, have seen virtually no change in their real wages since the 1970s. Poverty, like wealth, is inherited. For the many Millennials who grew up poor, the future doesn't look much brighter, no matter how hard they work.

The gender and race pay gap is also due to occupational segregation: black women (and Hispanic women and to a lesser extent, women generally) are pushed into lower-wage jobs. According to the economists Francine Blau and Lawrence Kahn, this process of occupational sorting is the single largest driver of the gender wage gap. A separate data analysis from Third Way found that of the thirty best-paying occupations in the country, twenty-six were male-dominated. Among the thirty lowest-paid occupations? Twenty-three were majority-female.

Wage gap skeptics argue that this is about "choice," and that women simply prefer, for example, care work, while men are more likely to do physically arduous and even dangerous labor. But that's not quite true. Researchers Asaf Levanon of the University of Haifa in Israel, Paul Allison of the University of Pennsylvania, and Paula England, who was at Stanford at the time, conducted one of the largest and most comprehensive studies of gender segregation, spanning fifty years and across occupations, and found that the feminization of an industry—the extent to which it is seen as "women's work"—decreases its prestige, and by extension its pay. When recreation jobs (camp counselor, park worker) started going to more women than men, pay dropped by 57 percentage points. The inverse also occurs: when men flooded into computer programming, dominating what was once a heavily female occupation, wages grew by 21 percent. When women take over any given role from men, it begins to be seen as lower-status, less valuable, and unworthy of competitive compensation, regardless of whether the day-to-day tasks remain the same. "It's not that women are always picking lesser things in terms of skill and importance," Paula England told the *New York Times*. "It's just that the employers are deciding to pay it less."

Occupational segregation—women in certain feminized jobs, men in different masculinized ones—rapidly decreased in the 1970s and '80s, as women swarmed into what were once predominantly male occupations, like law and medicine. But that leveled off in the 1990s and 2000s.

And so here's the mixed news about Millennial women's professional futures: many of the job categories that are growing the fastest are in female-dominated fields. Good, right? More work for women! The bad news is that precisely because these fields are female-dominated, they are also accorded lower status, lower pay, less job security, and fewer benefits.

Also: men won't do them, and that's a huge problem. Even the relatively more progressive men of the Millennial generation still very much tie work to masculinity and are hesitant to take jobs that read as female: nurse, teacher, childcare or eldercare worker, home health aide. "Much of men's resistance to pink-collar jobs is tied up in the culture of masculinity," wrote Claire Cain Miller for the *New York Times*. "Women are assumed to be empathetic and caring; men are supposed to be strong, tough and able to support a family." The fastest-growing industries in America are in education and health care, jobs that are male-dominated at the top but include a vast network of low-level "women's work." Women make up more than three-quarters of America's public school teachers; according to the Bureau of Labor Statistics, women account for nearly 75 percent of health care practitioners and nearly 90 percent of home health workers. But even though entry-level health care jobs that require some training but not a college degree offer better pay and job security than similar manufacturing jobs, men aren't taking them. The minority of men who *do* take them are more likely to be men of color. This suggests that gender segregation of jobs isn't going away anytime soon. And that means that low pay for women generally, and black and Hispanic women in particular, will persist for Millennials and for the generations after us.

This isn't just a female problem. Though the gender wage gap is at least decreasing, albeit glacially, the racial wage gap is actually *growing*. The median black employee makes 28.5 percent less than the median white employee, which is actually worse than it was in 1979, when a black worker made 20 percent less than a white one. It's grown for Hispanics, too, who made 19 percent less in 1979, and now make 30 percent less. Broadly speaking, wages have gone up across the board, but they've gone up more than twice as much for white workers than for black or Hispanic ones. And when you look at real wages, they've actually gone *down* for the poorest black and Hispanic employees, while poor whites have seen their wages grow at least a little. The 2020 recession has already done the most damage to young people of color, suggesting that this downturn will only exacerbate the racial wage gap.

Though the gender wage gap is at least decreasing, albeit glacially, the racial wage gap is actually *growing*.

In other words, it straight-up pays to be male, it pays to be white, and it pays the most to be a white male. White men benefit financially from both occupational segregation—being tracked into masculinized higher-status and higher-paid jobs—and from discrimination within fields, getting about a 10 percent pay bump from each factor, a team of economists found in a working paper published by the Washington Center for Equitable Growth. All that adds up to a pay premium of more than 22 percent overall.

Everyone else loses out in about the order you'd expect, but the proportions vary: looking only at occupational segregation and within-occupation penalties, white women lose out by a bit under 10 percent, mostly due to within-occupation penalties;

black men lose out by more than 10 percent, but mostly because of occupational segregation; and black women are penalized by closer to 20 percent, due to a heavy heaping of both, but a little extra on the occupational segregation side. In 1968, when all the Boomers had been born, their generation was more than 80 percent white. By contrast, nearly 40 percent of Millennials are racial or ethnic minorities. As a racially diverse generation with more women in the workforce, these wage discrimination statistics do not bode well for Millennials. In short: wage discrimination makes our racially diverse generation a poorer one.

Behind Bars and Out of Work

While women have been steadily entering the workforce for decades, men have been dropping out. That's partly due to the loss of traditionally masculine low-skilled work like manufacturing, which we heard a lot about in the aftermath of the 2016 election. The bottoming-out of the blue-collar economy, some pundits argued, led to widespread economic anxiety that pushed white voters to rally behind Trump. Those pundits were wrong about voters' motivations; multiple studies found racism and racial resentment were more significant factors than money. It is true, however, that even when the economy was allegedly booming, stunning numbers of working-age men were unemployed or underemployed. One well-known factor that has put so many men out of work is the decline in traditionally male jobs. A lesser-known one: the fact that we've taken millions of men out of the workforce and put them behind bars.

Ray is one of the scores of Millennial men of color caught up in an aggressive and unforgiving criminal justice system. Ray grew up in New Orleans, before Hurricane Katrina turned him and his family into some of the nation's early climate refugees. Nearly everything they had was gone after the storm, and there was no promise that if they rebuilt they wouldn't be wiped out again. So despite the fact that Ray had a budding career in the New Orleans film industry, he and his mother decided to resettle in Houston, Texas, when he was nineteen.

Ray was a pretty straitlaced kid. He sometimes drank with his friends, but he didn't use drugs, and he had never so much as smoked a joint. His parents both worked hard and were strict with their children. But Ray also made the choice to commit a serious, although nonviolent, crime for which penalties are extremely steep.

So when the cops burst through his front door with their guns drawn, he was surprised—not that he had gotten caught, necessarily, but that they were treating him like a dangerous and violent menace to society. He tried to be as compliant as possible, worried that he or his mother could easily be shot.

That was just the beginning of a process that seemed designed to send a single message: you are no longer a person. "You're shuffling from cell to cell like cattle," Ray says, "because they don't really see you as human at that point. The cells get more and more crowded as you move along. And then they get uncrowded, and crowded again, and you get to booking and it's cold and it's nothing but concrete around, and you don't know what the person next to you did or if they're mentally stable. At this point all you want is a bed."

Ray's mom was his biggest advocate, but Texas's cash bail system was brutal. Because he was new to the state, he says, they upped his bail from $10,000 to $30,000, even though he had a spotless record. His mother had to come up with $3,000 in cash.

They spent thousands not only on lawyers but on all of the other little indignities that add up in a justice system that makes you pay for part of your own prosecution and surveillance and demeans you in the process. "I didn't do drugs but I had to take drug tests, and pay out of pocket for those," Ray says. "It was humiliating. You have to stand in a bathroom in front of a mirror with your privates out, while somebody is evaluating whether your urine stream is legitimate."

While women have been steadily entering the workforce for decades, men have been dropping out.

Ray initially tried to fight the charge, but he was worn down by a system that incentivizes plea deals. Told he could be facing more than a decade in prison even as a first-time offender, he agreed to a plea that would let him out and put him on probation. It was framed as a second chance, but in reality, Ray says, "the court at that point looked at me and said he's a predator, we can't save him, just go ahead and give him a plea deal. We'll let him walk, but he's not going to be able to shake this."

And he hasn't.

"Since I've been discharged and completed my sentence, I've applied for jobs and they love me—I ace the interview and they say, 'You've got the job, just fill out the paperwork and we'll complete the background check.' And it's like, background check, shit," Ray says. "That's game over for me in lots of instances. And it's heartbreaking. I know I could offer a lot to that company. But they don't want to take a chance on me."

This is exacerbated, Ray says, by the fact that he's black. "When you're a white person and you get locked up, they try to find ways to salvage you, to make you whole again," Ray says. "When you're black and you've been through the criminal justice system, they toss you to the side like refuse. They say you messed up, you're not economically viable, and we're going to make sure everyone knows that you're not hirable because you did this thing. You're treated as a second-class citizen."

The formerly incarcerated often face totally legal discrimination. Even when discrimination based on previous arrests or incarceration isn't legal, it still happens. As a result, the Prison Policy Initiative found that people who have spent time behind bars face an unemployment rate of 27 percent. They are ten times as likely as the general population to be homeless. And in eleven states, people with certain felony convictions lose their right to vote indefinitely, which means that there's no traditional political avenue through which to advocate for their interests. They are rendered, by the state, something close to nonpersons.

That Millennial hustle? "I can't even be an Uber driver because of my conviction, which would have been a nice little side hustle," Ray says. "Most of these little side hustles people do, like Postmates, I wouldn't be above doing that, but now I'm limited because they can't vet me." He's done hard manual labor, but quickly realized he was going to destroy his body, and that it just wasn't a sustainable lifelong option. Now, he has a decent job at a call center, but he's still making less than he would be if he didn't have this conviction hanging over him. And he knows that when employers hire people with records, they often see them differently—as if those who committed a crime in the past should have to settle for less in perpetuity, should be grateful for whatever they can get. "If employers were forced to pay a higher wage, maybe I could make a decent living," Ray says. "That's the only way it's going to happen. It's not going to be me getting a job that pays me that on its own volition. It's like, 'You need to go get one of those minimum wage jobs where all the felons and human refuse have to go to work.'"

Emily Galvin-Almanza is an older Millennial and the cofounder and executive director of Partners for Justice; she also serves as senior legal counsel at The Justice Collaborative, a prison reform advocacy group. She has seen firsthand the devasting impact of mass incarceration on her generation (and on those older and younger), including ruinous debts that often saddle criminal defendants—even, in some states, if they're found not guilty. "You could owe sixty thousand dollars for the cost of being jailed pre-trial and represented by a public defender," Emily says. "I've seen people financially ruined. I've seen people unable to find work. People need a lot of help talking about a prior incident. If employers will even interview you, you have to be very good at talking about your priors—here's what happened and here's how I've changed."

And then there's prison itself, which takes a physical and psychological toll. "The health consequences are massive," she says. "Prison health care is astonishingly bad. I mean this on a physical and a mental health level. Let's say you are receiving mental health medication and you have a stable combination—and it's hard to find a combination of medications that works for most people. You go to prison and they're going to put you on the meds *they* want, or sometimes no meds, or sometimes bad meds." That can do lifelong damage. And while it's common, Emily says it's not the worst she's seen. "I know a woman who gave birth in prison and instead of providing her with the C-section she needed, they broke her hip," Emily says. "She delivered through a broken pelvis while shackled."

Many, if not most, of the women giving birth in prisons today—often without comprehensive care, let alone choice in the delivery room—are Millennials. Statistics here are hard to come by, but Millennials just may be the most incarcerated generation in America (although Gen Xers took a big hit, too). Even though incarceration rates have gone down in the last decade or so, the United States still imprisons more people than any other country in the history of the world, both in terms of raw numbers and in terms of proportion of the population. Most of these people are under thirty-five. A disproportionate number of them are black and brown.

Millennials are also heavily policed. A 2011 study published in the journal *Pediatrics* found that nearly one in three young people—today's Millennials—said they had been arrested before their twenty-third birthday. While the imprisonment rate has fallen dramatically for black Millennial men, it was so high to start that even its current rate—4.7 percent—remains outrageous. And even today's lower incarceration rates are 500 percent higher than they were forty years ago.

Boomers, of course, did not escape incarceration. One need only look at the enforcement of Jim Crow laws, the history of the civil rights movement, and the entirety of American existence to understand that black people have always been heavily policed on American soil. The Fugitive Slave Act gave law enforcement formal permission to track down black people seeking basic freedom and fleeing for their lives. In the *New York Times*'s 1619 Project, Supreme Court litigator and Equal Justice Initiative founder Bryan Stevenson wrote that in 1664, Maryland effectively sentenced all resident black people to hard labor for life, enslavement that "would be sustained by the threat of brutal punishment." And while the Thirteenth Amendment is read as ending slavery, it also "made an exception for those convicted of crimes," Stevenson wrote. "After emancipation, black people, once seen as less than fully human 'slaves,' were seen as less than fully human 'criminals.'" In place of slavery came "Black Codes" regulating free African Americans, "making the criminal-justice system central to new strategies of racial control." This is also the argument legal scholar Michelle Alexander makes in her book *The New Jim Crow*: There is a straight line from slavery to what she calls the "racial caste system" of Jim Crow to the modern-day prison system. The kind of widespread policing, military-style tactics, and high rates of incarceration that Millennials of color across the country have endured are a continuation of this brutality.

Jeffery Robinson is the deputy legal director and director of the Trone Center for Justice and Equality at the ACLU. Growing up in the 1960s in Memphis, Tennessee, he says, "the lessons I was learning as a child were the same lessons my father learned as a child and his father learned as a child. And that was: Be very, very careful. White people will kill you for no reason whatsoever. Our lives are at risk. If you ever encounter a police officer, here are the things you do not to get killed." Jeff remembers being eleven years old and watching the National Guard roll down the street, .50-caliber machine guns perched on the backs of their jeeps—it was 1968, and African Americans had been protesting on behalf of sanitation workers, and faced violence and arrest for their efforts. "My dad took me to the court hearings, and I saw these lawyers representing people who have been arrested," Jeff says. "Some of them were people I had been raised to respect and look up to: teachers, ministers. I saw these lawyers and I thought, Oh my God, that looks so cool."

In the '80s and '90s, "they were giving forty-, fifty-year sentences like it was ice cream and cake."

He graduated from Harvard Law in 1981 and watched the war on drugs and the rising tide of incarceration from a front-row seat: he spent most of his career as a criminal defense lawyer. In the '80s and '90s, he said, "they were giving forty-, fifty-year sentences like it was ice cream and cake. The judges thought they were doing the right thing, the prosecutors thought they were doing the right thing, and defense lawyers were saying, 'This is insane. This is going to destroy this person's family. This is out of line with the seriousness of the conduct.'"

In other words, Jeff says, it's not true that we were collectively blind to the harms of mass incarceration as it was scaling up. Some people—many of them Boomers—were in fact sounding the alarm. But their warnings went unheeded.

That meant Millennials were brought up in a nation in which widespread jailing, particularly of black and brown people, was the norm. "If you look at that famous statistic that one in three black men between eighteen and thirty-five will be incarcerated in his lifetime, that statistic is nationwide," Emily says. "So if you're looking at a community like Compton or the Bronx, you're looking at a community where those numbers are actually much higher. If you're a young man growing up in one of those hyperpoliced, hypersurveilled neighborhoods, you're living in a world where most, if not all, of the adult men you know have had experience with the criminal legal system or have been put in the cage at some point in their life, where the likelihood of that happening for you feels inevitable, and where that feeling of inevitably feels even more significant given the way that police interact with young people in these communities."

This is a recipe for criminalization of children, distrust, and trauma.

"For young people, every day when you leave the house, there are officers who you know, who have fucked with you every single day from the time you were maybe ten or eleven years old," Emily continues. "Growing up in the world where cops are stopping you, searching you, making fun of you, punishing you if you talk back, threatening you, arresting you for no reason, on a daily basis, it creates a very different perspective on authority, on the system, on who it's there to protect. You have a whole generation of people who have grown up with no belief in the whole 'serve and protect' claim, but who do know that the cages are there waiting as a trap."

Many Millennials also carry the trauma of having a parent behind bars—even as they face that possibility themselves. From 1991, the late-middle of the Millennial birth boom, to 2007, when the youngest Millennials were just entering middle school, the number of American kids with a mother in prison more than doubled. According to the Center for American Progress, one in four black Millennial children, and one in three of those born in the nineties, grew up with a family member behind bars (for white Millennials, it was closer to one in ten). Incarceration affected black Baby Boomers, too, 26.4 percent of whom said they also had a family member incarcerated at some point in their lives. But more often than not, these Boomers were adults (fewer than 15 percent of black children had a family member in jail in the 1950s and 1960s, when Boomers were born).

This makes for a generation of wounded and destabilized kids growing up in homes that have been torn apart. Families where a parent is or has been incarcerated are less likely to have other markers of financial stability and social mobility, the things that enable them to participate in the broader economy, plan for the future, and maybe even get ahead: buy a car, open a bank account, own a home. And that's not compared to the population generally; it's compared to families who are similarly situated in terms of socioeconomics, neighborhood, health status, demographics, and behavioral characteristics.

Young children who have a father sent to prison are more likely to be depressed and to act out than kids who don't. Kids with an incarcerated parent are six times more likely to be incarcerated down the line. Their education suffers, and they grow up poorer. For significant numbers of Millennials, and especially Millennials of color, these challenges shaped their lives.

So why did this happen? A lot of people point to for-profit prisons as one major factor fueling mass incarceration. And that's partly right—turning incarceration into a profitable industry, with shareholders who wanted to see industry expansion every quarter, was a predictable recipe for rank abuse and a massively expanded prison system. But for-profit prisons, odious as they are, remain a relatively small percentage of corrections institutions nationwide. The push for mass incarceration has been less about money and more about power. And power, in the United States, has always been tied to a system of racial hierarchy that puts white people on top, sows fear of racial minorities, and promises that white safety is contingent on black subjugation and confinement. "You have a generation of politicians who could use 'tough on crime' as a really reliable political theme," Emily Galvin-Almanza explains. "Scaring people into feeling unsafe and then telling them you can make them safe is one of the most effective ways to get into power."

Now that we're older and have a little more power, Millennials are taking up the charge to end private prisons, shift the focus to treatment and rehabilitation, and fight crime using community solutions rather than primarily punitive systems. In late May 2020, a police officer pressed his knee into George Floyd's neck for more than eight minutes, cutting off Floyd's ability to breathe and eventually killing him while onlookers objected and recorded. Video of Floyd's death sparked a national outcry. Protesters, most of them under forty, took to the streets and braved extreme police violence to say *enough*. And this was not the first battle in a war against abusive policing and incarceration that has seen important, if incremental, successes. That statistic Emily cited, that one in three black men would go to jail? That was from 2001, near the peak of America's incarceration of black men. Since then, and to the credit of prison reform advocates, it's fallen by 20 percent. Still, Marc Mauer, executive director of the Sentencing Project, told the *Washington Post* that even low estimates still put one in four black men in jail at some point in their lives. Jeff Robinson raised his young nephew, and when the boy turned thirteen, Jeff recalls a painful conversation. "I'm telling him some of the same things my father told me: If the cops come up to you, make sure your hands are out of your pockets. Say 'Yes, sir, no, sir.' Ask if you can reach for your identification. Don't make any sudden movements. And I'm sitting here telling him this stuff, and inside I'm going, *This is fucking pitiful.*"

The systems that incarcerated so many, it turns out, were far easier to build than they are to dismantle. But Millennials are working on it, brick by brick.

Making the Mess of the Millennium

The scourge of mass incarceration may seem unconnected to Millennials' culture of overwork, or to the rank inequality and financial precariousness that shape our decision-making. But all three can be tied to one person: the first Boomer-elected president, Ronald Reagan.

While Boomers split their votes between Reagan and Carter in 1980, they went overwhelmingly for Reagan by 1984, the first presidential election in which the whole generation was eligible to vote. And the youngest Boomers voted for Reagan in larger numbers than did older ones. Many Boomers do not think this was an error: they still tell Pew pollsters that Reagan was the best president of their lifetimes. True, they are an incredibly polarized generation, split down the middle between conservatives and liberals. (Nearly as many Boomers said Democrat Bill Clinton was their favorite president.) But the conservatives have usually come out on top, as they did with Reagan.

Here's what Reagan did: famously promising "trickle-down economics," he enriched the top, slashing tax rates for the wealthiest Americans and tipping the lives of everyone else into instability. While top marginal income tax rates exceeded 90 percent in the 1950s and '60s (and decreased to 70 percent in the 1970s), Reagan slashed them through the 1980s: by the end of his time in office, the rate for the highest earners was just 28 percent. His political heirs, George W. Bush and Donald Trump—both Baby Boomers themselves, and both elected by Baby Boomers—have done the same, while tax havens further allow companies to squirrel away hundreds of billions of dollars. In his many books and articles on the subject, Nobel Prize–winning economist Joseph E. Stiglitz draws a straight line from the Reagan tax cuts to the extreme wealth inequality that now plagues America—a gap that is only growing for Millennials, due to wealth-hoarding at the tip-top and stagnating wages.

At the same time, politicians have refused to raise the federal minimum wage, which has also contributed to stagnating wages and the shameful fact that an American worker can have a full-time job and still live in poverty. And while a great many Boomers were born into families that grew incrementally more affluent thanks to a glut of fairly paid blue-collar jobs and the strong unions that ensured decent pay, predictable schedules, and basic safety standards, conservative Boomer adults have gutted union power. In 1983, the Economic Policy Institute found, nearly a quarter of workers were in unions. Today, it's barely over one in ten. That same Boomer-inherited hyperindividualism that eventually manifested as Millennial rise 'n' grind hustle culture began, when Millennials were children, to dismantle the collective bargaining power of unions and their ability to find strength in numbers. Now, most American workers are on their own, with disastrous results.

That a lot of potential workers are behind bars or on parole can also be traced to Boomer fave Reagan. Boomers (and disproportionately black Boomers) were impacted by mass incarceration, too, while white Boomers were the political force that fueled it. Let's be clear: Boomers did not invent racism or the policing and punishment of black people; in America, that predated them by approximately three hundred years. But the majority-white Boomer generation maintained, and in many devastating ways exacerbated, the centuries-long project of criminalizing black people and placing them in bondage. Prison populations began increasing in the 1970s after President Richard Nixon launched his war on drugs, but they truly took off in the 1980s, 1990s, and 2000s. Reagan set the forces in motion, nearly doubling the prison population during his tenure in the White House, and those numbers grew exponentially, including under Clinton and George W. Bush (to be fair, incarceration rates started to go down, very slowly, under Boomer president Barack Obama).

Finally, the federal and state governments have been frustratingly inconsistent when it comes to enforcing the civil rights legislation that enabled many Boomers to get a little piece of the American pie. That legislation wasn't Boomer-made—their parents and those a few years older can mostly take credit for it—but Boomers were entrusted with the enforcement of civil rights rules outlawing discrimination based on race or gender in jobs, housing, and education. There have certainly been some valiant efforts. Overall, though, Boomers have eviscerated, rather than expanded, the basic protections that sought to make sure all Americans had a fair shake at work, in school, and in finding a place to live.

Millennials are living with the consequences.

Millennials make up close to a quarter of the US population, but hold just 3% of the wealth. When Boomers were our age, they held 21%.

The precipitous rise in education costs since the 1990s means that the average Millennial owes $33,000 in student loan debt, and even in their early thirties still owes $15,000. When the average Boomer was a young thirtysomething, their educational debts amounted to just $2,300 in today's dollars.

We are both more likely than our parents to have a degree and more likely to live in poverty. One in five Millennials, and one in four black Millennials, lives in poverty. If not for the social safety net, we would be vastly impoverished.

Just 32% of Millennials own their homes, compared with 75% of Boomers.

Millennials are the best-educated generation in American history: more than a third of us hold a college degree, compared to just one in ten young adults in 1960. And yet Millennials are worse off financially: we earn, on average, 20% less than Boomers did at our age.

When weighing debt against income and assets, Millennials are the brokest adults in American history, and on track to be the first American generation to do worse than our parents.

MONEY

Call us Generation Debt.

Millennials are overeducated and underwater. Our generation is the most credentialed in American history, and the most broke. Our degrees came with hefty price tags, and our earnings haven't caught up to our qualifications. Sixty-one percent of Millennials have gone to college, and close to half hold a postsecondary degree. By comparison, only about a quarter of Boomers hold a four-year degree. In 1960, when the oldest Boomers were starting high school, US Census data shows that just one in ten Americans older than twenty-four had completed a college education.

But Millennials are paying for those degrees, and we're paying a lot more than Boomers did. Take your average Boomer born in the first year of the baby boom. If this average guy went off to a public four-year college in 1964, he paid around $7,900 (adjusted, like the rest of these figures, to 2020 dollars) in tuition, fees, and room and board for the year. Opting for a private school would mean paying just under $16,000.

Now take your average Millennial born in 1980, our generation's first year. If she started at a four-year public college in 1998, she was looking at about $12,250 in tuition, fees, and room and board for that year alone; a year of private school education would set her back more than $31,500. And her Gen Z cousin, born in the first year of his generation? He paid a massive $20,900 as a freshman at a public school in 2015. If he opted for a private four-year college, he was looking at an astronomical $47,000 for his freshman year alone. That's nearly a 300 percent increase in private education costs compared to what the freshman Boomer paid.

Upon finishing college, older Millennials were hit hard by the Great Recession of 2008, which thrust huge numbers of us into unemployment and ground our earning potential to a near halt. All of this hit black and brown Millennials even harder: non-white American families had less wealth to begin with, which meant more debt for their children, and racial discrimination made entering and remaining in the workforce even more challenging for African American and Hispanic Millennials.

Let's dispel the myth that a college education makes you wealthier. It is true that having a college degree will get you higher wages than if you had only graduated from high school (or if you had not made it that far). But that's largely because the wages of Americans without college degrees have collapsed, making college graduates better paid by comparison. In 2019, the Stanford Center for the Study of Poverty and Inequality found that the median earnings of a twenty-five-year-old college-educated Millennial man were more or less on par with what college-educated Gen Xers and Baby Boomers men earned at the same age. But Millennial men without college degrees were bottoming out, making close to $10,000 less a year than Baby Boomers made at the same age. "It's not that going to college amounts to striking gold for most people," the center's director, David Grusky, told the *Stanford News*. "The big news is that if you don't go to college you're likely to do worse than ever. What makes college attractive is mainly that it offers some protection from that fate."

And consider this: if not for the social safety net, Millennials would be the most impoverished generation in modern American history. That same Stanford report found that while the number of Millennials living in poverty at thirty looks, at first glance, to be on par with Gen X and better than Baby Boomer and Silent Generation thirty-year-olds, that's only because Millennials receive a lot more in SNAP (food stamps) benefits, unemployment, and Social Security and SSI (Supplemental Security Income, cash assistance for the aging and people with disabilities). "Were it not for resources coming from government programs," the authors write, "the millennial poverty rate at age thirty would be the *highest* across the four generations."

And even with those benefits, more Millennial households live in poverty than any other generation. Millennials at age twenty-five—even those with high levels of education—are more likely to be unemployed than twenty-five-year-olds in any generation before. Despite being better educated, nearly half of us

Sixty-one percent of Millennials have gone to college, and close to half hold a postsecondary degree. By comparison, only about a quarter of Boomers hold a four-year degree.

have worse jobs than our parents did, and are, as a result, downwardly mobile. "By every metric, this generation is the most educated in American history," writes Malcolm Harris, in *Kids These Days: Human Capital and the Making of Millennials*. "Yet Millennials are worse off economically than their parents, grandparents, and even great-grandparents."

Millennials are behind. We have waited longer than our Boomer parents did to get married, have children, or buy a home—and we may never do any of that. And despite what you've heard from yelling TV commentators, we're not actually choosing to be broke, insecure, and alone. We already weathered what was supposed to be a once-in-a-lifetime Great Recession, beginning our working years in the worst job market in nearly a century. Now, we're facing a second global crisis, which may be even more shocking in its magnitude and devastating in its impact. We're watching the economy crash around us with the growing, gnawing fear that we might never be okay.

Degree-Rich, Cash-Poor

When Maddie Campbell was growing up, the path ahead was clear: go to college, get married, work a well-paying job, live in a nice house in an upscale suburb. That's what her parents had done: Maddie's mom had grown up in Dallas, Texas, and as a child she would point out one particular big house in her neighborhood. "I'm going to live there someday," she would say.

In 2007, Maddie's mother moved into her dream house. It was six bedrooms plus a guest house on two acres of land, a shimmering, palatial fantasy come to life. Maddie's father was a freelance video producer, and he did well—few people had the pricey equipment required for video production, or the resources to buy, for example, the one-terabyte data storage unit he purchased in 1994 for $600,000. Maddie's mother was a writer, mostly for high-end home and leisure publications.

A year later, the recession hit.

Video production work dried up as personal technology developed at a head-spinning pace. That massive one-terabyte data storage unit that had, just a decade before, set Maddie's dad apart as a member of the technologically elite? Now you can buy an external hard drive with that much memory at Best Buy for $50—and it's small enough to fit in your back pocket. The first iPhone was released in June 2007, and suddenly, it seemed like everyone was carrying around their own tiny personal computer, complete with a video camera and editing tools.

"Before it was like, is my mom going to go to Neiman's or Nordstrom today?" Maddie (who is using a pseudonym to protect her privacy) says. "Now, my parents have to decide between paying bills or buying groceries."

The house went into foreclosure. The bills mounted, and the good life ground to a halt. The reversal of fortunes was stunning not just in its significance but in its speed. "One Christmas when you're eleven or twelve, you're getting all these awesome new tech gifts and fancy stuff and you live in a nice house," Maddie recalls. "And the next Christmas it's like, we're jamming out on socks."

Maddie, a younger Millennial, was just entering high school when her parents were wiped out by the economic downturn. She watched their resources dry up, and her own—her college fund, mostly invested in the stock market, bottomed out. The family began a series of downwardly mobile moves: from their six-bedroom Texas estate into a two-bed, one-bath rental apartment in St. Louis, Missouri, then to a vacation rental in Orange Beach, Alabama, and finally to a house in Jacksonville, Florida. The reverberations of the recession fundamentally shaped Maddie's view of the world, as they did for much of her generation. "I've witnessed a lot of instability culturally as I've grown up," Maddie says. "It makes me want to help other people as much as I can with what I do have. But it also makes me very concerned for my clear and immediate future."

Like many people her age, Maddie grew up believing that a college education was the clear path to financial stability. That assumption wasn't necessarily wrong. The American economy shifted radically during and after the Cold War, with rapidly expanding opportunities in technology and the sciences, and in what became known as the "information economy": jobs that required high-level knowledge, expertise, and proficiency. By the time Maddie and other Millennials were in their early years of primary education, clear divides had already emerged between the relatively prosperous college-educated "haves" and the struggling high-school-or-less have-nots. For the middle class, a bachelor's degree, not a high school diploma, was increasingly the new baseline for a decent job. Troops of college admissions professionals filled out a higher education bureaucracy that created additional and allegedly meritocratic hoops for high schoolers to jump through—the SAT and the ACT, admissions packets and essays, interviews and volunteerism requirements—and also worked to advertise college as a necessary leg up for a broad cross-section of American young people. If Maddie wanted the trappings of the pre-recession good life she grew up with, she knew—like so many of her peers—that college was the best way to get there.

In 2014, Maddie headed off to the University of Kansas, part of a massive student wave: between 2000, when the oldest Millennials were coming of age and graduating from high school, and 2019, when the youngest were finishing their university years, college enrollment went up by more than 3.7 million students. In 1980, fewer than half of graduating high school seniors were college-bound. By 2009, 70 percent of them were.

1980　　　　　　　**2009**

In 1980, fewer than half of graduating high school seniors were college-bound. By 2009, 70 percent of them were.

That's a stunning shift. In a single generation, a significant majority of graduating high schoolers heeded the advice of those who claimed to know best: that if we wanted to succeed, we had to go to college.

For the wealthy and to a lesser extent the middle class, that promise was true. If you were born into a wealthy family in the 1970s and you went to college, you had about a 50-50 chance of finishing. If you were born into similarly privileged circumstances in the 1980s and went to college, you had a 60 percent chance of getting a degree and enjoying the attendant boost in pay, health, and even happiness.

But the same isn't true of students who grew up poor. While many more young people who grew up in low-wealth households are attending college—among Millennials, close to half enrolled—they have the same depressing graduation prospects they did decades ago: only about 12 percent actually graduate. And low-income college students are predictably more likely to take out loans to pay for college, leaving many of them deep in debt with nothing to show for it. Those numbers are even more stark for African American students, who are more likely to withdraw from higher education than they are to complete their degrees in six years.

It's not that poor students are less able to hack it at college; it's more likely that they're working and even raising children while trying to attend classes, and can't do it all. The archetypal college experience of the 1978 classic *Animal House* or late-nineties television drama *Felicity*—living in a dorm or a Greek house, playing Frisbee on the quad, and gaining the freshman 15 from binge drinking and eating dining hall food—is for the privileged few. While 62 percent of Americans think most first-year college students live on campus, in reality just 13 percent do, according to a 2018 report from Higher Learning Advocates, an education advocacy group. About 30 percent of college students are the first in their families to go to college. More than a quarter have children. Among financially independent students, 40 percent live at or below the poverty line. Unsurprisingly, most of these students work. A report by the Georgetown University Center on Education and the Workforce found that while some 70 percent of college students generally work for pay while also attending classes, about a quarter work full-time, and those full-

In a single generation, a significant majority of graduating high schoolers heeded the advice of those who claimed to know best: that if we wanted to succeed, we had to go to college.

time workers are more likely to be low-income. And students who worked more than fifteen hours a week received poorer grades than students who worked less, and were more likely to drop out. Students who drop out are the most likely to default on their student loans.

Americans now owe $1.5 trillion in student loan debt.

Maddie is one of them. Just weeks into her first year at the University of Kansas, she was raped by a football player after a Halloween party. For two years, she unsuccessfully tried to tamp down the residual effects of the attack—anxiety, depression, post-traumatic stress disorder. When one of her rowing team-mates told her that she had been raped by the same guy, Maddie cracked. The two women reported their assaults to KU, but Maddie says that the school did little to help her, let alone level swift and appropriate consequences against her attacker (KU eventually settled the Title IX lawsuit Maddie filed against them, but with no admission of liability or wrongdoing). Here Maddie was also depressingly representative of her generation: nearly one in four undergraduate women in 2015—Millennials—experienced sexual assault on campus, a study by the Association of American Universities found. Struggling academically, Maddie withdrew from school, moved home, and, she says, spent the next year "lying on the couch in the fetal position." Leaving college meant that Maddie's loans came out of deferment; she needed to re-enroll or figure out a way to pay them. So even though she didn't feel ready, she went off to New York University.

Between two years at the University of Kansas, a year off, and two years at New York University, Maddie accumulated about $100,000 in student loan debt. Her parents, who have their own loans and took several out on Maddie's behalf, owe twice that.

This makes Maddie something of an outlier. A CNBC examination of Federal Reserve data shows that among Millennials in their twenties who hold educational debt, the average amount owed is more than $22,000. Close to 70 percent of 2019 graduates from four-year colleges owe money on a student loan, and the average grad owes nearly $30,000. But about one in ten Millennials owes, like Maddie, student loan debt in the six figures. When Boomers were in their early thirties, just 17 percent of them had educational debt to begin with; and among those who did, the average amount owed was about $5,600 (yes, that is adjusted for inflation).

Millennials were also raised on the narrative that going to a *good* college mattered. And "a good college" was often assumed to mean "a private college," which meant more expensive. All of this meant higher college costs and greater student loan debt.

The big question is: Was it worth it? By one calculation, yes: yawning income inequality means that higher education is more necessary than ever, not to live in luxury but just to white-knuckle it into the middle class. You see this play out in the difference a degree makes. In 1980, when the first Millennials were born and Boomers were young adults, a bachelor's degree earned you a 42 percent pay bump, while an advanced degree got you

62 percent more. By 2018, as a result of collapsing blue-collar wages, a person with a bachelor's degree earned, on average, 77 percent more than a person with a high school diploma or less, and someone with an advanced degree earned 129 percent more. Today, a person with a college degree makes roughly the same amount as someone with only a high school education in 1989. Meanwhile, the cost of a four-year college education increased by 200 *percent*, and graduate degrees became 350 percent pricier. Wages, though, have not increased in real terms since the 1970s, which means we're making the same but spending much, much more. For many Millennials, the burden of student debt may wipe out whatever income boost their degrees gave them.

Was it worth it? Well, you do the math.

Boom Times

It's November 8, 1965, and President Lyndon B. Johnson is standing at a podium in the gymnasium of Southwest Texas State College, his alma mater. Men in jackets and women in knee-length dresses sit ramrod straight in the folding chairs covering the gym floor. The bleachers are filled to the top with onlookers. It's the president's first public appearance since his kidney stone and gallbladder surgery, and it's an event: when he arrived on the San Marcos, Texas, campus, the school band greeted him with a rendition of the "Lyndon Baines Johnson March." Now, as he announces one of the most significant achievements of his presidency, Johnson promises that his Higher Education Act will redefine America's future, as his education at Southwest Texas State did for him. "Here the seeds were planted from which grew my firm conviction that for the individual, education is the path to achievement and fulfillment," he intones in his Texas drawl. "For the nation, it is a path to a society that is not only free but civilized; and for the world, it is the path to peace—for it is education that places reason over force."

Several decades, hundreds of thousands of students, and $2.6 billion later, the act hasn't brought world peace, but it was nonetheless an unmitigated success in enabling hundreds of thousands of Americans to go to college. Even in 1965, Johnson understood the power of his legislation, which funneled millions of federal dollars into public colleges, offered scholarships and eventually low-interest loans to students in need, and established a National Teacher Corps to serve under-resourced areas. With his wife, Lady Bird, and one of his college professors nearby, Johnson told the packed gym that his ambitions were nothing short of radical. This legislation "will swing open a new door for the young people of America," he proclaimed. "For them, and for this entire land of ours, it is the most important door that will ever open—the door to education. This legislation is the key which unlocks it."

That new door did indeed swing wide open. Baby Boomers flooded into higher education in record numbers. Public colleges and universities were affordable—a summer job could cover most of the expenses—and newly generous federal and state government grants covered most, if not all, of the rest.

For Millennials, this sounds unbelievably luxe. While educational assistance still exists (if you paid part of your college expenses with a Pell Grant, a Stafford loan, or a federally funded work-study job, you can thank the Higher Education Act), when Boomers were going to college, there was more free money to go around, and no expectation that students would take on an extraordinary debt load: grants made up a greater share of financial aid dollars than loans.

Well-deserved credit for this easy access to higher education goes to Boomers' parents and elders. The newfound prosperity after World War II meant that the US experienced an unprecedented baby boom alongside an extraordinary economic one. It was a moment of expansion and optimism, at least for the white families who had long seen American law and policy cater to their needs. A new economy, one requiring skilled labor, was emerging. By the time Boomers came of age, profound cultural shifts were also well underway, with young people—some of them older Boomers, some of them a generation older than that—pushing for an end to race and gender discrimination, and for greater equality overall. It's hard to overstate just how far of a jump Boomers made in a single generation. In 1960, just a few years before the Higher Education Act was signed, more than 40 percent of American adults hadn't gone to school *past eighth grade*. The average American had a tenth-grade education. Fewer than 10 percent had a college degree. By the mid-1980s, when the last of the Boomers were graduating from college, the proportion of Americans with a college degree had tripled.

The Higher Education Act was just one part of Johnson's Great Society program, an ambitious agenda to combat poverty and make America a leader in education, health, and development. States did their part, too, contributing more than half of public education funds by the mid-1970s. In 1989, when most Boomers were in their twenties and early thirties, just 17 percent of twentysomethings held educational debt. And there was a clear relationship between the financial benefits of a college education and any debt incurred: the higher pay that came with a college degree justified the debt Boomers took on.

Boomers have been, from the time they came of age and for most of their adult lives, the largest American generation in history (until Millennials overtook them sometime between 2016 and 2019). Public policy radically evolved to meet their needs and cushion their entry into adulthood, even as the booming economy of their childhoods took a turn for the worse as they entered the job market. No, Boomers didn't always have it easy in their early years of independence. But their parents had scrimped and saved and set up a system of public works that worked for them, helping to keep Boomers afloat and later enabling them to prosper, even as the economy suffered. But as Boomers came to power in city, state, and federal government, something shifted: while they hoarded resources for their own families, any sense of obligation to open doors for the next generation of young people seemed to recede. Boomers entered adulthood with few financial constraints and climbed steadily up the socioeconomic rungs, doing far better than their parents.

And then they pulled the ladder up behind them.

The Great Student Loan Plunder

Contrary to idealized images of Boomers as the Woodstock hippies, feminists, and civil rights activists of the 1960s and 70s, most of those agitators and culture-makers weren't Boomers at all. While some of the very oldest participated in these movements, most of the generation actually came of age later, and younger Boomers in particular wound up much more conservative. Those famous bra-burning feminists protesting the Miss America pageant in New Jersey? That was in 1968, when babies born at the peak of the boom were just eleven years old (and for the record, no bras were actually burned). The generation-defining Woodstock festival? The oldest of the Boomers might have been in attendance—they were in their very early twenties—but the youngest hadn't started kindergarten. When Martin Luther King Jr. gave his famous "I have a dream" speech in the shadow of the Lincoln Memorial, the youngest Boomers weren't even born.

By the early eighties, Boomers made up a plurality of the electorate. And the first thing they did was usher Ronald Reagan into office, drawn in by his promise of lower taxes and trickle-down economics. Just days before the 1984 election, the *New York*

Times ran an article titled "Making Mark on Politics, 'Baby Boomers' Appear to Rally Around Reagan." It included a thirty-six-year-old Merrimack, New Hampshire, homemaker named Mary Beator, who seemed to be speaking for many in her cohort when she said, "I'm tired of being the middle class that pays for all of those giveaways."

"I guess I have more to lose now," she continued. "I've gotten attached to my creature comforts. I've started having a vested interest in the status quo, because I am the status quo."

It was, as Ronald Reagan put it, morning in America.

That fertile financial landscape Boomers enjoyed was about to be razed for their children. The first thing Reagan did was declare war on Johnson's Great Society, kneecapping or wholly obliterating many of the same programs that enabled Boomers to do better than their parents. Johnson's Great Society, tellingly, sold its antipoverty programs on the image of *white* poverty: When Johnson went on a national tour to promote the program, he first dropped in on communities across Appalachia; *Life* magazine illustrated Johnson's crusade with images of white families living in squalor in eastern Kentucky. Reagan, eager to erase Great Society gains, portrayed poverty as a black problem fueled by sloth, criminality, and crack cocaine. That made anti-poverty programs, and progressive social programs generally, less popular among the whites who were the majority of the electorate.

> **"I've started having a vested interest in the status quo, because I am the status quo."**

When he took office in 1981, Reagan cut taxes and ran up the national debt, leaving that bill to be paid off down the line. His administration quickly set about dismantling various aspects of the Higher Education Act, making it harder for college students to qualify for need-based aid. And while Reagan slashed grant-based aid, guaranteed student *loan* aid continued unabated—that is, the government gave away less money for higher education but made it easier for students to borrow. With decreasing public investment in education and loans increasingly available to make up for the significant grant shortfall, tuitions went through the roof, and in response, the federal government raised the ceiling on the amount of loans students could take out. This was where the seeds of today's student debt crisis were planted.

In 1989, Dan Quayle became the first Baby Boomer to join the executive branch as George H. W. Bush's vice president. At the end of Bush's term, Congress made another round of disastrous changes to the Higher Education Act. Tuition and enrollment continued to surge, but Congress failed to expand Pell Grants and instead increased the amount that parents and students could borrow. And while federally subsidized loans had been subject to need requirements, a new category of unsubsidized loans became available regardless of financial need. Borrowing exploded.

In 1992, voters elected the first Baby Boomer president: Bill Clinton. As a candidate he had promised to do something about the growing student debt crisis, and as president he tried to fundamentally alter the system by making the government the direct lender, administering rather than simply guaranteeing the loans. The Clinton plan came under fire from privatization-happy Republicans; the conflict threatened to torpedo his direct-loan plan entirely.

And so Clinton played ball with the GOP, signing a bill that preserved his direct-loan program in exchange for privatizing Sallie Mae, the federal middleman that had been established in 1972 as a way to offer federally backed student loans to a greater number of students. Clinton's compromise gave educational institutions the choice of whether to rely on direct federal loans for student aid or go with Sallie Mae. Making the government the direct lender would be cheaper, Clinton believed. He gambled that as students and schools relied on his direct-loan program, Sallie Mae would quickly cease to be relevant.

This bet backfired spectacularly. Sallie Mae transitioned from government-sponsored enterprise to private entity driven by shareholder profit. Unfettered by government restriction, it could be its own federally backed lender, collection agency, and private lender, increasingly offering students a mash-up of low-interest federal loans and higher-interest private ones (offering fewer opportunities for loan forgiveness), and then chasing down any delinquents. The company's aggressive marketing arm also convinced colleges and universities the nation over to rely on Sallie Mae over direct federal lending, sometimes offering financial incentives to get schools to abandon the direct-lending program. A Republican-dominated Congress, on the other hand, formally barred the Department of Education from advertising their own direct-loan program. That the government's direct-

MONEY | 85

lending program was an inefficient bureaucratic mess didn't help. Within just a few years, Sallie Mae had cornered the market on student lending. The company made billions.

By 1999, Boomers made up a majority of the House of Representatives. One of those Boomers, Lindsey Graham, then a congressman from South Carolina, was one of the first to make a novel argument: that private student loan debt should not be dischargeable in bankruptcy. This proposal soon found support. It was added to the Bankruptcy Abuse Prevention and Consumer Protection Act, sweeping legislation that radically overhauled American bankruptcy laws and was widely backed by credit card companies. When the bill landed on Clinton's desk, though, he vetoed it, reportedly because his wife talked him out of signing it. Hillary, the *New York Times* later reported, had been briefed on the law's potentially disastrous effects by a law professor named Elizabeth Warren.

A little more than five years later, though, the Bankruptcy Abuse Prevention and Consumer Protection Act gained bipartisan support in Congress. By then the new president in the White House was a business-friendly Republican: George W. Bush. He signed the bankruptcy overhaul bill into law in 2005, and students who took on private loans could no longer discharge them in bankruptcy. From 1999, when the bill came under consideration, and 2005, Sallie Mae, now a private company, spent $9 million lobbying Congress.

By 2015, more than 42 percent of twentysomethings (Millennials all) owed money on a student loan. Millennials owed much,

The average Millennial owes $33,000 in student loan debt. When the average Boomer was the same age, their educational debts amounted to just $2,300 in today's dollars.

much more than what their parents took on, and if those obligations pushed them underwater, the 2005 bankruptcy bill meant that they now couldn't treat their educational loans like nearly all forms of consumer debt and declare bankruptcy. Between 1980 and 2011, the cost of college increased sixfold (even adjusting for inflation, the price of tuition and fees at a four-year institution nearly tripled). At the same time, grants dropped. According to a Demos analysis, the maximum Pell Grant in 1980 covered about 70 percent of a college student's expenses at a four-year school. By 2011, it only covered a third. And while state financial aid was 100 percent need-based in 1980, that dipped to 73 percent by 2011. Private student loans filled the gap.

The 2005 bankruptcy bill was one final rung torn off the battered educational ladder that helped so many Boomers break into the middle and upper classes. And then, as the Bush presidency wound down, the Great Recession hit.

In the swirl of the 2008 financial crisis, the promise that college was the path to financial stability, let alone prosperity, was looking a little thin. But it was already clear that folks without degrees were doing even worse.

So instead of dealing with an unfriendly job market by gritting our teeth through underemployment and running up our credit cards to make ends meet, record numbers of us went to college. In 2000, 36 percent of eighteen- to-twenty-four-year-olds were enrolled in a two- or four-year degree program; by 2011, 42 percent were, a number that has now leveled off.

At the height of the recession, and in its wake, we also flooded into graduate school. Graduate school enrollment swelled 39 percent between 2000 and 2017. While only a small percentage of Millennials have graduate degrees, we still hold more graduate degrees than any other generation. And the costs are stark: according to New America, the average graduate of a professional program—the kind required to be, say, a lawyer or a doctor—leaves with $152,654 in cumulative student debt.

But college and graduate school had fundamentally changed. Systematic underinvestment by the federal government coupled with coffers emptied by the recession and newly generous student lending led states to slash funding for public college; as a result, tuitions rose. By 2018, state dollars spent on two- and four-year colleges had dropped by $6.6 billion, adjusted for inflation, from 2008. At the same time, tuition rose by more than

$2,500 a year, shifting the financial burden onto students. And as any college student can tell you, tuition isn't the only unbearable cost. Just about every aspect of going to college is several magnitudes more expensive today than it was for our parents. Textbook prices have increased more than 800 percent in the past thirty years; the average college student pays $1,200 for books every year. The cost of room and board has doubled, far outpacing inflation, and living on campus now costs nearly as much as renting on the general market. For Boomers, this wasn't the case: the cost of on-campus housing stayed more or less steady from 1964 to 1980, their prime college years. As of 2015, a student at a private four-year college could expect to pay nearly $11,000 annually for room and board; a student at a four-year public university paid more than $10,400.

There was no escape from rising costs. Public colleges and universities, once charged with educating middle- and low-income students in their own states, began acting more like private colleges. Out-of-state students paid more than in-state ones, which meant greater revenue. Public colleges thus began recruiting beyond their borders, often shifting need-based aid set aside for in-state students to "merit aid" aimed at attracting out-of-state ones.

For younger Millennials like Maddie Campbell, college was still on the horizon when the recession hit. But the landscape quickly became a lot less inviting, and many students had fewer tools to navigate it. Students whose college funds were invested in the stock market suddenly found themselves with numbers that didn't quite add up to tuition demands; others saw their parents, desperate from being plunged into debt themselves, drain those funds for survival.

Student loan debt, now not dischargeable in bankruptcy, had also been made lender-neutral—that is, as a result of the Bush bankruptcy law, students could take out loans to pay for education at sub-par for-profit institutions and would be unlikely to ever be able to discharge them. For-profit colleges operate by their own set of rules. Public colleges are funded largely by taxpayers and private educational institutions by tuition dollars and donations. Not-for-profit institutions are controlled by boards of trustees and exist primarily for education and research. For-profit colleges, by contrast, are basically corporations: they exist to make money, and are funded in part by investors who want to see returns. While most students who enroll in public or private colleges graduate in five years, students who enroll in for-profit institutions are far less likely to earn their degrees. Just 30 percent of graduates from for-profit colleges finish in less than five years.

But students pay whether they graduate or not, and now they could fund even a for-profit education by taking on student loans. A new moneymaking opportunity had blossomed, and predatory for-profit institutions proliferated, all on the backs of students who were young, unsophisticated, and disproportionately both nonwhite and the first in their family to go to college. These for-profit institutions, which educated a relatively small number of students at the turn of the millennium, more than quadrupled their enrollment in a decade. They charged high fees and offered few financial resources, while sometimes defrauding students with false claims about job placement and costs. Susan Dynarski, a professor of public policy, education, and economics at the University of Michigan, found that almost a million Millennials who had taken out loans to attend for-profit institutions went into repayment in 2011. About a quarter of them defaulted.

By 2010, student loan debt surpassed credit card debt.

"Boomers definitely benefited from accessing higher education, and that education translated for some of them into opportunities for rising and higher incomes," says Reid Cramer, who is a nonresident fellow at New America, the former director of its Millennials Initiative, and the author of *The Emerging Millennial Wealth Gap*. "And conversely, Millennials did everything they were supposed to do in a recession, which is go back to school and invest in yourself so that when the economy recovers, you're prepared to take advantage of that. They did that, they have more credentials than any other age group, but it hasn't translated into rising incomes."

Casualties of the Recession

Entering adulthood in five- and sometimes six-figure debt and looking for work just as a recession hit, the older half of the Millennial generation was screwed from the start. It took us longer to get work, and when we were hired, we were paid less—partly because of the economy, and partly because more of us entering the workforce were female, and black and brown, all categories of people who are systematically underemployed and undercompensated. The recession didn't just damage our immediate ability to support ourselves, nor even just our long-term moneymaking potential; it fundamentally undermined our faith in the promise that a good job would mean we were taken care of.

But with little other choice, we adapted. Many of us took jobs where we could find them, often as temps or interns or contractors. We might have resented it, but these insecure positions became the new normal—and so we weren't alarmed as crappy gig economy jobs with no benefits, basic worker protections, or even consistent hours proliferated. We even learned to make it seem like maybe we were choosing it all, that we preferred the flexibility offered by our #hustle. We learned the only people we could rely on were ourselves.

And, well, our parents.

The stereotype of the Millennial living in the parental basement is partly true: While most of us do in fact live independently, more young adults live with their parents today than at any time in the twentieth century. More than half of Millennials receive some sort of financial help from their parents, whether that's Dad paying a cellphone bill or Mom keeping the kids on her insurance until they turn twenty-six (thanks, Obamacare!). This reliance isn't because Millennials are lazy. It's

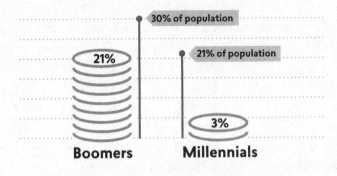

Percentage of Wealth

30% of population

21% of population

21%

3%

Boomers   **Millennials**

Millennials make up close to a quarter of the
US population, but hold just 3 percent of the wealth.
When Boomers were our age, they held 21 percent.

because we have more debt in a job market with more competition, less certainty, and fewer opportunities than Boomers had at our age.

And, unlike our Gen X predecessors, we didn't rack up credit card debt. More of us lived within our means and didn't open up credit card accounts at all. But that hurt us, too: we have the lowest credit scores of any other adult generation, and now we're getting rejected for mortgages, apartments, loans, and new credit cards as a result.

Now we're facing down the triple whammy of inflated housing costs, recession-suppressed incomes, and overwhelming student debt.

That was Maddie's trajectory. After graduating from NYU in 2018, Maddie wanted to stay in New York but quickly did the math: between student loan payments, exorbitant rents, and limited openings in her field of study, it didn't add up. So she moved back home with her parents in Jacksonville. She estimates she has applied to at least seven hundred full-time jobs in two years. She hasn't gotten a single one. But student loans don't wait for stability. To make her loan payments, she works gig jobs: she drove for Uber for a while and then delivered food for Uber Eats. She walked dogs for Wag and Rover. She babysits, house-sits, pet-sits. She's pretty good at video editing and her dad has the software, so she sometimes makes "In Memoriam" videos for funerals when people in her community pass away. Still, she hunts for work.

> There's nothing fun or glamorous about the gig economy, with its low wages, no benefits, and absurd demands.

"I hate the job search," Maddie says. "It's starting to grind me down." There's nothing fun or glamorous about the gig economy, with its low wages, no benefits, and absurd demands. "I would 100 percent not characterize myself as one of those 'rise 'n' grind, gotta hustle' types, no thank you," she says. "My ideal life is I live in a renovated Airstream van by the beach and I tour the country doing comedy. I want nothing to do with the hustle."

But ideal or not, hustle she does, because that student loan bill still comes every month.

And it's not as if Millennials who didn't go to college fared any better. The Great Recession meant wages stagnated across the board and nosedived for people with a high school degree or less. While the recession hurt everyone, Pew found the average decline in weekly wages was double for high school graduates compared to graduates of four-year colleges.

College-educated Millennials may be doing better than our peers without degrees, but the outlook is still bleak. According to Pew, "The median net worth of households headed by Millennials (ages twenty to thirty-five in 2016) was about $12,500 in 2016, compared with $20,700 for households headed by Boomers the same age in 1983."

And Boomers are pulling even further ahead while Millennials are languishing. You would expect that older folks, who have had decades to save, invest, and pay down their mortgages, would be wealthier than younger ones who are just starting their adult lives. Indeed, in 1998 the wealth gap between young workers and those within a decade of retirement age was significant: households headed by Americans aged fifty-two to seventy were worth about seven times as much as those headed by Americans twenty to thirty-five. In the ensuing twenty years, though, that wealth gap has nearly doubled, and Boomer households today are worth twelve times as much as Millennial ones. In fact, the average net worth of today's young households has *decreased* by $2,600. For those headed by fifty-two- to seventy-year-olds, it's ballooned by a whopping $452,400. In other words, today's young adults are worth less, adjusting for inflation, than people in that same age range were worth in 1998. The over-fifties are worth almost twice as much as that same age bracket was worth in 1998.

"A rising tide in our country is lifting some boats more than others," says Signe-Mary McKernan, vice president of labor, human services, and population at the Urban Institute. "Wealth inequality has worsened over the past fifty years. When we start to look at what groups are affected and what groups stand out, young Americans are one of the groups that stand out."

The average Millennial is worth just $8,000, less than adults of any generation in three decades. Even though the oldest are pushing forty, we make, on average, just over $35,500 a year— 20 percent less than Boomers made at our age. The massive wealth gap between Boomers and Millennials doesn't look like it will ever be bridged, even as Millennials age.

"Millennial families are barely breaking even with families the same age over three decades earlier," McKernan says. "At this point [in their lives], the Baby Boomers and Silent Generation were doing at least double as well as the previous generations."

While we scramble to support ourselves, we're also footing the bill for our Boomer parents' golden years. Americans are living longer, and as huge numbers of Boomers age, Social Security and health care costs are skyrocketing. "Folks my father's age like to say they've paid for those benefits, so they should get them in full," wrote Jim Tankersley for the *Washington Post*, in a 2015 article titled "Baby Boomers Are What's Wrong with America's Economy." "But they haven't. The Urban Institute has estimated that a typical couple retiring in 2011, at the leading edge of the Boomer wave, will end up drawing about $200,000 more from Medicare and Social Security than they paid in taxes to support those programs. Because Social Security benefits increase faster than inflation, Boomers will enjoy bigger checks from the program, in real terms, than their parents did."

Meanwhile, Boomer entitlement programs have been bolstered by Boomer politicians (and conservative Boomer voters) at the expense of investments in the young. When Boomers were entering the job market, the federal government spent $3 on future investments— things like research, education, and infrastructure—for every $1 it spent on entitlements like Medicare, Medicaid, and Social Security. Now those numbers are reversed. Entitlement spending will reach $5 for every $1 investment by the time Boomers are fully retired. At the same time, Boomers look at how Millennials are struggling and blame us for our alleged bad decision-making.

Americans are living longer, and as huge numbers of Boomers age, Social Security and health care costs are skyrocketing.

Here's the thing: Millennials are happy to invest in our parents and our elders. We want them to have stable retirements. We want them to be able to afford the medications they need.

We just want our country to invest back in us, too, instead of sticking us with the bill.

MONEY |

Less White = Less Rich

The Great Recession may have defined Millennials' economic lives, but the heart of the story is about race. Because Millennials are a more diverse generation, we are a poorer generation.

"We have a racial wealth gap," New America's Cramer says. "It's been exacerbated by the Great Recession, and if you use that race lens, it appears there's been no progress in America over the last thirty or forty years. It doesn't look like we had a civil rights movement. It doesn't look like there was a president Barack Obama."

American wealth is profoundly racialized. White families have a lot more than nonwhite families. Part of the reason Millennials are so broke is that fewer of us come from the white families that have consolidated, and can draw upon, generational wealth. The United States was built on chattel slavery, creating a formal system of white political, economic, and legal supremacy. Even after that evil institution was outlawed, American law and policy continued to formally and informally privilege whites, from the Homestead Acts to the Chinese Exclusion Act through Jim Crow and the New Deal (the Social Security Act, for example, excluded industries where black workers were concentrated, leaving 65 percent of African Americans ineligible when the act was passed in 1935).

It's no secret that the average white American family starts with an economic advantage over the average black American family. But our national narrative is one of steady improvement, of narrowing racial gaps and moving ever closer to equality. It turns out to be a little more complicated. There was, unsurprisingly, a significant racial wealth gap when Baby Boomers were growing up in the shadow of Jim Crow. In 1963, according to the Urban Institute, the average white family in America had $140,663 in wealth (assets like a home, retirement accounts, and savings minus debts), while the average nonwhite family had $19,504—a gap of more than $121,000. But by 2016, when Millennials were coming of age, this gap had widened into a preposterous chasm. The average white family is now worth over $700,000 more than the average black or Hispanic family.

American wealth is profoundly racialized.

This wealth disparity, accelerated by our vanishing investments in social and economic programs, is primed to keep growing. In the years since Boomers came of age, and as America has grown more diverse, family wealth has built on itself, and family poverty has become more entrenched. Lower-income families, a disproportionate number of whom are families of color, have less in savings, so their children need to take out more in student loans to go to college. And because of ongoing racial discrimination in hiring and pay, when those students enter the job market, they wind up making less in salary to pay those loans back. Black and Hispanic students are also less likely than white and Asian students to stay in college through graduation, in part because they are more likely than white students to be supporting themselves and supporting their families while they pursue their degrees.

As a result, many Millennials of color entered the workforce with student debt but no degree, already in a financial hole, and finding themselves only qualified for lower-paying jobs.

And it gets worse. For-profit educational institutions, which helped build the wealth of Trump education secretary Betsy DeVos and graduate far fewer students than not-for-profit schools, target and disproportionately enroll students of color: while black students make up 13 percent of enrollees at public colleges, they are 21 percent of students at for-profit schools.

Many students at for-profits are tempted by the promise of flexibility. And indeed, some of them do graduate and thrive, but they tend to be the exceptions. Nathalie Nguyen, a thirty-two-year-old law student in Sacramento, decided to go to a for-profit law school because, she says, "the curriculum is catered to working people or people who went to school late in life and have decided to do a career change. You don't need a bachelor's degree to attend. When I was looking at schools, I was taking more into consideration the tuition and what I could do to offset the costs." As the daughter of Vietnamese immigrants who could not afford to pay for her schooling, and already $80,000 in student debt from undergrad and graduate school, Nathalie couldn't afford not to work, which took most full-time law schools off the table. But the law school she went to is only California Bar accredited, meaning she can't practice anywhere else in the United States. She will also have about $40,000 in law school debt on top of her existing educational debt when she finishes.

The school she chose promised the diversity and working-class flexibility she needed, at a lower price than the private nonprofit options. It may, on its face, sound as though educational institutions that cater to underserved communities are performing a necessary service. But many are pricey, sub par, and fail to meet the needs of their constituencies. Just 22 percent of students enrolled at for-profit four-year colleges graduated from the same institution within six years (by comparison, the six-year graduation rate is 76 percent for students at private nonprofit schools and 65 percent for public ones). Among black and Hispanic students who took on student loan debt to pay for a for-profit college education—many of whom were promised the flexibility they needed to work and support family members while going to school—two-thirds never graduated. But they're more likely to take on student debt: 88 percent of graduates of for-profit colleges leave school in the hole, owing an average of $39,950. Nearly half of those borrowers default within twelve years.

In 2016, 70 percent of white students graduated college with debt. For black graduates, it was 85 percent. Those black graduates then entered a labor market that undervalues their skills and underpays them. The average white Millennial household brought in $60,800 in income in 2016—50 percent higher than the income in Hispanic Millennial households, which averaged $40,500, and 63 percent higher than black Millennial household income, which was $37,300. Income is not the only driver of wealth, but it of course has an impact. "Each dollar in income increase yields $5.19 in wealth for white American households, but only 69 cents for black American households," wrote Mel Jones, in a 2015 article on the racial wealth gap for the *Washington Monthly*. And educational debt doesn't necessarily decrease even if you're paying your bill every month: The Roosevelt Institute found that twelve years from the day she started school, the average black woman's student loan balance is 13 percent *higher* than what she took out to pay for school. White and Latino borrowers, by contrast, had managed to pay down significant portions of their loans (black men saw their student debt unchanged).

Despite indebtedness across racial groups, white Millennials are wealthier than their nonwhite counterparts. When you add up cash and assets (things like a home and retirement savings) and deduct liabilities (things like student loan and credit card debt), white Millennials were worth, on average, $26,100 in 2016, a New America analysis found, while Hispanic Millennials were worth $14,670 and black Millennials just $5,700.

Income also requires having a job, something that is less likely for young people of color. Young workers overall face higher rates of unemployment, but young black and Hispanic workers fare worse: sixteen percent of them are unemployed, twice the rate of unemployment of young whites.

While Millennials are struggling, Baby Boomers are the richest generation in American history. Boomers are projected to pass some $68 trillion down to their descendants over the next twenty years or so. This massive wealth transfer means that by 2030, Millennial wealth is projected to grow to five times its current balance.

At least the eventual passing-down of Boomer wealth will level the playing field, right? Of course not. Centuries of racial discrimination will allow white Millennials—who make up just 56 percent of our generation—to inherit many times more than their black and brown peers. That's in large part because black and brown Millennials' parents weren't cut in on the American dream, despite Boomers being born smack in the middle of the civil rights movement. Boomers have always been an overwhelmingly white generation, but a few decades of immigration made them marginally more diverse: while 82 percent were white in 1968, by 2015, that proportion had dropped to 72 percent. But whatever their numbers, those white Baby Boomers have maintained lifelong advantages that they are able to pass on to their children. They are far more likely to own their homes, and to own more expensive homes, than Baby Boomers of color. White families are also more likely to have a whole assortment of assets that their black and brown peers don't. About 60 percent of white families have retirement accounts, while large majorities of black and Hispanic households do not—62 and 69 percent, respectively, do not have any retirement assets.

"White families are about five times more likely than African American and Hispanic families to inherit money or receive a large gift," the Urban Institute's McKernan says. "And when they do receive that gift or that inheritance, it's larger. So this disparity contributes to the wealth gap—this is money that can be used for major family investments, like college or a down payment on a home."

More than one in four white families report having received an inheritance, compared to just one in ten black and Hispanic families. And white heirs receive ten times as much money as black ones.

For black and brown families, the obligations often run in reverse: it's children who are supporting older family members.

Millennials in America are more likely than Boomers, Gen Xers, and even Gen Zers to be immigrants.

According to a Clark University poll, 86 percent of African American parents and 74 percent of Hispanic parents expect their children to support them in old age. That's not out of selfishness but necessity. While white families are typically able to systematically save and draw upon generational wealth, black and Hispanic families are much more likely to be living paycheck to paycheck. Across income levels, black and Hispanic families report significantly lower abilities than white families to cover a $400 emergency. While more than a third of white families making less than $40,000 a year said they could pay $400 with either cash on hand or a credit card they could pay off at the end of the month, only 20 percent of black families said the same. Among wealthier Americans, 83 percent of whites making more than $100,000 a year could easily cover a $400 emergency, compared to just 63 percent of African Americans. In other words, income inequality isn't the biggest driver of insecurity; wealth inequality, heavily driven by race, is. White Americans, whether they are low-income or higher-income, have more wealth and resources than Americans of color, and those benefits and the stability they bring are passed on to their children.

This is Justin Pinn's reality. Though he attended George-town on a full ride, he worked two or three jobs at a time while in school, and still managed to rack up significant credit card debt. Scholarships didn't cover all of his needs in Washington, DC, and there were bills to pay and people to help back home. "It's not lavish expenditures" that people ask for, Justin says. "It's, 'Hey can you help me with my light bill, this medical bill.'" As the kid who made good, what can he say—no? Of course he helps out. "I am blessed and I can make up for this in my thir-ties," Justin says. "My salary is going to increase. That's the story I'm telling myself. But at the same time, I haven't been able to put money away for a house."

Millennials in America are also more likely than Boomers, Gen Xers, and even Gen Zers to be immigrants, Pew found (while Gen Zers are more likely to be the children of immigrants). With that often comes a series of financial obligations not just to par-ents but to siblings and extended family members both at home and abroad.

It may be tempting to read these statistics and conclude that black and Hispanic families are perhaps just making bad decisions: not saving enough of their wages, not buying homes as early and often as they should, not getting college degrees at comparable rates. If only it were that simple. In fact, controlling for income, black families save more and spend less than white families, suggesting that financial profligacy is not driving the wealth gap. Nor is education the "great equalizer" that self-styled race-blind commentators say it is. The Samuel DuBois Cook Center on Social Equity crunched the numbers, and they're outrageous: A white household headed by someone with a college degree sees, on average, a greater income than a black household headed by someone with a *graduate* degree. A black household headed by a person with a bachelor's degree still earns less than a white household headed by a high school dropout.

Black and Hispanic Millennials, then, need to have even more credentials—more degrees—than their white peers to be hired for the same jobs and make anything close to the same amount of money. And with less access to family wealth to pay for those degrees, black and Hispanic Millennials take on more debt. This puts them further in the hole, requiring them to spend more years in school, with the attendant student debt, to see anywhere near the same payoff down the line, which in turn pushes back their ability to save for retirement or buy a house. Put plainly, Millennials—and especially Millennials of color—have to work harder for less.

"I don't think there's been a full accounting of what our country has put Millennials through," Justin says. "From [Boomers'] perspective we have so many opportunities, but they don't realize the floor wasn't underneath us. We've had to build our own floor. We were in a hole. I look back at credit card bills and this and that and I'm making headway, but I think back and it's like, wow, those expenses were racked up because of a recession and because my parents didn't have work—it was just what you had to do."

Black Millennials are less likely to own their homes than black members of the Silent Generation, who were born in the 1920s and '30s.

Millennials are paying almost 40% more for their first homes than Boomers did.

Millennials are less likely to own a home than any previous cohort except the Greatest Generation, who came of age at the close of the Great Depression.

As of 2016, more young adults lived with a parent than lived with a spouse—nearly a third of eighteen-to thirty-four-year-olds still lived in a parent's home. More than one in five lived with a roommate. Nearly a third of Millennial men live with a parent.

Three-quarters of Millennials are renters, and more than one in ten of them say they plan to rent for life.

Nearly half of Millennials spend at least 30% of their income on rent.

HOUSING

One of the reasons Millennials are so broke is that we are much less likely than our Boomer parents or Gen X siblings or even our Silent Generation grandparents to own our own homes—and we don't own our own homes because we're broke.

Close to half of Boomers were homeowners by age thirty-four; today, 75 percent are. By contrast, only 37 percent of Millennials owned a home by age thirty-four. Today, only 32 percent of us are homeowners. Some of this decline is a cultural shift, and some of it is an economic one. First things first, though: it wasn't exorbitant spending on avocado toast that left Millennials without enough money to buy houses.

Millennials have broken away from what several young people I talked to characterized as "The Script": graduate from high school, go to college, get a job, get married, have kids, retire. We are marrying and having children later, and often reversing the order of those things—or forgoing one, the other, or both. Some of us like the flexibility of renting, how it means we're not pinned down and can move at will; others can't afford to buy

Just 32 percent of Millennials own their homes,
compared with 75 percent of Boomers.

alone, and wait for a serious partnership to buy a house. And like most of the other hardships our generation faces, Millennial diversity curtails our options: Asian, Hispanic, and particularly black families have been systematically screwed by the US housing market, leaving them with less generational wealth to pass along. Black and Hispanic Millennials are particularly unlikely to own their homes.

There are very real financial barriers to Millennial homeownership. The first is that the country's absurd housing market has everyone trapped: Boomers are living longer and aren't moving out of their houses, often because they can't afford to. And even if they were, there's a mismatch between where and how Boomers live—in big houses in the suburbs—and the Millennial appetite for smaller homes close to cities, where jobs are increasingly consolidated.

In the meantime, we're stuck paying sky-high rents that make saving for a down payment difficult and push homeownership even further out in the distance.

Different Strokes

Baby Boomers might have appeared to initially reject the *Leave It to Beaver* suburbia of their childhoods in order to avail themselves of the free love (and cheap dope) of the 1960s and '70s, but they quickly reined it in. Boomers generally married in their early twenties and were even more likely than their parents to sprawl into single-family suburban homes, where they raised their kids with abstinence-only education and the antidrug program D.A.R.E.

Millennials are a different kind of generation. Like Boomers, we're marrying later than our parents, but we're marrying *way* later. We are, on average, nearly thirty when we tie the knot. A growing number of us will never marry at all. This marital reticence is one factor shaping our housing decisions. Sixteen percent of first-time home buyers have never been married, and about a quarter of Millennial homeowners bought their house with their significant other and married them sometime after. But being married still increases your chances of buying a home by 18 percentage points. With half of adults under the age of thirty-five still single, and those of us who do marry doing so late

HOUSING |

into our twenties and beyond, it's no wonder Millennial home-ownership rates lag.

Our generation's diversity is also a leading factor. African Americans, Asians, and Hispanics have been alternately left out and pushed out of the American housing market. Our nation was founded on chattel slavery, which designated black people as property. The country carried out centuries of housing discrimination, including redlining of black neighborhoods. Racial segregation and discrimination in endless other forms made it much more difficult for African American and other families of color to build wealth. The results of these policies now ripple out to children and grandchildren. We know that there is a direct link between having a parent who was a homeowner and being a homeowner yourself: children of homeowners are 9 percentage points more likely to buy their own place as adults than are children of parents who rented. This is in part because of passed-down values, including the belief that buying is better than renting, but it's more because of the real passed-down dollars and the knowledge of *how* to buy: how to save, how to boost your credit, how to fill out all the mortgage forms, what a good interest rate is, how to refinance. And more directly, homeowners can pass on their actual homes to their descendants, making homeowners of the younger generation without those young people having to do much of anything.

This has all been very good for white families, and less good for people of color, including the significant proportion of Millennials of color. Today, white Millennials are almost three times as likely as black Millennials to own their homes. And it's getting harder for African Americans: according to New America, the homeownership rate for black Millennials is lower today than it was for African Americans of the same age in 1960. An African American member of the Silent Generation, born between the late 1920s and early 1940s, and living, as an adult, in an era in which Jim Crow laws were still enforced, was more likely to own a home than a black Millennial is now.

But all is not lost. Just as the Silent Generation remade America into a network of suburbs interconnected by a national highway system, today's Millennials are similarly redefining what it means to live a good life. We're pushing for more affordable housing, better public transit, and more green spaces. We're rejecting the Walmart-ification of America, and we are patronizing small businesses and local bars and restaurants. We spend more of our young adult lives in cities, and even when we leave them, we want many of their amenities to come with us. There are enormous challenges facing our generation as we get older and can't afford to own homes. But we're creating opportunities, too.

City Mice

Antonia Dean hadn't planned to move to New York City. But when she finished Harvard Law, instead of clerking for a judge or practicing at a big firm like many of her peers, she decided to pursue a career she actually wanted to do, and got a job in the beauty industry. It was a dynamic and challenging field, and even though she would have preferred to live in a more affordable city, there aren't many other places in the world where the beauty industry thrives. Plus, New York was New York: full of bars and restaurants, music venues and museums, and richly diverse.

"I'm definitely more of a city person in general," Antonia says. "I like being able to walk places, public transit, etcetera. Also diversity is a big consideration for me. As a black woman, I honestly wouldn't feel safe living in a small rural environment without other black people and people of color."

Millennials are city creatures. Data on where Millennials actually live is surprisingly varied, but one 2018 Gallup poll indicates that a third of Americans under fifty live in cities, and the younger the respondents were, the more likely they were to be city dwellers. Among Americans under thirty, most of whom were Millennials in 2018, more than half live in cities, large or small. While the move from suburbs to cities actually started with Gen Xers, Millennials have kept the trend strong. Over the past thirty years, a greater share of young people have become urban dwellers, and a greater share have stayed in cities even as they age out of their twenties. This "youthification" of cities, Richard Florida wrote for CityLab in 2019, began in the 1990s as Gen X-ers flooded into New York and San Francisco, and, later in the decade, Seattle. By the 2000s, what were once midsized cities began to see boom days, too, as young people moved in droves to places like Miami and Washington, DC. These are now some of the most expensive places in the country to live.

For a cohort that is highly educated and single for longer periods than any generation before them, the incentives for city life are obvious. First there are the jobs: cities offer more of them. According to the Brookings Institution, the fifty-two largest metropolitan areas in America accounted for two-thirds of the country's job growth from 2010 to 2016. Rural areas? Just 5.3 percent. The high-paid professional roles available to people with college and graduate degrees tend to be concentrated in urban areas, which is one reason urban dwellers are much more likely than rural residents to hold a bachelor's or advanced degree. There are more lawyers working in New York City's ten largest law firms than there are in all of New Mexico, and in each of more than a dozen US states. And even though America's cities are much pricier than its rural reaches, Millennials who live in urban areas are more financially secure and more likely to be employed than those who live in rural communities.

Millennials are city creatures.

"People think, Oh, these Millennials want to live in New York and LA and eat avocado toast and go to brunch," Antonia says. "But it's also that a lot of the jobs that would pay well are clustered in those places. If you want to work in the beauty industry, you have to live in New York. If you want to work in media you have a handful of places you can go. Our economy has really changed. Our industries have condensed, and there are fewer players and fewer options."

Cities have always been a draw for the young and ambitious. What sets Millennials apart is that more of us are flocking to them, and we're staying longer than our parents did. Millennials, unlike every other adult generation, are actually happiest in big cities, and least happy in small rural areas. We're staying in urban areas longer partly because we're marrying later. The young (and not-so-young) and single understandably want to be around other people who are young (and not-so-young) and single, of course for dating and sex, but also for fun, friendship, and creative endeavors. Delaying parenting means we have a long stretch of unencumbered years. Women in particular are freer than ever to live alone, date around, and postpone or forgo marriage and childbearing and even monogamy; we also have more education and are more likely to work outside the home. And we find that when we do marry, those single years have shaped us into more fully formed creatures with deep friendships, enriching hobbies, important community ties, cherished routines, and, if we're lucky, meaningful jobs. Is it worth giving all of that up for a stand-alone house with a wraparound lawn?

Plus, contrary to stereotypes about Millennial laziness, we work really hard, and we don't want to add hours of commuting via car. We're concerned about climate change, which may disincentivize the old model of the two-car middle-class family (plus, as you've read, we're broke, and a lot of us can't afford car payments, gas, and repairs—a monthly Metro card or bus pass is a lot cheaper). Today's young urbanites say that when it comes to city living, access to public transport matters more than anything else.

Interestingly, our Boomer parents may be looking at our urban lives, seeing the benefits, and following suit. A growing number of them are moving into large buildings with generous amenities, perhaps looking for a little more culture and adventure themselves as they wind down their careers and hit retirement age. Close to 80 percent of Americans now live in urban areas.

Millennials largely say that big-city life is pretty great. So why are we starting to leave?

The Rent—and Everything Else—Is Too Damn High

Jimmy McMillan has run for governor of New York State, senator, and mayor of New York City (twice). He has been both a registered Republican and a Democrat; his primary affiliation is himself. When he ran for Senate in 2010, he received more than 40,000 votes, despite the fact that his party, of which he is founder, chairman, and leader, only had three members. (McMillan himself was not one of them. That year, he was registered as a Democrat.) McMillan is what one might call a character: he sports narrow black-framed glasses and a mullet that begins about 60 percent of the way back on his otherwise bald head. His mustache is a soft W, winding its way from his nose down under his apple cheeks and up to meet the sides of his glasses in front of his ears. A white goatee splits, inexplicably, into two cotton-ball tufts on his chin. McMillan, who endorsed Trump for president and now lives in Flatbush, Brooklyn, was born in 1946, making him an older Boomer. But in one important respect he's speaking Millennials' language. McMillan is a single-issue candidate and the head of a single-issue party: The Rent Is Too Damn High.

Close to 80 percent of Americans now live in urban areas.

Preach.

Antonia spent most of her eleven years in New York living in Harlem, a traditionally African American neighborhood. She arrived in 2007, just before the financial crash hit. The economic downturn temporarily depressed housing costs but did not stem the tide of Millennial urbanization and the related gentrification of what were once middle-class black enclaves. Antonia found an apartment; a few years later, her college boyfriend, who eventually became her husband, moved in. He worked on Wall Street, and she had worked her way up to a good job in beauty, but between her high student loans ($100,000) and New York City rent, they still lived paycheck to paycheck. "Rents just kept going up," Antonia says. "You have to have somewhere to live, and we wanted to have a steady cost of living, and not be thinking about, *Are we gonna move this year, can we get anything better for this price, is it worth it, that new building is going up.*" Buying a house was appealing but felt close to impossible. And moving out of the city felt daunting, too, with both of their jobs tied to New York.

Median Monthly Rent

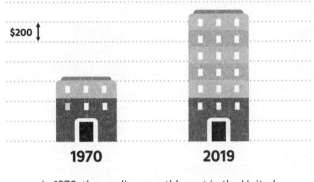

$200 ↕

1970   **2019**

In 1970, the median monthly rent in the United
States was a little more than $600, in 2019 dollars.
By 2019, it had doubled, to more than $1,300.

Across the country, rental costs have exploded. In 1970, the median monthly rent in the United States was a little more than $600 a month, in 2019 dollars. By 2019, it had doubled, to more than $1,300 a month. Nearly half of Millennial households spend more than 30 percent of their income on rent: "rent-burdened," the Urban Institute calls them. In this respect, Boomers didn't get off unscathed. By some measures, the minority of Boomers who are renting are dedicating an even higher proportion of their income to rent than Millennials are.

Antonia faced a quintessentially Millennial problem: simultaneously in debt and living in one of the country's most expensive cities, she was both vulnerable to the vagaries of the rental

Median Home Price

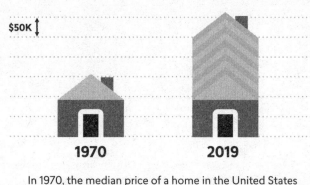

$50K

1970   2019

In 1970, the median price of a home in the United States
was $23,400, or $154,184 in 2019 dollars. But by 2019, the
median home cost more than twice that: $321,500.

market and couldn't afford to buy a house. Homes are indeed
much, much more expensive today than they were for our parents. In 1970, the median price of a home in the United States
was $23,400, or $154,184 in 2019 dollars. But by 2019, the median
home cost more than twice that: $321,500. Millennials pay almost
40 percent more than Boomers did for their first home.

"The cost to build homes has increased so much since the
[2008 financial] crisis, it's more difficult for Millennials to find
affordable homes," says Jung Hyun Choi, a research associate with the Housing Finance Policy Center at the Urban Institute. Builders focus on more expensive projects, and as a result,
she says, there are simply fewer affordable starter homes to go

around, making all of them more expensive and making it more difficult for young buyers to find a home in their budget. "Because of restricted supply, rental costs have also increased a lot," Choi says. "For Millennials, it's more difficult to save for homeownership, because their income remaining after paying for rent has decreased over time."

The National Association of Realtors found that a median-income household in Los Angeles, New York, Oakland, and San Francisco would need to save for a decade to afford a median-priced home in those cities. According to a Freddie Mac survey, 82 percent of renters today say that renting is more affordable than buying, the highest number on record. Homeownership looks so far outside the realm of possibility for so many that more than 12 percent of Millennials say that they plan to rent for the rest of their lives.

But it wasn't rent alone that eventually drove Antonia from New York; it was children. "Our first child was born when we were in a one-bedroom apartment that was spacious when I moved in there by myself, but by the time there were two adults, a child, and a dog, it was not spacious at all," Antonia says. "So we moved into a two-bedroom. Then we had a second child. By the time we left New York, we were paying more for two kids at a reasonable home-based childcare place than we were paying in rent."

The Deans moved into a three-bedroom rented row house in Philadelphia, where Antonia's parents live. The city boasts a vibrant cultural scene and world-class restaurants, but the rent and, more importantly, childcare, are a fraction of what they had been in New York. As a result, the couple was able to save, and a little more than a year after moving, they put a down payment on their first house.

Like Antonia, Mollie Cohen D'Agostino also moved to an urban center after graduating from school, except she headed west, to the San Francisco Bay Area. She was drawn in by the job prospects of pre-recession San Francisco but fell in love with the vibe and the political activism of Oakland, which is where she settled, living with several roommates in a series of shared houses. In 2005, she paid $250 for a glorified closet on Eighteenth Street and Martin Luther King Jr. Way, a location so desirable that she guesses rent today for that same tiny room would easily top $1,000 a month. "I moved into the crappiest little room, and then when a vacancy appeared, I would move into a larger room in that same house," Mollie says. "In one house I lived in three of the five rooms because I kept moving up to bigger and better rooms." She worked at a nonprofit and frequented the local bars, cafes, and music venues; she became active in city politics, and biked all over town to get around. When she met the boyfriend who would eventually become her husband, he moved into the spacious room she had acquired over years of moving up in the roommate hierarchy in yet another share house, and they eventually moved into their own place together.

Mollie and her husband left the city before having a baby, but, just as Antonia and her husband had experienced on the East Coast, preparation for a life with kids (or at least *a* kid) was the chief reason. Living in Oakland, "we talked about having kids but we didn't think it was possible," Mollie says. Then she got offered a job in Davis, a smaller community about an hour northeast of the Bay. She had never seriously considered life in a small town or a suburb, but her husband owed six-figure student loan debt and she owed $40,000 from graduate school. When they added in their hopes for a future family the scales tipped away from Oakland. They ended up in Woodland, a suburb about ten miles from downtown Davis (yet another city they couldn't afford).

"It's not as exciting as the Bay Area, but it felt like we could have a kid and buy a house and all these things that were not possible in the Bay Area," Mollie says. "We moved because of the housing crisis, and I feel like we made the right decision. But that means we did wait to make some life decisions. We might have had a kid sooner if we had a better financial situation." Now, Mollie is thirty-six and the mother of an infant.

As Millennials get older, get married, and have kids, we may resist following in our parents' suburban footsteps, but more of us are decamping for something more affordable. That means smaller cities and, yes, the suburbs—and even exurbs in the nation's priciest areas. Like Antonia and her husband, many of us are moving to smaller metropolises, making Phoenix, San Antonio, Fort Worth, Seattle, and Charlotte the fastest-growing cities in America.

Others are going the small town and suburban route, but we're not heading to the same suburbs Boomers chose. Davis, where Mollie works, is a college town, which means there are jobs; Millennials who move out of cities often still find themselves living in places like Woodland, which is at least adjacent to an urban center. Millennials, the *Wall Street Journal* reported, are also flocking to a handful of small Sunbelt communities where jobs are concentrated, in turn creating clusters of highly credentialed high-income residents. Once relocated, they push for city amenities, in what might be called the Brooklynization of America: in small towns and cities across the US, you can wander into coffee shops with exposed-brick walls and eat locally sourced produce served in artisan-crafted ceramic bowls, all under the glow of the ubiquitous Edison bulbs.

Big things like transport are slower to change, though, than eatery aesthetics. "One thing that has been a real bummer about living in the suburbs is I really like cycling, and envisioned myself being this bike commuter transit advocate person," Mollie says. Her work is seven miles away, which is a long round-trip bike commute for anyone, but especially when one has a family to get home to. More reliable public transport or, even better, an affordable home in a bike-friendly small city—that would be the dream.

Those who remain in the most popular cities make serious concessions if they're not at the top end of the economic scale. More than one in five Millennials live with a roommate, making us more than twice as likely to do so than Boomers were when they were young. We're much less likely than Boomers to live with a spouse, but much more likely to shack up: while 12 per-

As of 2016, more young adults lived with a parent than lived with a spouse—nearly a third of 18- to 34-year-olds still lived in a parent's home.

cent of Millennials live with an unmarried romantic partner, just 1 percent of Boomers did when they were young adults.

We're also much more likely to live with our parents than either Boomers or Gen Xers were as young adults. The statistics are frankly not great, because we use pretty out-of-date assumptions about housing and family life to measure who and how people today live (it means something very different to live at home as a twenty-year-old college student than as a thirty-year-old man, for example). But according to census data, 31 percent of eighteen- to thirty-four-year-olds in 2016 lived with their parents. Another 21 percent lived with a roommate or relative; just 8 percent lived alone, and 27 percent lived with a spouse. In 1975, a quarter of that same age cohort still lived with a parent, and just 11 percent had a roommate or lived with a relative. The majority were married.

Younger Millennials are still in school, and a great many college students who are teenagers and early twentysomethings live at home while they finish their education or work their first jobs—they're still getting launched. But Gray Kimbrough, the economist and Millennial myth debunker, looked at older Millennials, those who are between twenty-five and thirty-four. What he found was striking: even in this cohort, within which there are very few full-time students, 20 percent of women and more than 25 percent of men lived with a parent. "The result is rather dramatic," Kimbrough says. "And it hasn't gone down as the economy improves. I think people are still struggling with how to figure out how to deal with the repercussions of the financial crisis."

With later marriage and childbearing, greater student loan debt, and, crucially, an absurd housing market, Millennials are living at home longer than any generation since before World War II.

While Millennials burdened with educational debt do delay homeownership, those who are college-educated are still more likely to own homes than those without a degree. In so many ways, Millennials who either didn't go to college, or didn't complete a degree, are worse off: priced out of homeownership, priced out of big cities, and facing a paucity of job opportunities offering a living wage. Think about it: if Antonia's dual-income professional household can't afford to comfortably raise two kids in Harlem, how could the guy who drives for Uber do so, or the health aide who works in the local nursing home?

Housing didn't become this expensive by magic, or even by the unfettered hand of the market. Real estate investors,

New York Times reporters Ben Casselman and Conor Dougherty reported, have scooped up a shocking number of affordable would-be starter homes with cash offers: investors bought close to half of the affordable homes in some of the country's most competitive housing markets in 2018. This, in turn, raises prices for everyone. It's more expensive to build houses now than ever before, and the profit margins are lower on affordable housing. A number of other factors are in play as well, Casselman and Dougherty found: with Boomers staying in their homes longer, supply is limited. Where supply isn't an issue, demand is lower. In areas where demand is high, supply is low and skews toward the higher end of the market; and in some of the fastest-growing cities, restrictive zoning laws limit buildings to single-family housing, artificially constraining supply and jacking up prices.

How did this all happen?

I'll give you one guess.

The NIMBY Boom

In defense of Boomers, it was really the members of the Silent Generation who made several fateful choices that, nearly a century later, would send us tumbling into an urban housing crisis.

The first was the midcentury development of suburbs, and the massive investment in the national highway system that connected them. While the earliest decades of the twentieth century brought government investments in affordable urban housing and efforts to tear down urban slums, suburbanization quickly took over the bulk of government housing resources in the postwar period. "It can be said with considerable truth that the vast landscape of suburban ranch houses and apartment complexes that sprawled outward from every US city during the late 1940s, 1950s, and beyond was—no less than the grimmest public housing project—'federally subsidized housing,'" writes Thomas W. Hanchett, a historian of the American South and an expert on urban history, in the anthology *From Tenements to Taylor Homes: In Search of Urban Housing Policy in Twentieth-Century America.*

The federal government directly funneled cash to suburban home buyers. Beginning in the mid-1930s, the Federal Housing Administration (FHA) backed bank loans that went disproportionately to white buyers, a practice the GI Bill expanded via the Veterans Administration (VA), removing virtually all lending risk and incentivizing banks to extend a greater number of mortgages with lower down payments—and in the case of VA loans, sometimes no down payment at all. The FHA wouldn't guarantee just any loan, though; there was a rating system that prioritized suburban dwellings, awarding better scores to large new homes with landscaped lawns and significant privacy, situated in homogeneous neighborhoods and primarily accessible by car. Developers, Hanchett wrote, also milked the federal cash cow, building thousands upon thousands of new single-family suburban units.

In determining which neighborhoods were desirable, the federal government color-coded them in the 1930s. Wealthy neighborhoods without immigrants or black people were the best, and those were colored in blue. Neighborhoods populated by African Americans and, to a lesser extent, Jews, Catholics, and immigrants from southern Europe and Asia were colored in red—redlined. "Neither the percentage of black people living there nor their social class mattered," Ta-Nehisi Coates wrote in his famous "The Case for Reparations" piece in the *Atlantic*. "Black people were viewed as a contagion."

This racism did not materialize anew in the 1930s. With slavery, black people were forcibly held as property and formally barred from owning private property themselves. Whites spent several hundred years systematically stealing land from black people, beginning before the Civil War and continuing into modern-day America, an Associated Press investigation found. The racist housing policies that were formalized in the 1930s propelled this particular arc of history forward. "With segregation, with the isolation of the injured and the robbed, comes the concentration of disadvantage," Coates wrote. "An unsegregated America might see poverty, and all its effects, spread across the country with no particular bias toward skin color. Instead, the concentration of poverty has been paired with a concentration of melanin. The resulting conflagration has been devastating."

It also gave whites an unearned advantage. The flood of affordable houses with remarkably low down payments gave

There is perhaps no character more closely associated with Boomer suburbia than the NIMBY phenomenon: the homeowner who places their property value and their desire for suburban sanctuary above all else, including the good of the broader community.

millions access to the kind of wealth that would have been previously unimaginable. In 1955, as the baby boom was ascending to its peak, 41 percent of houses in the United States were purchased with federal mortgage assistance. By 1970, Hanchett wrote, some 11 million Americans owned homes thanks to the FHA and VA programs. But these preferential mortgages went almost entirely to male-headed white families. African Americans were systematically excluded at nearly every turn: from receiving federal assistance, from being approved for a mortgage, from being sold a house in their neighborhood of choice, from enjoying federal investments in the neighborhoods they already lived in. Women were also at a disadvantage: the FHA's own manual forbade lending to female-headed families, and said that "if a neighborhood is to retain stability, it is necessary that properties shall continue to be occupied by the same social and racial classes." Racial deed restrictions were ruled unconstitutional in the 1948 *Shelley v. Kraemer* Supreme Court case, but that ruling hardly stopped housing discrimination and segregation, so much of which happened—and continues to happen—informally but systematically. The 1968 Fair Housing Act at least gave people who could prove discrimination the ability to bring their claims to court, but proving discrimination is a high bar, and one most individuals can't clear.

In 1969, Jeff Robinson, the ACLU lawyer, moved with his family from their majority-black neighborhood in Memphis to an entirely white one. The Robinsons' old house was about to be razed and replaced by a shopping center, and the Robinson parents wanted to keep their kids in the Catholic school Jeff had integrated when he was in second grade. They made several offers on homes, always at the asking price, and were consistently rejected—once, the Realtor told them that he had gone fishing and accidentally dropped their contract in the water. The family found out later that when white families put their homes on the market, their white neighbors would encourage them to sell to white buyers, promising that even if they had to sell at a loss, the neighbors would make up the difference in exchange for not having a black family move in. And that's how the Robinsons eventually got their house: they put in an offer at the asking price, white friends of theirs offered less, and when the white friends got the house, they turned around and sold it to the Robinsons.

"I remember after we moved in the FBI coming and meeting with us in our home and telling us if something happens, stay away from the windows, and here are the numbers you can call," Jeff says. "There was vandalism at the house for the first few weeks after we moved in. My dad, who was about five foot five and a hundred thirty pounds dripping wet, would sit on the carport in a lawn chair with a shotgun across his lap."

Jeff was twelve.

Decades later, Jeff's dad asked Jeff and his brother if moving into the white neighborhood was the right thing to do. They told him yes. "It's one thing to talk to your kids about how you should do what's right and you should not let people disrespect you because of the color of your skin and you're just as good as anybody else," Jeff says. "It was one thing to preach it. It's another thing to see your parents live it. To this day, I think my parents' decision to do what they did with that house, and the way they tried to raise us, is one of the most significant acts of courage I've seen in my entire life."

As some African Americans slowly and with exceptional bravery pushed across the neighborhood color barrier, whites moved further away. And that white flight to suburbia was also federally subsidized by massive investments in suburban life, including sewer system and highway construction, tax incentives for developers, and tax breaks for homeowners. A hefty investment in a national highway system was approved in 1956, a year before the peak of the baby boom. By the time most Baby Boomers were in their teens, 42,000 miles of expressway crisscrossed the nation, built by bisecting and sometimes bulldozing urban communities of color. The highways made it easier to ferry better-off whites to the city's sprawling and racially exclusive suburban outskirts, neighborhoods that also enjoyed significant government investment. Black and immigrant families remained concentrated in neglected urban communities. Middle-class homeowners also enjoyed significant tax breaks not on offer to renters.

For the white Boomers who grew up in the prosperous blue-lined enclaves or the growing suburbs, their unearned advantages were intentionally obscured. "Because of the way I grew up as a middle-class white person, I had no training or education that would allow me to recognize the roles that my racial biases were playing in the decisions I was making and the way I was understanding political choices," says Joy Ladin, a poet, writer, and college professor who was born in 1961. "My family was explicitly liberal. We were pro–civil rights and pro-integration. But that didn't prevent me from going to an all-white school. And it didn't prevent me from not even being aware that I was going to an all-white school. It wasn't until I read that great piece in the *Atlantic* about redlining and housing policy that Ta-Nehisi Coates wrote that I was like, oh my god, that's why we lived in this house that was much nicer than we could afford."

There is perhaps no character more closely associated with Boomer suburbia than the NIMBY ("not in my back yard") phenomenon: homeowners who place their property value and their desire for suburban sanctuary above all else, including the good of the broader community. One hallmark of NIMBYism was invented well before the baby boom, but Boomer NIMBYs of the

1980s took it to the extreme: zoning and land use restrictions. These restrictions first began sprouting up in New York City around the turn of the twentieth century, an attempt to stymie Manhattan's proliferating skyscrapers, Amanda Erickson reported for *City Lab*. They took a decidedly racist turn in San Francisco when they were used to restrict public laundries, which were overwhelmingly Chinese-run, in a transparent effort to shutter the businesses of Chinese immigrants. The laundry law was overturned by the courts and New York's skyscrapers continued to rise, but zoning laws, in more sophisticated form, were here to stay.

Through the first half of the twentieth century, racial covenants formally excluded nonwhites from white suburban communities. After those efforts were struck down by the courts, zoning regulations took their place. Zoning laws were leveraged to bar affordable housing from being built in wealthy areas, and to restrict the construction of apartment buildings and condos in neighborhoods where white-owned single-family homes dominated. Though racially neutral on their face, these laws reinforced racial segregation, solidified white wealth, and pushed black families further into financial insecurity. And in today's diverse and growing city centers, these ill-conceived laws are creating a new wave of disaster: housing shortages, outrageous rent hikes, and gentrification that pushes out longtime residents. In Los Angeles, 75 percent of city land is zoned for detached single-family homes. In my hometown of Seattle, which is currently booming courtesy of big tech companies including Amazon, Microsoft, and their legions of Millennial workers, 81 percent of the city is restricted to single-family housing. Zoning laws, which have been not just kept in place but radically expanded by Boomers, make it nearly impossible to build the number of residential units needed to house all the people now in cities.

This whole ball of incentives, rules, benefits, and overt and covert discrimination resulted in a housing ownership landscape that is overwhelmingly white. As a home became, and has remained, the most significant investment most families make in their lifetimes, the entrenchment of racial discrimination in the housing market perpetuated and magnified the concentration of American wealth into white hands.

For a moment, things seemed to be looking up. In the 1990s and early 2000s, black homeownership was on the rise. By 2004, it was nearing 50 percent, an all-time high—still lower than the proportion of white families who owned a home, but a mark of significant progress. Some of these gains came from government programs like the Community Reinvestment Act (1977), which sought to reverse the history of discriminatory lending and promote homeownership, lending, and investment in traditionally underserved communities; in the '90s, the Clinton administration scaled it up with new regulations to root out racial bias from lenders and investors. But too much of what looked like progress came about because black families were about twice as likely as white ones to be targeted by shady subprime lenders. Predatory lenders retained the right to adjust interest rates to farcical degrees; these adjustable-rate mortgages offered initially low interest rates, only to ratchet them up (often beyond what the homeowner could pay) a few short years later. Some mortgages were even interest-only, which meant that people might spend their whole lives paying the mortgage on their house only to own zero percent of it. And families of color were targeted across income levels. Jacob William Faber at New York University found that in 2006, African American and Hispanic families making $200,000 a year were more likely to be offered subprime loans than white families making just $30,000.

Then came the financial crash.

Families of color lost somewhere in the neighborhood of $200 billion because of the housing market collapse and the mass foreclosures that followed. The Obama administration attempted to cauterize some of the wounds, requiring, for example, that areas receiving federal aid dollars make efforts to racially integrate their neighborhoods. Those were swept away when Trump came into office. By 2019, the gains of the 1990s and early 2000s were wiped out, and black homeownership hit an all-time low, even as homeownership among white, Hispanic, and Asian families grew. Today, prospective black and Hispanic buyers are denied mortgages at twice the rate of their white counterparts.

While redlining was theoretically done away with a half-century ago, its impact persists: three-quarters of neighborhoods so designated are still financially hurting today. Even when you control for income, loan amount, and neighborhood of the prospective house, African Americans are still far more likely to be denied loans than their white counterparts. And African American renters pay more in rent than white renters, even for the same kind of housing in the same kind of neighborhood.

The residual effects of generations of racist policies have affected the exceptionally diverse Millennial generation more than any other. White people in the United States still hold most of the nation's wealth. Black Millennials were also badly hit by the housing crisis, and are the least likely to own their homes today. Appallingly, Millennials see the largest racial gap in homeownership of any previous generation. Our parents, our grandparents, and even our great-grandparents saw less of a racial gulf between young white homeowners and young black ones.

Yes, Millennials have different values than our Boomer parents. But here's what grates: white Boomers saw their preferences and values met with government recognition, response, and investment. They saw massive public works projects that worked for them. Now, Millennials are trying to navigate a constricted housing market and a nation with outdated urban infrastructure, so much of which is out of line with what we want and what we need to remain gainfully employed, financially stable, and moderately happy. But Boomers, well into their sixties and seventies, retain significant control over American politics; Millennials haven't enjoyed our fair share of political influence, which means we haven't seen the kinds of investments we need. And Boomers aren't loosening their grip anytime soon.

Millennial mortality is up almost 20% compared to our Gen X predecessors. For white Millennials, it's increased almost 30%.

Drug-related deaths among young adults have shot up more than 300% in just 20 years—largely due to the opioid crisis—and yet Millennials are significantly less likely than the general population to receive treatment for substance abuse.

American families spend more than twice as much on health care today as they spent in 1984, when Boomers were young heads of households.

Millennials use less health care than older generations but have more medical debt.

Millennial moms pay about three times as much to have their babies as new moms did in 1996. When Boomer women were having babies, the cost was close to zero; today, the average C-section costs close to $50,000.

HEALTH

Millennials are the wellness generation. We fill up yoga studios, CrossFit gyms, and SoulCycle classes, and guzzle coconut water and green juices. We download meditation apps and can expound on the purported benefits of rose quartz and Himalayan salt lamps. Millennial workplace team-building might be a group hike or a Tough Mudder. We believe time to exercise and eat well is a right; we want to prepare healthy meals with organic produce and hormone-free meat; we drink more water than soda; we know we should be eating more whole foods, mostly plants. We grew up with in-school antidrug curricula and then moved to cities that ban smoking in bars. We made seltzer great again. We are the generation of #selfcare and #MotivationMonday.

So why are we so unwell?

Millennial Madness

Maddie Campbell, the dog-walking Uber-driving Millennial living with her parents in Jacksonville, Florida, has one big thing working in her favor: she has health insurance because of the Obamacare mandate that young people can stay on their parents' plans until they're twenty-six. "I have a couple of different disabilities, I have PTSD, I have chronic illnesses," Maddie says. Even so, if she wasn't able to get insurance through her parents, "I really think I would be chillin' without health insurance, and trying my best not to get sick."

For a great many Millennials, "don't get sick" is the plan. For others, it's too late.

Millennial mental health is especially worrying. Older Millennials may be the most depressed thirtysomethings in American history. A Blue Cross Blue Shield analysis of health data found that we are significantly more likely to suffer from major depressive disorder than Gen Xers were when they were in their midthirties, and women are about twice as likely as men to be diagnosed with depression. That older Millennials may be more likely to be *diagnosed* with depression may mean that we're more depressed, or it could mean that we are more willing to seek help for it—or some combination of the two. A portion of any population is simply biologically predisposed to depression. For another (overlapping) piece of the population, though, depression is also situational, sparked by stress and exacerbated by brain chemistry. For all the jokes about Millennials being triggered snowflakes, in truth we really are more aware of the importance of mental health: younger Millennials, a Harris poll on mental health and suicide found, were more likely than older adults to report having seen a mental health professional in the previous year, and almost twice as likely to say that seeking mental health care was a sign of strength.

So it's particularly worrisome that we're also less likely to be insured. While we might be more open to seeking mental health care, we're a lot less able to afford it. One in five Millennials struggling with major depression, a condition that can shave nearly a decade off one's life, goes without treatment. And 85 percent of people with depression are also struggling with at least one serious additional issue, whether substance abuse or chronic hypertension or Type 2 diabetes or a range of other afflictions.

Right now, Maddie's insurance covers part of her therapy bill, so she only pays $35 per session. But $35 is a lot when your net worth is in the negative, and all of your disposable income is earmarked for paying down your debts. Maddie is happy with her therapist, but cost forces her to pass on other critical care. "My PTSD was initially so intense, I tried so many different things," she says. "I tried TMS, transcranial magnetic stimulation, and it worked pretty well, but it was super-expensive every session . . . It made me a lot better, but I couldn't afford to go every week."

We like to think we can separate out the psychological from the physical, but mental versus physical health care is a false dichotomy: mental health struggles have physical effects, and physical illness can hamper psychological well-being. Rates of suicide in America are soaring among Boomers and Millennials alike, and Boomers have the highest rates of any generation. Suicides in the US have long occurred among older people at higher rates than younger ones—when Boomers were coming of age, the suicide rate for people sixty-five and up hovered around 20 per 100,000—but rates are higher for the over-sixty-five cohort now than they were in the 1970s and 1980s. For Millennials, it's not much better: suicide rates among eighteen- to thirty-five-year-olds shot up 35 percent between 2007 and 2017.

Millennials have also been hit particularly hard by the opioid crisis. Between 1999, when the oldest Millennials were turning nineteen, to when the youngest were becoming adults in 2017, drug-related deaths increased by 329 percent. Opioid-related deaths grew by 500 percent, and overdoses from synthetic opioids surged a ghastly 6,000 percent. Out of every 100,000 people between the ages of twenty and thirty-four, nearly 35 now die of a drug overdose every year.

These deaths—drug overdoses, suicides—are what the economist Anne Case and the Nobel laureate Angus Deaton have called "deaths of despair," and they are the primary reason the Millennial mortality rate is 20 percent higher than it was for Gen Xers at the same age. For white Millennials, a Stanford Center for Poverty and Inequality analysis of census data found, the mortality rate has shot up almost 30 percent. And these deaths stem from problems our health care system is particularly inept at addressing. An Ohio State University study found that people with

Millennial mortality is up almost 20 percent compared to our Gen X predecessors. Out of every 100,000 people between the ages of 20 and 34, nearly 35 now die of a drug overdose every year.

drug-use disorders pay much more for care than those without. They were much more likely to wind up in an out-of-network hospital and to rely on out-of-network care, even compared to patients with congestive heart failure, an emergency condition. And those with substance addictions paid an annual $1,242 more for out-of-network health care than people with diabetes. Inpatient rehab programs run into the tens of thousands of dollars, and many insurance plans refuse coverage; even those that do may not cover a second (or third) stint in rehab, though rates of relapse are high for most addiction disorders. Drug rehab facilities also routinely turn away pregnant women.

So what's driving Millennial depression, anxiety, and an uptick in death by suicide and overdose? Some researchers (and critics) have suggested that "helicopter parenting," that hallmark of suburban Millennial childhood, left us unprepared to solve our own problems; that we were told we were special, and now we can't handle the disappointment of realizing we're not; that Mom and Dad had such a hand in navigating our conflicts, arranging our schedules, and even doing our homework that once we're out in the world and expected to do those things on our own, we simply can't handle it.

Maybe. Anecdotes certainly abound of parents calling their kids' college professors to complain about a bad grade, or young people not knowing how to productively fight with a friend. Intensively parented kids very well may turn into anxious and less resilient adults. But when you look at the tangible challenges Millennials face, our allegedly overinvolved mothers seem like the least of our problems.

One of those problems is money: it may not buy you happiness, but financial stress ties closely with depression. As incomes rise, the incidence of depression goes down. When about a third of Millennial-headed households live below 200 percent of the federal poverty level (FPL)—in other words, are poor or low-income—you can bet our mental health is going to suffer.

It can be difficult, and perhaps impossible, to untangle medical causes of mental illness from social ones. We know that for many people, pharmacological tools to treat chemical imbalances in the brain are profoundly useful and even lifesaving. But when you look at the vast landscape of challenges that so many Millennials face, in a world imbued with so much suffering, and where that suffering is more visible than ever, perhaps it is entirely rational to feel depressed and anxious. Perhaps these conditions reflect social problems as much as individual brain chemistry.

"Problems are now more often believed to be questions of personal brokenness than they used to be," says Satya Doyle Byock, a Portland, Oregon, therapist who works primarily with Millennials. In the past, she says, human beings faced the same big existential questions we do today—who am I, why is the world what it is—but had a greater number of common and respected social outlets through which to examine those questions, whether it was religion or philosophy or prayer or contemplation. Now, there's a sense that anxiety, depression, and malaise are issues of individual psychological dysfunctions to be individually fixed, not rational responses to irrational conditions worth collectively addressing. "Yes, there are sometimes medical solutions to mental health issues, and thank god," Satya says. "But we are still human beings on a planet that is dealing with severe chaos, catastrophes, and suffering. Why would we not be trying to sort that through in our bodies and our souls?"

Millennials are, perhaps more than any other cohort, also suffering from a kind of generation-wide cognitive dissonance. There is a profound gap between the expectations we were raised to hold and the reality we now experience. Growing up, we believed that if we followed the rules and did the right things—go to school, get a job, be a decent and kind person—we would be rewarded and life would be, if not amazing, at least good, stable, and predictable. And, well, it wasn't. A lot of us are entering our thirties underemployed, indebted, and living in our child-hood bedrooms. That sucks, and we know it. "I deeply believe the things I learned as a child are true and important," Dave Rini, a thirty-six-year-old Millennial in Boston, told me. "And then I see how they operate in the real world, and I don't know how to deal with that."

Millennials want to live lives of purpose, but we don't have a road map for what that might look like. And as we struggle to piece together meaningful lives among the shards of a shattered economy, we are also bombarded with messages that we're weak, sensitive snowflakes whose efforts at introspection are narcissistic and embarrassing. "We neglect the amount of trauma that Millennials have grown up with," Satya says. "In almost every clickbait article and every discussion, there is a lack of acknowledgment of the rise of school shootings, the amount of imprisonment and incarceration, of immigration trauma, sexual abuse, rape, family abuse, family trauma, 9/11, growing up when your country is going to war for seemingly no reason. There are massive existential issues and personal traumas that Millennials are dealing with, and [they are] simultaneously being mocked for being so self-involved."

"We neglect the amount of trauma that Millennials have grown up with."

When Millennials come to her office, Satya says, they are always quick to recognize their own privilege and to note how lucky they are and how, despite being in a therapist's office, they don't really have any right to complain. I had the same experience reporting this book: nearly all the Millennials I talked to, regardless of how severe their struggles, noted that they were privileged in some way; most were almost apologetic for suggesting that their pain might matter. "Millennials have been so mocked and ridiculed in culture that to actually want to look at one's own suffering is immediately ridiculed by the mocking ingrained voice inside of everyone's head," Satya says. "We have been trained to make fun of our own introspection."

And while the internet has increased awareness of mental health struggles, it's also fueled them. "With Instagram, for example, the comparison of oneself to other people is extremely toxic," Satya says. "Everyone says, 'I don't know why I'm the only one who doesn't know what I'm doing.' Everyone thinks they're the only one who doesn't have their shit together. Part of that is just standard blindness of self and others. But another part, of course, is that people put their best self up on the internet—or the new thing is that you put your most vulnerable self up, and so now it's an authenticity competition. The resulting comparison is exceedingly toxic." And conflict online is even worse than comparison. Anonymity, or even being behind a screen using our real names, can make us crueler than we might be with a person face-to-face, but our nervous system reacts to that feeling of attack all the same, even if it's "just" coming from social media. "For younger people it's even worse," Satya says. "We at least have some impulse control. The younger you are, the shame, mockery, fitting in—it's all so much more magnified with the internet."

The Unwell-est Wellness Generation

Millennials' physical health is in decline, too, and at a faster rate than our predecessors'. We are increasingly sedentary: in 2011, more than half of us sat for more than five hours a day, as compared to about a third of us in 2007. And we're more isolated, spending significantly less time interacting with other human beings in person rather than through a screen. Less than a third of us talk to our neighbors, compared to 40 percent in 1995.

Older Millennials report higher rates of substance abuse, high blood pressure, Crohn's disease and colitis, and higher cholesterol than Gen Xers did at the same age. By contrast, Baby Boomers are the longest-living generation in American history. Boomers who have made it to sixty-five still have about two decades ahead of them: men will live to be, on average, nearly eighty-six, and women nearly eighty-eight.

Comparing life expectancies is complicated work, because once a person lives past a certain age—in wealthy nations, fifty or sixty-five—they're a lot more likely to keep living into old age. Given that a good chunk of the Millennial cohort is still under the age of thirty, and that we're surrounding ourselves with the traditional trappings of adulthood later, it's tough to look at our life expectancy compared to Boomers. What we do know is this: our health is trending in the wrong direction.

This is ironic, given the value Millennials place on our health. Compared to previous generations, we exercise more and eat healthier; we smoke less. And we have a more nuanced view

In 2011, more than half of us sat for more than five hours
a day, as compared to just over a third of us in 2007.

of what it means to be "healthy." While Boomers pretty much say that being healthy means "not falling ill" and not being over-weight, Millennials are more likely to say that "healthy" is defined by eating well and exercising. And yet our health outcomes are still poor.

Young people aged thirteen to thirty-five reportedly spend some $150 billion of their limited resources a year on nutrition, fitness, and health. As we have entered our twenties and thirties, Millennials have fueled an explosion of boutique fitness classes: the $25 yoga or barre class, $30 or more for SoulCycle and spinning, sometimes even more than that for personalized Pilates or boxing. We're also partly responsible for the surge in organic, locally sourced, and sustainable produce, and we want it for our kids, too. (Who demanded the now ubiquitous gourmet organic baby foods? Millennials.) We're more concerned about the environmental impact of how we eat, which is part of why we're the force behind growing global veganism (between 2015 and 2018, the number of vegans in America increased by 600 percent). Even those of us who haven't gone whole hog in forgoing animal products are pushing plant-based diets and the kind of "flexitarianism" that pops up in #MeatlessMonday campaigns and encourages reduced meat consumption.

Yes, there is a big class gap here. Flexing for Instagram from a chic boutique fitness studio in $140 Alo yoga pants is a particular way of signaling wealth; so is sipping a $12 Moon Juice, buying a $495 "intimate wellness solution" from Goop.com (it's basically a very expensive vibrator), or going on a $1,395 Sakara cleanse before your wedding. But while the luxury market has embraced high-end wellness products, the push for health as Millennials define it has crossed class lines. Walmart sells organic produce. The YMCA and affordable gyms like Planet Fitness offer yoga classes. Local green thumbs have planted community gardens and health-conscious entrepreneurs have opened vegan cafés in neighborhoods long neglected by chain restaurants and big grocers. Even in the midst of coronavirus stay-at-home orders that shuttered gyms and exercise studios, public health messaging was clear: stand up, walk around, and get some exercise.

It's easy to scoff at "wellness" as a trend at best and a Millennial money pit at worst. But I suspect there's something else going on here. Millennials are facing a broken health care system with poor outcomes and high costs. And a system that assumes widespread employer-based insurance is badly underserving a generation of freelancers. As with so much else about Millennial life, the old systems have failed us. And so we're trying to figure things out for ourselves.

Dead Broke

Maddie Campbell needs a filling. She can tell—her tooth hurts, and it's not getting better. But her dental insurance doesn't cover everything she needs done. "I can't afford the filling I know I need," she says. "So I'll just chew with the other side of my mouth now."

In 1970, health spending amounted to $355 per person. By 2018, that amount had increased thirty-one-fold: We now spend $11,172 per person on health care (even when adjusting to 2018 dollars, health spending has shot up more than 500 percent since 1970). Nationally, we spend more than $3.5 trillion on health care every year. Our out-of-pocket spending (that is, what we spend on health care not counting our insurance premiums) has also gone sharply up, from about $119 per person per year in 1970—$770, with inflation—to $1,150 per person in 2018. And when you add insurance, it gets worse: the average American household now drops nearly $5,000 per year *per person* on health care, including insurance premiums, prescription drugs, and medical supplies. In 1984, when Baby Boomers were giving birth to the babies who are now older Millennials, household health care spending was half of that.

For Millennials having children, the numbers are no better. The cost of having a baby has tripled since 1996: A vaginal delivery will run you $30,000, while a C-section is more than $50,000. If you have employer-sponsored health insurance, lucky you, but you'll still be on the hook for an average of $4,500 in out-of-pocket costs. That is close to the *total* cost of having a baby in Switzerland or France, which is largely covered by the state. Women in those countries pay virtually nothing for their deliveries. That used to be true in the US, too: as recently as the early 1990s, Elisabeth Rosenthal reported for the *New York Times*, American women's out-of-pocket childbirth expenses were close to zero—unless they opted for special extras, like a private room with a TV.

Nor do these extortionate sums translate into better outcomes for mothers and babies. The US maternal mortality rate has more than doubled since the years in which Millennials were being born. Two-thirds of US maternal deaths are preventable, and African American women are especially vulnerable: they are two and a half times as likely as white women to die bringing new life into the world. Black babies, regardless of their mother's income level or educational attainment, are also far more likely than white babies to die before their first birthday. The baby of a poor white mother without a high school diploma is more likely to survive than the baby of a black woman with a graduate degree. Millennial women, and black Millennial women in particular, are dying from a health care system that is not only woefully inadequate but deadly racist.

Racial disparities in health care and health outcomes are significant. There is, first, just straight-up racism: white health care providers are less likely to recognize black patients' pain, and one study by University of Virginia researchers found that a shocking 40 percent of white first-year medical students, and a quarter of white medical residents, believed that black people's skin was thicker than white people's. And then there are the many outcomes of centuries-long racism that are slow-drip factors leaving many people of color in poorer health and more vulnerable to disease. Communities of color are more likely to live near polluted areas, where they're breathing in carcinogens, and less likely to have easily accessible local grocery stores where they can get fresh fruits and vegetables—all of which contributes to higher rates of disease, including asthma, diabetes, heart disease, and cancer. Redlining meant systematic underinvestment in what are now often low-income neighborhoods, which in turn means fewer high-quality health care providers. Discrimination in home buying means that African Americans, who are less likely to own their homes, are more vulnerable to housing instability and evictions, which we know fuels ill health. Our absolutely asinine system of tying health insurance to employment means that the same communities facing disproportionate rates of unemployment or underemployment because of discrimination, incarceration, poverty, and ill-health are also less likely to have private insurance coverage. "Black people are poorer, more likely to be underemployed, condemned to substandard housing, and given inferior health care because of their race,"

Keeanga-Yamahtta Taylor wrote in *The New Yorker* in 2020. "These factors explain why African-Americans are sixty per cent more likely to have been diagnosed with diabetes than white Americans, and why black women are sixty per cent more likely to have high blood pressure than white women."

We saw this all come home to roost with the COVID-19 pandemic, which hit communities of color, and African American communities in particular, extremely hard. "The old African-American aphorism 'When white America catches a cold, black America gets pneumonia' has a new, morbid twist," Yamahtta-Taylor wrote. "When white America catches the novel coronavirus, black Americans die."

During the coronavirus epidemic, long-overlooked employees who stock drugstore shelves, take vital signs, ring up grocery purchases, and make deliveries found themselves thrust to the front lines of the outbreak and deemed "essential." A *New York Times* analysis found that a majority of these "essential critical infrastructure workers" were women. Three-quarters of the health workers infected with COVID-19 as of April 2020 were women. The *Times* didn't offer a racial breakdown, but many of the jobs deemed most essential—nurses and health aides, grocery and fast-food counter workers—are disproportionately filled by women of color. African Americans are about 13 percent of the US population but make up 30 percent of health aids and nursing assistants. Of that 30 percent, 88 percent are female.

Millennials, too, were likely to be on the front lines, because we are disproportionately employed by the kinds of businesses that didn't close. We're 49 percent of restaurant and food service workers, 46 percent of pharmacy and drugstore workers, 46 percent of warehouse and storage workers, and 45 percent of gas station workers. And the black Millennials who are more likely than their white peers to work in the gig economy? Many of them spent the shelter-at-home periods working for the various services that send a shopper out to get your groceries and drop them at your door—often without the most basic safety supplies, let alone health insurance.

No wonder so many Millennials say our health care system doesn't work.

We are the least likely adults to be insured. Almost half of young Americans don't have a primary health care provider; around 15 percent of Boomers say the same. And despite the fact that our health care spending is lower overall, we are the group most likely to have medical debt, even though we are more likely than Boomers to know the cost of our care before we receive it. But that's a double-edged sword: we're also twice as likely as Boomers to forgo care we need to avoid the bill.

Millennials are 49 percent of restaurant and food service workers, 46 percent of pharmacy and drugstore workers, 46 percent of warehouse and storage workers, and 45 percent of gas station workers.

We may also opt for substandard care to fill the gaps. That's what Maddie is doing now. She has polycystic ovary syndrome, which can cause hormonal imbalances, heavy bleeding and irregular periods, and endometriosis, a chronic and painful condition where uterine lining grows outside of the uterus.

One treatment for both is hormonal contraceptive pills, which Maddie's doctor tells her to take continuously, and so she gets her prescription filled in three-month supplies. The brand that causes the fewest side effects costs $150 per month. That means she's regularly dropping $450 she really can't afford on medication, often putting the cost on a (now maxed-out) credit card. "I just went to the doctor yesterday and he's going to try to put me on a cheaper birth control that may give me horrible mood swings," Maddie says. "But if it's nine dollars, I'd rather pay that and feel shitty and have my symptoms mostly managed than feel great and have to spend so much money every month."

These are the choices Millennials are forced to make in one of the most prosperous nations in the history of the world.

There is no singular cause of our swelling health costs and worsening outcomes (especially for women giving birth), but a look at the component parts of this mess is revealing: the architects, and the beneficiaries, are mostly Boomers.

To put it succinctly: 1980, the first year Millennials were sliding into the world, was a tipping point. According to Austin Frakt, the director of the Partnered Evidence-Based Policy Resource Center at the V.A. Boston Healthcare System, associate professor with Boston University's School of Public Health, and a senior research scientist with the Harvard T.H. Chan School of Public Health (lots of titles for this guy), the US was humming alongside our economic peers until we peeled off—for the worse—in 1980, when our health spending began to radically outpace that of other nations. In the years that followed Ronald

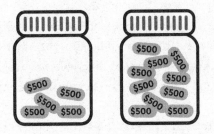

American families spend more than twice as much on health care today as they spent in 1984, when Boomers were young heads of households.

Reagan's election to the presidency, Frakt wrote for the *New York Times*, deregulation allowed the market to control medical costs, which meant that they ran wild. (Other developed countries kept costs down with price controls, and expanded national health systems.) The American insurance system comes with a massive administrative sector—people whose job it is to deny or accept claims, manage billing, and negotiate between insurers and providers—all of which drives up costs that are passed on to the patient. And of course, insurance companies are in the business of making money. Who do you think they're making it from?

Even though health spending was up, health outcomes were not. Nineteen eighty, Frakt writes, was again a major turning point. While our economic peer nations have seen their populations get healthier and healthier over time, and while their life expectancies have steadily increased, Americans didn't keep pace. Why? Because America simply does less for its people, and especially for its poor. A series of Boomer and Boomer-elected presidents have further slashed holes in the American safety net and in welfare benefits for the vulnerable; as a result, Americans die younger and more often than people in economically similar countries.

Bill Clinton tried at least to patch up some of the more obvious holes. His wife, Hillary Rodham Clinton, took charge of reforming what he called "a health care system that is badly broken." Republicans and those who profited from the existing health care system immediately opposed the effort, despite the fact that the reform plan was moderate and market-friendly; it didn't help that the plan was complicated, and communication to the public poor. As soon as the plan was announced, conservative media outlets, organizations, and politicians launched a broad attack aimed at convincing Americans that it would be a radical government expansion that would make their health care worse. When Republicans triumphed at the ballot box in the 1994 midterms, Clinton-era health care reform was dead in the water.

Clinton and others did succeed in establishing, in 1997, the State Children's Health Insurance Program (SCHIP, today CHIP), which covered children of families who made too much to qualify for Medicaid but too little to afford insurance themselves. The number of uninsured children fell to its lowest in American history up until that point, and long-standing racial disparities in health coverage began to shrink. Today, more than half of black and Hispanic children, and more than a quarter of white children, are insured through CHIP. A whole lot of Millennials had health care as children because of CHIP, and today, a lot of Millennials' own children can go to the doctor because of it.

But once young people aged out of CHIP—at nineteen—we were up a creek. From 2003 to 2010, the number of uninsured young people rose; by 2010, 29 percent of Millennials—20 million of us—didn't have health insurance. Because companies cut benefits, and because of the Great Recession, eighteen- to thirty-four-year-olds (mostly Millennials) made up nearly half of the uninsured workforce in 2010, even though that same group was only 36 percent of workers.

We caught a bit of a break when Barack Obama pushed through the most significant change to the American health care system in Millennials' lifetimes. The Affordable Care Act ("Obamacare") is far from perfect, and nowhere near the universal systems enjoyed in many of our peer nations. Health care and insurance both remain ludicrously expensive, and a great many Americans are still one health catastrophe away from bankruptcy. But it filled some of the more egregious gaps, especially for Millennials. In the first three years of Obamacare alone, 2.3 million young adults either stayed insured or became insured through a parent's plan. Basic preventive care, including contraception, was mostly free. Insurers could no longer discriminate based on preexisting conditions, which a Department of Health and Human Services analysis found could have denied insurance to as many as 46 percent of twenty-five- to thirty-four-year-olds. The many of us who freelance or work in the gig economy had more options. Some 8.7 million women gained maternity coverage. Because of Obamacare, the number of uninsured Millennials halved. If conservative states had taken the option to expand Medicaid, the number of uninsured Millennials would have decreased further still.

And then came Donald Trump.

The Trump administration, and the Republican Party more broadly, have gone out of their way to gut Obamacare. Unable to repeal the act wholesale, Trump instead destroyed whatever he could. He cut the advertising budget, so fewer people knew how and when to sign up each year, and he shortened the amount of time Americans had to complete those sign-ups. Trump also cut funding for the trained navigators who helped consumers and businesses understand their options, eligibility, and the enrollment process. Predictably, enrollment dropped, and lots of people who needed and wanted health care coverage didn't get it. Trump also ditched the individual mandate, a critical component of Obamacare that brought down insurance premiums by forcing younger and healthier (less costly) people to get insured. He made it harder for poor people to get Medicaid, and easier for states to kick poor people off. He cut federal payments that incentivized insurance companies to remain on the Obamacare marketplace. And he let more people stay on crappy, skimpy plans that are intended to be short-term precisely because they have enormous deductibles, meaning you could have insurance and still go bankrupt if catastrophe hit.

When catastrophe did hit, in the form of a pandemic, Trump didn't stop his efforts to undermine Obamacare's gains. Democrats and health insurance companies alike pushed the president to reopen the Obamacare enrollment window—after all, the numbers of sick people were growing, and the CDC's worst-case predictions in March 2020 had 214 million people sick and as many as 1.7 million dying. Unemployment was exploding in a nation where health coverage is tied to employment, leaving tens of millions of people newly uninsured in a world convulsed by a highly contagious and often deadly disease. Still, Trump refused to reopen Obamacare enrollment, which would have allowed people without insurance to get it and people with substandard insurance to level up. All the while, Republicans had a lawsuit pending before the Supreme Court aimed at dismantling Obamacare without offering a replacement; Trump was a public supporter, although his administration offered no real plan of its own, even in the midst of a massive deadly outbreak. The individual financial reverberations, including personal bankruptcies, will be felt for years to come.

To no one's surprise, health care premiums have gone way up under Trump. Nearly 70 percent of Americans say they worry about being able to afford unexpected medical bills. Some Millennials are staying in jobs they hate because they can't afford to lose their insurance; others are quitting jobs they love because adequate insurance isn't on offer. And many employers increasingly treat health insurance as a perk rather than a requirement. Between 1989 and 2011, the percentage of recent college graduates who got health insurance through their jobs was cut in half. And the insurance we do have is worse: 82 percent of employer-sponsored plans now have deductibles, compared to 63 percent ten years ago, and average deductibles have gone up from $826 to $1,655.

No wonder so many Millennials want what our Boomer parents have: Medicare. Or at least something like it. Or at least *something*.

A majority of Americans now say they want a universal health care system, and Millennials are leading the way. A Morning Consult/*Politico* poll found that 70 percent of us support a universal health care plan where health coverage comes via the government. Early in the 2020 Democratic primary, a Hill-HarrisX survey found that about 60 percent of Millennial Democratic voters said they would be more likely to support a candidate who backed a Medicare for All plan. While voters on Super Tuesday broke for Joe Biden over Bernie Sanders, there was a glaring age gap: 58 percent of voters under thirty, and 41 percent of voters under forty-five, cast their ballots for Sanders. Health care was at the top of a lot of voters' minds, and those who put health care as their number-one issue were more likely to vote for Biden. But voters who said that they wanted a single-payer system as opposed to our current private employer-based one broke for Bernie by a significant margin.

Not every Millennial wants a Sanders-style Medicare for All plan. But we largely do want better health coverage, and as a generation of freelancers, contract workers, and part-timers who have lost jobs again and again, we've seen firsthand the absurdity of tying health insurance to employment. You would think this would be common ground (and perhaps, in the aftermath of coronavirus, massive layoffs, and widespread illness, it will be). After all, older Americans *love* Medicare, their universal health care program. Three-quarters of Medicare enrollees said they were satisfied or very satisfied with the program in a 2019 consumer survey. They oppose any cuts or even changes to the program, and overwhelmingly say that it's important to them and their families. All of which is great: Medicare is wonderful, and even though caring for aging Boomers on the government dime is really, really expensive, we prioritize it and we can afford it. Millennials agree that keeping it funded and functional is the right thing to do. We don't want to take Medicare away from our parents and our grandparents.

A majority of Americans now say they want a universal health care system, and Millennials are leading the way.

We just want in. Boomers, unfortunately, don't seem interested in sharing. Consider this a plea: We don't want to take your health care, and we know that you're struggling with our broken health care system, too. We want you to have affordable prescriptions. We want you to go to the doctor when you're sick. Boomers, you're our parents and grandparents, bosses and mentors, friends and neighbors. We love you, we really do. We want you to be healthy and live for a long time.

Do you want the same for us?

60% of Millennials say we know our food choices affect the planet, and a full quarter of us have gone vegetarian or vegan.

By 2100, some 2 billion people on earth could become climate refugees.

Only about half of Boomers believe climate change is caused by human behavior; 70% of Millennials do.

A third of young people say worries about climate change made them have fewer children than they would have wanted—or that they elected to have no children at all.

Nearly 80% of the US Senate is fifty-five or older, an age group that makes up the largest chunk of climate deniers. The number of senators who are Millennials? Zero.

CLIMATE

Every generation has its shocks, hardships, and upheavals. The Greatest Generation had World War II. The very small Silent Generation spent their childhoods in the Depression, saw the devastation of the nuclear bomb, and in early adulthood faced Cold War fears and McCarthyism as young adults. Baby Boomers came of age with the war in Vietnam and a Cold War that threatened nuclear conflict; as young people, they saw the assassination of some of America's most visionary leaders; and as they hit adulthood, they saw America's postwar prosperity come to an end as a recession weakened the economy.

Millennial life, too, has been defined by a series of disasters and traumas. September 11, 2001. The 2008 financial crash. Mass incarceration. The largest global refugee crisis since the Second World War. COVID-19. Another financial crash.

But while the traumas of the past had end dates, if not full resolution, we are the first generation to come of age under the looming existential threat of climate change. Millennials the world over list climate change as their number-one concern, ahead of income inequality, unemployment, personal safety, terrorism, political instability, and war.

Boomers, perhaps more than any other generation, should be able to relate. After all, they grew up during the era of duck-and-cover (as if that school desk would protect you from nuclear annihilation) and the pervasive dread that any chunk of America could be wiped out at any time. But as the Cold War drew to a close, Boomers were ultimately able to raise their kids in a world that felt newly prosperous.

It was also a world that felt newly prosperous and optimistic. But that prosperity came at a cost, and it's one that Millennials, Gen Zers, and our children are left to pay. Even the oldest Millennials grew up hearing about the ozone layer and greenhouse gases, the depletion of the Amazon and global warming. Our parents knew, too, and so did those in positions of power. After all, Earth Day was a product of the 1970s. Boomers hit adulthood in the era of Superfund cleanup site battles. And by the 1980s, scientists had been clear that danger loomed, but that there was a path forward if everyone acted, fast. No one moved. Boomers in America have done little to nothing to stop the effects of climate change. Worse yet, the disproportionately white, disproportionately Boomer Republican Party made climate a political issue, sowing disbelief in the broad scientific consensus that climate change even exists.

Boomers in America have done little to nothing to stop the effects of climate change.

The goal was to enable big business to continue reaping massive profits—by mortgaging our futures.

Every young person on earth now faces the planet's impending doom. But Millennials have faced this existential threat for a lifetime—the first generation to do so. And that has reshaped adulthood as we know it.

It's Getting Hot in Here

Steph Larsen is forty-one, and so is technically an Xennial—born in the overlap between the Gen X and Millennial generations. But even though she was born just outside the generation's bounds, she thinks of herself as more of a Millennial than a Gen Xer, in part because technology is such a big part of her life. It lets her do her job from anywhere. And it allowed her to become one of the growing number of people around the world who left a place she loved because of the pressures and impending disasters of climate change.

After spending her twenties and thirties in school, building a successful nonprofit career, and adventuring, Steph met her husband in Missoula, Montana, got married, and moved onto a farm. They had sheep and yaks, and looked forward to raising their two children in a place where they could play endlessly under the big Montana sky.

But in the four years they lived on their farm, they watched the weather fluctuate wildly and unpredictably. When 2017 rolled around and brought with it a deliciously wet spring, "everyone was so happy because we're gonna have plenty of water, the wildfires won't be as bad this year, great," Steph says. "And then it didn't rain from June until October. All of this greenery that had grown so lushly in the spring totally dried up and burst into flames.

"We were in the thick of it," Steph says. "We couldn't go outside for six weeks. We couldn't take our daughter outside. We had to get air filters. It was awful." With no snow pack in the winter to ski and fires all summer long, Steph says, "We looked at each other and said, if this is the sign of what's to come ... what are we doing here?"

Steph, a geographer by training, set to work finding a region that fit their family's desires: arable and affordable farmland, in a place at least somewhat sheltered from a changing climate. There was no perfect answer, she knew that. But there had to be somewhere better than where they were. "I said, climate change is going to affect all of us," Steph says. "What concerns me the least? Where am I going to be the safest?" They settled on upstate New York, a long way from their beloved Montana, but addressing other quintessentially Millennial concerns: their new town was closer to family, and New York State offered more generous children's health insurance, which helped to make raising two kids financially feasible.

It is this mash-up of encumbrances—the threat of climate

change, the cost of childcare, the difficulty of finding comprehensive health care coverage, the burden of debt—that drives so much of Millennial decision-making. We may not yet have reached a point where a significant proportion of Millennials are making serious life decisions based on climate change alone. But we are already past the point of Millennials taking climate change into account when deciding where and how to live.

Aaron Bos-Lun, now thirty-one, is originally from central Pennsylvania, "an area that the *New York Times* discovered existed in the 2016 election," he says. "I never saw a future for myself there." He couldn't imagine remaining in a town where he had never met an openly gay person. As an adolescent, he learned his great-uncle's best friend, Eugene, in Wisconsin had been gay—but when Eugene came out, Aaron's great-uncle cut him off. He had died of AIDS-related complications before his thirtieth birthday. "Growing up," Aaron says, "the thing I knew about being gay was lose your friends, lose your family, die."

After college, the small-town Rust Belt life did not appeal. "The dynamic you now hear about with the storefronts shut down and the glory days of the mill fifty years ago, none of that ever connected with me," Aaron says. "Why was that so great? I never saw the life with the wife and the kids."

And so off to Miami he went.

It was a big, vibrant, and diverse city with a large and lively gay community, and Aaron finally felt at home. "I have this super-gay life," Aaron says. "Half of my friends are gay. Part of me feels like I've arrived." This is a prototypical Millennial desire:

A host of large global cities—Miami, Beijing, Jakarta, Chicago, Dubai, and New Orleans among them—could become uninhabitable by 2100 due to flooding, heat waves, pollution, and rising tides.

to live in a place where one feels seen, accepted, and embraced. "This is where I came into my own in so many ways and made sense of the world," Aaron says. "It's the America I want to live in. It's open. It's not about what your family did three generations ago. The immigrant ethic and the openness is something that creates good conditions for someone like me. No one talks about the glory days of fifty years ago because there was no mill fifty years ago. No one thinks that way."

"I'm so invested in my life here," Aaron says. "And at the same time, there's this big ticking clock."

It's counting down to climate catastrophe.

In eighty years, Miami could be wholly unlivable; many people will likely be forced to leave their homes much earlier than that. In this, Miami joins a host of large global cities—Beijing, Jakarta, Chicago, Dubai, and New Orleans among them—that could become uninhabitable by 2100 due to flooding, heat waves, pollution, and rising tides. For some smaller communities, Miami's future is already the reality. When the federal government allocated some $48 million in 2016 to resettle people living in Isle de Jean Charles, Louisiana, residents of that small island became America's first climate refugees.

As inhabitants of a relatively prosperous nation, people in the United States have been more insulated from the damage of climate change than poor people in poorer countries. Between 2008 and 2018, natural disasters turned some 265 million people globally into internally displaced persons. Many of these disasters were exacerbated by rising temperatures, and future ones are on target to become more common and increasingly worse.

Researchers predict there will be at least 140 million and as many as a billion climate refugees by 2040.

In recent decades, a whole slew of disasters have become more severe, from heat waves to wildfires to droughts to extreme rainfall to cyclones and hurricanes, all caused in significant part by changing temperatures fueled by human behavior. Every year, global sea levels rise about a fifth of an inch, and that rate increases annually. With vast swaths of earth set to be uninhabitable or at least starkly inhospitable in the near future, researchers predict there will be at least 140 million and as many as a billion climate refugees by 2040, when the youngest Millennials are in their midforties, and before any of us hit retirement age (not that we'll ever be able to retire).

In 1997, about half of Americans told Gallup pollsters they could see that the effects of global warming had already begun. Twenty years later, more than 60 percent reported seeing the negative effects of climate change.

Aaron is one of them. "Climate change is threatening the places that have become home for me," he says. "What do you do? I don't know. You organize. You tap into what's going on. You hope, hope, hope that at some point we pull our heads out of our collective asses, or we watch a major city go underwater."

Already, he says, many of Miami's most under-resourced neighborhoods face significant flood risks; meanwhile, others that are on higher ground are increasingly targeted by developers who want to buy up elevated land for the wealthy, even if it means pushing the poor into more environmentally hazardous locales.

Miami residents, Aaron says, are acutely aware of the looming threat. And so they are organizing. "I can't imagine leaving here," he says. "I want to be part of defending it. I don't know what that looks like and when we start to take it seriously, and it requires a lot of federal help. But I can't imagine leaving."

Aaron and his neighbors will stay and fight another day, and hope that in a decade, the federal government will do more so that they will not be forced, like Steph was, to pack it in and move to more hospitable ground.

Green Diaper Babies

Where to live is just one major Millennial life decision being shaped by climate. Another biggie: whether or not to have kids, and what it means to live a good and meaningful life.

I met Elena Valeriote on an organic farm in Tuscany, where she works for most of the year. Originally from Southern California, Elena, twenty-five, has led a largely itinerant existence, traveling extensively and living mostly out of a suitcase. The choices she has made since college can be traced, in part, to her dedication to the natural world, an ethos she shares with many other Millennials who prize conservation and value experiences over things. "There's a movement toward anti-consumerism that I think is fabulous," Elena, who also writes about food, travel, and sustainability, says. "I'm much more into an experience that is impermanent and lived, instead of a thing that will eventually be in a trash can or landfill."

For Elena, caring about her impact on the health of the planet also means not having kids, and encouraging others to deeply consider their own choices and reflect on what it means to parent, connect, and nurture. "The question first is why is it fundamentally the default that people have children?" Elena asks. "I don't think that should be a default choice. I think that should be the most serious and important choice a person makes in their life. I think I will find deeper meaning in my life and be able to do more good by mothering people who are not my biological children."

Lots of older folks tell Elena she'll change her mind on the kid thing. After all, some people in their teens or twenties say they'll never have kids, only to find themselves parents in their thirties or forties. Steph, who moved from Montana to New York, always wanted kids but, as a young fire-and-brimstone environmentalist, dedicated herself to only having one child—and then went on to have two. "My twenty-year-old self would have admonished me for that," Steph says. "We've talked about adoption and growing our family that way someday. Honestly I wish that adoption were easier. And I wish that people didn't have such an obsession with biological children."

In 2018, US birth rates hit a 30-year low.

But that may be changing. In 2018, US birth rates hit a thirty-year low. Lots of people who say they don't want children aren't changing their minds. And some people who do want children, or who are agnostic on the issue, aren't having them. Others are having fewer. There is some evidence that Elena and Steph aren't alone, and that Millennials are taking climate change into account when they decide whether or not to have children, and how many to have.

The explanations for why birth rates have dropped are both complex and poorly understood (more on that later), but climate concerns do seem to be playing a role. *Business Insider* found that 30 percent of Americans think climate should at least be a minor consideration in childbearing decisions. The younger poll respondents were, the more likely they were to say that climate change should be a factor in reproductive decision-making. When the *New York Times* partnered with the research firm Morning Consult in 2018 to ask young women about their childbearing decisions, they found that, among those who had or planned to have fewer than their ideal number of children, a third listed climate worries as one reason for deciding to bring fewer into the world.

On one hand, it is heartening, particularly from a feminist perspective, to see childbearing as increasingly optional rather than framed as the primary marker of women's adulthood or our life's purpose. But it is also troubling to see people who want to have children, or want to have more children, feeling fatalistic enough to delay or even cancel their plans to grow their families.

Meehan Crist, forty-one and the writer in residence in biological sciences at Columbia University, is both a science writer and a new mother. She says it's nearly impossible to divorce our global history of eugenics and racism from conversations about the environment and childbearing. There was a turning point, she says, around 2018, when all of a sudden it felt like these conversations were happening *everywhere*. "In terms of kids, I hear three things," she says. "One is, how will having a kid affect the planet? Another is, how will having a kid affect the kid in a time of ecological collapse? And finally, how will having a kid affect me? For some people, it's too painful to imagine watching a child they love growing up in what will be our future."

But mostly, she says, "I see a lot of what feels like flailing."

We don't quite have the language to talk through how some of the most intimate choices a person makes weigh against the threat of climate change. We have barely just developed the language of reproductive justice, which grew out of concerns from women of color who have seen restrictions not just on their right to abortion but on their right to bear and mother their own children. One thing we do know is that conversations about population growth are set against an ugly reality of racist reproductive abuses, including forced and coerced sterilizations of women of color. When we talk about limiting reproduction to save the planet, what a lot of people rightly hear is that certain groups of people—typically those with fewer resources, and typically poor black and brown women—will be deemed less deserving of making their own fully free reproductive choices.

The truth, Crist says, is that to be broadly effective, individual choices have to extend to the political and policy realm. And that means laws that adequately regulate big companies. According to an analysis by Richard Heede at the Climate Accountability Institute, more than a third of all carbon dioxide and methane emissions since 1965 have come from just twenty fossil fuel companies. Topping the list are Saudi Aramco, Chevron, Gazprom (a state-owned Saudi company), Exxon, National Iranian Oil Company, BP, and Shell. And those big companies are often the same enterprises pushing the personal responsibility narrative, while refusing to take sufficient responsibility for their own actions. In 2005, Crist wrote in an essay for the *London Review of Books*, BP spent $100 million on a media campaign that including pushing the concept of an individual carbon footprint. The "education services" section of their website encourages kids to calculate not just their own carbon footprint but that of their school. "In other words," Crist wrote, "the narrative that you, personally, are responsible for the climate crisis has been carefully crafted and drilled into you by the fossil fuel industry."

When environmentalists and activists encourage others to forgo something as fundamental as childbearing because of climate concerns, "you have to ask what kind of humanity it is that we are preserving for the future," Crist says. "I am concerned about the thoughtless version of that: *This is the way I can make an impact*. Without thinking about what we are doing to our sense of possibility in the future. That to me seems like a massive failure of imagination."

And yet many of the Millennials I talked to said they viewed forgoing children as a kind of compassionate choice, given the global outlook (if, given Millennials' dire financial straits, they talked about having kids at all). Natalie Liddle, a twenty-seven-year-old living in small-town South Carolina, has been with her boyfriend, Sebastian, since high school. But, she says, "in terms of our plans for the future, we don't talk a lot about having children. We have this silent assumption that we are just not even going to talk about until we, excuse my French, have our shit together."

But when Natalie thinks about it by herself, she gets stuck. "It's a wonder thinking that someday we will have full HD *National Geographic* footage of these beautiful wonderful creatures that inhabited our earth, and we will have to explain to our grandchildren and potentially our children, why these creatures don't exist and why we didn't do anything about it," she says. And she has a point: the World Wide Fund for Nature reports that human beings very efficiently obliterated 60 percent of mammals, birds, fish, and reptiles between 1970 and 2014. A million more animal and plant species are threatened with extinction.

Human beings obliterated 60% of mammals, birds, fish, and reptiles between 1970 and 2014.

Sometimes Natalie finds it easier to ostrich: stick her head in the sand and pretend this isn't happening. The whole concept of irreversible climate crisis simply feels too big and too terrifying to fully consider. When she does think about it, some clear conclusions come into sharper focus. "Why do we have kids?" she asks. "We have kids to try and achieve the only path to immortality we have, which is carrying on a piece of us in the world. But if the world is not going to be habitable for much longer, then what right do I have to bring another into that?"

Still, as a caveat: While I spoke with dozens of Millennials about their reproductive decisions and heard, mostly from women, that climate was a factor they were considering, one suspicion kept nagging at me. Was this all really about the environment, or do a lot of Millennial women still lack the language—and believe they do not have permission—to express ambivalence about childbearing? That isn't to say that women say one thing and mean another, but not a single woman I spoke with said she didn't want children *only* because of climate change concerns. Instead, many listed climate change as one of several anxieties. In a culture where women who don't want children are seen as selfish and cold, maybe pointing to something outside of one's own desires takes a little of the heat off. After all, forgoing kids because you don't want to bring them into a difficult world is easily framed as compassionate, and therefore appropriately feminine. Forgoing kids because you like your life as-is and just kinda don't want them? That's a very different thing, more easily vilified as "selfish."

Whatever reproductive decision anyone makes, and whatever the complex and unspoken motivations, it's hard to argue with Natalie that there are significant moral questions to weigh when looking toward a future that is bleak, and getting bleaker. In 1980, when global warming was just coming onto the national radar screen, the average global temperature was 0.3 degrees Celsius over the twentieth-century average. Today it's almost a full degree higher. Environmentalists (and rational people generally) are struggling mightily to keep global temperatures from rising any more than 1.5 degrees Celsius. This was the motivation behind the Paris accord, which aimed to at least keep global temperatures from rising more than 2 degrees Celsius and, ideally, to keep the rise to no more than 1.5 degrees Celsius. Things are already going to be pretty brutal. But if we get to a two-degree rise, it gets exponentially worse: fresh water supplies dry up, crops wither, punishing heat waves wreak even more havoc and death, droughts plague some areas while extreme rainfall destroys others, species are eviscerated, and oceans rise to dangerous levels as polar ice sheets melt.

In 2018, the year Meehan Crist, the Columbia University writer in residence, says all of a sudden everyone seemed to take notice of climate concerns, the United Nations did the equivalent of pulling the emergency fire alarm: it released a report saying that we have just twelve years to make major changes. Not twelve years to make changes that will stop climate change—that flaming hell ship has sailed—but just to slow it down enough to prevent the most cataclysmic and ruinous outcomes that will result in massive, post-apocalyptic death and destruction. A few years have now ticked by with little progress. By 2100, 2 billion people could be forced from flooding homes.

Doesn't sound like a great place to raise a kid, does it?

For some Millennials on the reproductive fence, the promise of a habitable future world would shift their choices. Erika Lindsey, a Bay Area native now living in Brooklyn, is one of them. "There's something about the reports that have come out that give a super-finite amount of time to make hard pivots that gave me pause about whether or not I wanted to bring children into that environment," Erika says. "I'm sure we're not that special, and there have been other points in history where people worried about this catastrophic change, but this feels like new territory, like a permanent substantial change. We've already seen the impact on climate refugees and clean water. It makes me extremely anxious about having kids."

This is tough, because Erika loves kids and used to be sure

she wanted them. Sometimes she can still picture a version of her life with kids. But she's also thirty-seven and doesn't have a serious partner or the kind of super-high income that makes raising kids in New York City marginally easier; having a baby on her own sounds tougher than what she wants right now.

She still might do it.

"If there is a shift in political leadership, and I know there are people working on reversing the impacts of climate change and fixing things, I will consider it," Erika says. "I'm sure most people would say they need a partner, and that would be great, but it's literally like more income and addressing climate change and I would figure it out. I do fully realize the impact that adding additional people to this world has on climate change—it's a contributing factor. But bold political leadership would get me to reconsider this decision."

Teaspoons in a Sinking Ship

Millennials are making tremendous personal sacrifices to stave off climate catastrophe. But we also know that all of the canvas bags on the planet won't save us. That will take serious policy change and much stricter regulations of industry. And that takes politicians dedicated to righting the climate Titanic—which, in the Trump era, with a Boomer-dominated Congress, Americans don't have.

And so, as in so many other aspects of our lives, Millennials are chugging along, stitching together a hodgepodge parachute of individual solutions and hoping it keeps us aloft. You can see this in how we eat: 57 percent of Millennials say they follow a special diet, and 44 percent of them say their dietary choices are a reaction to climate change. Americans, it should be said, are meat hogs: we eat an average of 214 pounds of meat per person per year, while Europeans eat 152 pounds, and even steak-loving Argentines average 190 pounds. But younger Americans—Millennials and Gen Zers—are shifting this trend.

We are a generation that believes how we eat matters. Sixty percent of us say we are aware of how our food choices affect the environment, which is perhaps why 63 percent of us are trying to incorporate a greater proportion of plant-based foods into our diets, and half of us buy with an eye toward less plastic and packaging. We are much more likely than older Americans to have eaten a plant-based meat substitute, like an Impossible Burger, in the previous year. As we've hit adulthood and are increasingly in charge of family food decisions, a quarter of Millennials have turned to vegetarianism or veganism, part of a broader dietary revolution that has fueled a 600 percent rise in veganism nationwide.

While Millennials are indeed a generation that prioritizes experiences over things and may choose a great trip over a new couch, we also understand that we have to balance our desire to see more of the world with our desire to make sure it's around for future generations. For a small number of Millennials, that

A quarter of Millennials have turned to vegetarianism or veganism—part of a broader dietary revolution that has fueled a 600 percent rise in veganism nationwide.

means a commitment to less air travel, something that's easier for our European counterparts, who are well connected by rail, than for Americans. For others, it means sustainable travel: visiting new places in a way that leaves a light footprint (no massive cruise ships), and staying in eco-friendly accommodations.

It's also notable that even in a sharply polarized country, climate change is much less of a partisan issue for Millennials than it is for Boomers. According to the Pew Research Center, Millennial Republicans are twice as likely as their Boomer counterparts to agree with the scientific consensus that global warming comes from human activity, and close to 60 percent of Millennial Republicans say that climate change is having at least some effect on the United States. Millennial Democrats are even more concerned: Ninety-one percent of them told Gallup that global warming is happening, and 81 percent say humans are to blame.

While just 31 percent of Boomer-and-older Republicans say

the federal government isn't doing enough to protect the environment, more than half of Millennial and younger Republicans say the government should do more, and nearly 80 percent say we should invest in alternative energy sources. According to surveys conducted by the Yale Program on Climate Change Communication, Millennials are also more likely than any previous generation to say that global warming is an issue of personal importance, and are more willing to donate to and volunteer for organizations fighting climate change, and to call their political representatives and tell them to do something about it. That last bit is key. While Millennials can try our best to cut down on red meat and live in cities where we can take the bus or ride a bike instead of driving a car, we know these efforts are like using a teaspoon to scoop water out of a capsizing boat: not totally useless, but nowhere near enough to prevent the inevitable.

Columbia University's Crist also says she notices generational differences in how people process and discuss climate change. "I think that older generations are experiencing the climate crisis with a sense of profound grief and loss, and much of mainstream media is eulogizing what we're losing," Crist, an Xennial, says. "Which I think is because people in those slightly older generations made decisions and built lives not knowing about the climate crisis, and so they have a lot to lose—when you're older you have more stuff, a job, a house."

Younger folks, by contrast, haven't built all of that up yet, nor made many of their biggest life decisions. "What they're seeing taken away from them is the possibility of the future," Crist says. "And they are rightfully so angry. Not at what they have being taken away, but at not ever having the chance to build and grow and flourish in the ways they imagine they would want to, because the world they grew up in is not going to be there."

It's telling that the few Millennials who do have a seat at the national political table are putting aggressive climate action at the top of their agenda. Millennial representatives like Alexandria Ocasio-Cortez aren't just grieving the loss of extinct species; they are demanding significant changes to climate policy *now*, not at some undefined time in the future when it becomes more convenient for big businesses. "Millennials and Gen Z and all these folks that come after us are looking up, and we're like, 'The world is going to end in 12 years if we don't address climate change, and your biggest issue is how are we gonna pay for it?'" Ocasio-Cortez said (hyperbolically) in an interview with the writer Ta-Nehisi Coates. "This is our World War II."

Young leaders like Ocasio-Cortez argue that the right policies could both mitigate the impending climate disaster and create new green jobs to make up for the ones that will be lost when fossil fuel industries take a hit. Millennials seem to recognize that when it comes down to it, saving the future of humankind is a little more important than protecting corporate profits (this same gap emerged during the coronavirus response, with younger, more progressive leaders firmly on the side of "save people," and older, more conservative ones like the president prioritizing saving the markets). And credit also goes to those even younger than us: Gen Z might be even more committed to climate activism, from Greta Thunberg to the Climate Strike to the young people of Extinction Rebellion.

Part of this is age: those of us who are set to inherit a burning, flooding earth are understandably more alarmed about its prospects, and more motivated to do something about it rather than kick the can down the road. And part of it is the overlap of age and race: African Americans and Hispanics in the US are much more likely than whites to say that climate change is a significant problem. Communities of color have long borne disproportionate burdens of toxic environments, and are likely to experience the ills of climate change sooner and more significantly than whites. Millennials are a more diverse generation than Boomers and Gen Xers, and so we are more likely by virtue of both age and race to have grown up seeing environmental devastation firsthand. There is also what researchers call the "white male effect": that is, white men are more likely than other groups to shrug off a variety of risks to the vulnerable, including climate change. Millennials have proportionately fewer white men in our generation than any before us, which may contribute to our acceptance of the scientific consensus on climate, and our determination to do something about it.

African Americans and Hispanics in the US are much more likely than whites to say that climate change is a significant problem.

For now, our individual ability to do something to save the planet is limited, although our choices reflect a pretty high level of climate savvy. Even though the US population is growing, per capita energy consumption is down. Per capita annual emissions are down, too, a dip that began in 2005, just as Millennials were entering adulthood. While petroleum consumption has largely stayed the same—due to artificially low gas prices and under-investment in public transport—coal consumption has also gone down.

Young people are doing our part. But we are also the ones who will be bearing future burdens. We know that individual decisions alone will not get this done. We need national and international regulations on big businesses, and for that, we need buy-in from Baby Boomer politicians. We needed it to start yesterday.

So why aren't the people in charge working harder to put out the climate fire?

We Didn't Start the Fire

The frustrating truth is that Boomers knew this was coming.

Some of the first people to know just how bad the climate crisis could get were the same ones leading us down the path to hell. Petroleum megacorporation Exxon has been aware of our coming catastrophe since at least the 1970s, and in the following few years, other big energy and fossil fuel companies began to draw the same conclusions. And what they projected were not just minor inconveniences or small-scale damage. James F. Black, a scientist on an Exxon research project in the midseventies, wrote at the time, "Present thinking holds that man has a time window of five to ten years before the need for hard decisions regarding changes in energy strategies might become critical."

Faced with stunning warnings coming from inside their own houses, big energy, petroleum, and fossil fuel companies used the same strategy as Big Tobacco: denial. Exxon spent the next half-century spewing carbon, posting massive profits, and rejecting its own experts' climate conclusions.

Luckily, scientists who aren't employed by fossil fuel companies are a little less tight-lipped when they see a crisis brewing. In 1981, NASA scientist James Hansen published a paper predicting that burning fossil fuels would in turn fuel global temperatures, making them tick up by 4.5 degrees Fahrenheit, or 2.5 degrees Celsius, in just two decades. This did not please the powerful and moneyed fossil fuel industry or their political benefactors: our Boomer-approved friend Reagan entered office and decreased funding for Hansen's department within NASA.

A few years later, on a sweaty June day in 1988, Hansen testified before Congress that high temperatures were not the result of normal fluctuations, but significant and troubling changes to the atmosphere: a warming climate caused by human behavior. Two years earlier, fewer than half of Americans had ever heard of the greenhouse effect; by 1990, two years after Hansen's testimony, three-quarters of them had. Congress held more hearings, and the Environmental Protection Agency made it clear: global warming is real, and it's here. By 2000, nine in ten Americans had heard of the greenhouse effect. It wasn't only scientists sounding the alarm: a lot of Baby Boomers spent their careers in public life jumping up and down and shouting at everyone else to pay attention to climate change. Former Vice President Al Gore, to give one notable example, has used his time out of office attempting to capture global attention for the "inconvenient truth" of climate crisis.

But that doesn't mean most Americans have listened.

Fossil fuel and energy businesses have a vested interest in sowing doubt about climate change. After all, the kind of large-scale emergency changes necessary to save the planet would cut into their bottom line, and older executives would apparently rather enjoy their riches now and let their rest of us—including their kids and grandkids—figure out how to survive in the roasting hellscape they plan to leave behind. According to a 2017 report by the Climate Accountability Institute, just 100 companies—ExxonMobil, Shell, BP, and Chevron among them—are responsible for 70 percent of the world's greenhouse gas emissions since 1988. American politicians sided with these 100 absurdly prosperous and planet-pillaging businesses over the health, well-being, and future of the 7 billion other people on the planet.

This is why you can't separate climate from the extreme wealth inequality that has divided Americans into an increasingly tiny pool of have-a-tons from a vast national ocean of have-not-muches. The refusal to act on climate change has exacerbated this inequality. In turn, the very few have a disproportionate say in the regulations that would slow climate change.

Just like the wealth inequality that leaves Millennials broke and desperate, the scourge of environmental degradation and rising temperatures lies at the feet of big businesses, the billionaires who run them, and their enablers in government.

And even as climate change makes life miserable for the poorest people in society, it has become a booming business for those keen to exploit it. Companies have sprung up to make global warming less painful for the rich—there are, for example, the private firefighters who are paid handsomely to risk their lives protecting the homes of the very rich in fire-prone California. Other companies, many based overseas, are profiting from the proliferation of air-conditioning units, a consumer good increasingly necessary to stay cool in hot temperatures but in turn contributing to them. Wealthy investors are scooping up farmland, knowing the world is going to be hungrier when there's less arable land to grow food and graze livestock on. And real estate speculators have swooped in to buy up the homes of lower-income folks who live on high (and dry) ground.

Under-regulated businesses are profiting from all directions: the equivalent of an arsonist who gets paid to put out the fire, collects the insurance money, and sells the house's scorched remains for a profit.

So why aren't we stopping them? It's not *just* that the worst polluters are politically influential via major donations, although of course some of them are. One issue is that these companies are big employers, and have successfully convinced a significant number of workers that any attack on dirty industry is a personal attack on them. Employees in the energy sector, understandably, worry that their jobs are on the line. But cutting emissions and regulating polluters doesn't have to mean economic devastation for the millions of workers in the oil, gas, and energy sectors. Green jobs are already among the fastest-growing in the nation, and while a transition to greener energy sources won't be easy or painless, the path can certainly be smoothed over for the average folks who need a paycheck. Instead, we are choosing to believe the fantasy that all is well and our futures will be fine.

Efforts to save the planet don't come cheap, but the bill for inaction will be even more devastating. A Morgan Stanley analysis estimated that doing the minimum to stave off the problem, including meeting the terms of the Paris Agreement and getting to net-zero emissions, will cost the world $50 trillion total by 2050. But the National Resources Defense Council projects that the devastation wreaked by a warming planet, including the destruction brought about by superpowered hurricanes, real estate lost to or damaged by rising sea levels, dizzying energy costs (air-conditioning and refrigeration in a hotter world doesn't come cheap), and the expense of bringing water to an increasingly dry nation, will cost the United States alone an additional $2 trillion a year, every year, by 2100.

Time is running out. And unlike with other instances of Boomer can-kicking down the road—racking up the national debt, failing to fully fund Social Security for the next generation—our climate emergency can't be dealt with later. Temperatures are rising, ice caps are melting, cities are flooding,

Nearly 80 percent of senators and two-thirds of the US House of Representatives are fifty-five or older. Just 7 percent of representatives in Congress are Millennials.

and the planet is burning. And Millennials, Gen Zers, and our kids are the ones who are going to be left roasting our sustainable veggie dogs in hell.

Boomers, Gen Xers, Millennials, and Gen Zers may each have different priorities and immediate desires, but no one wants to see the kind of suffering we're on pace to experience. Getting on the same page about fighting climate change, though, means agreeing on the same set of facts about climate change. And that's not happening.

Three-quarters of Americans ages eighteen to thirty-four agree that global warming is caused by human activities—the broad and nearly undisputed global scientific consensus—but only 55 percent of those over fifty-five do. About the same proportion of Boomers and those older than them tell Gallup that they are regularly concerned about global warming, compared to 70 percent of American adults under thirty-five.

And yet those of us with the biggest stake in the issue don't have a seat at the table.

Millennials and Boomers each make up about 22 percent of the US population. And yet nearly 80 percent of senators and two-thirds of the US House of Representatives are fifty-five or older—Boomers, and a few Silents hanging on. Just 7 percent of representatives in Congress are Millennials. There is not a single Millennial in the US Senate.

Crist, for her part, sees a generational shift in how younger people approach the imminent perils of a changing climate. No, Millennials don't have the same sense of wonder and awe about things to come as previous generations. We may have grown up fascinated by the promise of technology and robots and outer space, but we no longer assume that the future will be shiny and bright. But that doesn't mean we've given up. "It's one thing to think we're going to have *The Jetsons* in the future," Crist says, which Millennials obviously do not. "It's another to think, 'Fuck you, we're going to survive.' It's a different kind of sensibility. Gimlet-eyed *optimism* isn't even the right word. It's gimlet-eyed hope."

Close to 40% of opposite-sex American couples now meet online; for same-sex couples, it's 65%.

Millennials use social media much more than members of any other adult generation. As of 2016, we were almost twice as likely as Boomers to use Facebook, about three times as likely to use Twitter, and four times as likely to use Instagram.

Millennials are isolated: one in five of us say we have zero friends and zero acquaintances.

Nearly 80% of Millennials bring work with them when they go on vacation. Most Boomers disconnect.

TECHNOLOGY

Millennials are the technological bridge generation, connecting the analog Boomers and Gen Xers to the digital Gen Z. Like Boomers and Gen Xers, and unlike the Gen Zers whose births might have been broadcast on Instagram, Millennials largely spent our childhoods without smartphones, tablets, or laptops. We have the context of a less-connected earlier era: a time when most experiences went undocumented, years when entertainment was not always at your fingertips, life before everyone sat around the dinner table tapping and swiping their phones after photographing their food. The older among us grew up without home internet; as adolescents, we were lucky if we had AOL dial-up. But once the technological innovations of the internet and the handheld computer arrived, we were quicker than older Americans to integrate them into our lives. It didn't hurt that we were younger: About half of Americans were using the internet by the year 2000, when the oldest Millennials were in college, and the youngest adults were the most likely to be online. When the first iPhone hit the market, Millennials were preteens, teen-

Millennials text about five times as often as Baby Boomers.

agers, and young adults, and we remain the most likely adult generation to own a smartphone.

While Boomers also grew up in an era of rapid technological advancement, the innovations of their time came with a sense of wonder and optimism: from the dawn of color television to the space race to the invention of the microwave oven, Boomer childhoods were marked by advances that promised brighter, better, aluminum-shiny futures, and these discoveries often delivered.

Millennials, on the other hand, have seen the great promises of digital technology and connection—often created by Millennials and then sold to Millennials—quickly turn sinister. The great hope that the internet and social media would make us better informed, better connected, and more empathetic has been thoroughly dashed as bad actors have exploited these tools for personal gain, while many technology companies have been slow, inadequate, and often shockingly blasé in response. The results have been devastating: the rise of authoritarian strong-men and the breakdown of liberal democracy; the proliferation of misinformation campaigns; sustained and sometimes coordinated acts of bullying and harassment, and victims who find themselves traumatized, financially ruined, socially isolated, even suicidal; and the widespread embrace and weaponization of rhetoric that fuels bigotry, violence, slaughter, and ethnic cleansing.

Do Millennials deserve all the blame for this? Of course not. But when it comes to the transformative power of technology and the internet, we royally screwed this one up. And now a lot of us are wondering how we fix the future.

The Great Promise

Millennials came of age in an era of almost unprecedented technological growth. From the internet to smartphones to social media, we have seen nearly every aspect of life revolutionized at breakneck speed. While older generations experienced these same shifts alongside us, the young tend to be quicker to adapt and adopt. And given that many of these changes occurred when Millennials were just entering adult life, they also shaped how we live as adults.

Communication is the most obvious shift. For young people, landlines are a thing of the past; even picking up our iPhones to place a call instead of sending a text is a rarity. A full 93 percent of Millennials own a smartphone, compared to 68 percent of Boomers. Millennials text about five times as often as Baby Boomers. The proliferation of social media has also kept Millennials connected, and helped us to forge new relationships in ways unimaginable when our parents were young.

Much of this is good. Though we don't spend our Sunday afternoons catching up with friends over hours-long phone conversations, we can easily check out, for example, what a huge number of our high school and college classmates are up to more than a decade after graduation, which helps to sustain long friendships and occasionally reignites new ones. The ease with which we can communicate with people who do not live in our immediate vicinity is revolutionary, allowing us to socially sort by interests and values rather than by previous vectors of division: class, location, race. This doesn't mean those previous factors are no longer in play—race, socioeconomic status, and location also shape one's interests and values. But social media platforms specifically, and the internet more generally, make it easier for all of us to find our own version of "our people." While Boomers see significant socioeconomic divides when it comes to social media use—the Stanford Center of Poverty and Inequality found that wealthier and middle-class Boomers are a lot more likely than poor ones to be on sites like Facebook, LinkedIn, and Twitter—for Millennials, the haves use social media only marginally more than the have-nots. These platforms also make organizing and information distribution more effective. Move-

Close to 40 percent of American heterosexual couples now meet online; for same-sex couples, it's 65 percent.

ments including March for Our Lives and Black Lives Matter, for example, were able to leverage this power to bring attention to what was happening beyond the spotlight of mainstream media attention.

The internet also makes it easier to find a partner for marriage, a date, sex, friendship, or conversation. Close to 40 percent of American heterosexual couples now meet online; for same-sex couples, it's 65 percent, a 2019 Stanford University study found. For the 60 years following World War II, the Stanford researchers found, couples overwhelmingly met through friends and family. That changed after 2009, and now couples are more likely to meet online than anywhere else. And while traditionalists worry that online dating may lead to an increase of assortive mating—people romantically sorting themselves and marrying within racial, socioeconomic, and educational groups—the Stanford researcher found that the opposite might actually be true: couples who meet online are actually more likely to have different racial and ethnic backgrounds, different religious beliefs, and different educational levels. And while those couples are not *more* likely to date across political lines than couples who meet in more traditional "real-life" settings, they're not less likely to do so, either.

Couples who meet online are more likely to have different racial and ethnic backgrounds, different religious beliefs, and different educational levels.

The Millennial embrace of nontraditional life paths may also be at least partly credited to the internet. Steph Larsen, the Xennial mother who moved her family from her beloved Montana to a farm in upstate New York because of climate change fears, grew up in a small Wisconsin city where getting married in your twenties and having babies soon after was the longtime cultural norm. But because she had the internet as she came of age, Steph says, "I took a completely different path than what I grew up being told was 'normal.' I said I'm going to travel, I'm going to pursue a career, I'm going to try out farming, I'm going to weigh whether I really want to be a parent or not." For Steph, internet access made her more curious about the world around her, and hungry for travel and new experiences. It also shaped her identity. "I remember when I was ten praying for God not to make me a lesbian. And now that kind of breaks my heart—I want to just hug that little ten-year-old and say it's fine, and it's gonna be fine," Steph says. "As I got to grad school, I realized, oh my gosh, I'm bisexual, there's this whole community of people who are attracted to different genders, let me try this on. I wish that I had had role models when I was younger that my kids will have because of the internet." If her kids have questions Steph can't answer, she can google it. If they have unusual interests, she can look them up. If their experiences diverge from hers, she and her husband can more easily find resources to support them. "If our daughter comes to us and says 'I'm a boy' and insists upon it, we can go research that and understand what it means to be trans in a way that previous generations couldn't," Steph says.

For Jolie Theall, a late Boomer who was born in 1959, the Boomers-as-tech-dolts stereotype doesn't quite hold—her kids, she says, call her for tech support. She started a software company in the eighties that continued to prosper through the nineties, until the financial crash of 2008 wiped her out. But she continued to work in tech long after. And the tech revolution hasn't just given Jolie a job; it has, in very tangible ways, helped confirm her identity and sense of self. Four years ago, Jolie came out as transgender. But as she began hormone therapy to physically transition, she also noticed that, for the first time in her life, she was having a hard time getting work. After a bout of unemployment, near homelessness, and then the COVID-19 outbreak, she wound up at her sister's house in rural Texas ("They're playing Fox News twenty-four-seven and I'm hiding in the back room with my RESIST hashtag t-shirt on." Jolie laughs. "It's an interesting dynamic."). But she also got a job—working remotely for a California college on their online learning initiatives. "I just got a doctor via telemedicine," Jolie says. "I'm working on finding an apartment in Austin with all virtual tours. The pharmacy that I'm working with is drop-shipping my meds; they did it on Friday and it's arriving Monday here in the boondocks. It's friggin' amazing."

Tech has also largely made work easier, more efficient, and safer, something that came into sharp focus when millions of people were forced to shelter, work, and socialize from home during the 2020 coronavirus outbreak. The virus's impact on the global economy was devastating. But imagine how much worse it would have been if we didn't have the internet to work, communicate, shop, and gather information.

That's certainly the case for Cassidy Theall, Jolie's twenty-nine-year-old Millennial daughter. She is a barber in New York City, an analog job if there ever was one. Coronavirus meant unemployment, but Cassidy says she was lucky she got on the state's unemployment rolls quickly, and received her stimulus check. "All of that, every single penny of that, is going toward rent and food," she said. I spoke with Cassidy in the midst of nationwide shelter-in-place orders; she was stuck in her apartment with her cat and her roommate. Technology, though, helped her eke out a little extra cash even at home, even in a job that is usually literally hands-on. "In this situation it's been a saving grace to all of us," Cassidy said. "We can FaceTime and communicate, and I can talk to my clients and see them face-to-face. I can help them with their haircutting needs and get paid for that." That's right: Cassidy used FaceTime to walk her clients through the process of cutting their own hair.

Even outside of pandemic times, technology often makes work better. If you're a lawyer researching case law, you no longer have to spend hours in the library thumbing through hardcover books; you can do a search on Westlaw, target the most relevant terms, and find what you need. If you're a nurse, you input medications and vitals not just on a physical chart but into a computer, which in turn keeps long records and decreases the chance of a high-stakes human error. Advertising your small business, doing inventory, reaching out to clients, applying for jobs, filing taxes—it's all easier.

This has, in many ways, worked in Millennials' favor. Millennial technological fluency—or the perception of it—is one reason this cohort, despite pretty poor job prospects overall, is flourishing in the tech industry, where the average age of workers is thirty-eight (it's forty-three in other industries). Millennials make up almost half of the tech work force, and we are much more likely than Boomers to judge employers on how they leverage technology. Boomers, and to some extent Gen Xers, aren't just getting left out of the tech labor pool; they are often facing active age discrimination, which is perhaps why so many tech workers say they're anxious about getting older and losing their jobs.

Millennials make up almost half of the tech work force.

That Millennial love of travel and experiences versus things? Another outcome of technological innovation. Travel is cheaper, more efficient, and more accessible than ever. International flights go for a fraction of what they cost when Boomers were young. The internet has negated the need for a travel agent (another industry felled by Millennials), as anyone with a smartphone can not only book a flight and hotel online but scour review sites for the best places to stay, eat, go out, and sightsee. We are a generation of people who fear we'll never be able to buy a house or pay down student loan debt, but at least the experience of going to a new place is a little slice of affordable luxury.

> **The tech revolution has, in so many ways, been a bright one for Millennials, who have reaped disproportionate benefits from all of the new ways we work, travel, meet, date, and learn.**

Millennials are more likely than Boomers to use their vacation days to travel, but Boomers are traveling more than they used to, and they have more disposable income to travel with. But Boomers tend to see their trips as disconnected vacations, while Millennials view travel as part of life. Boomers set out-of-office messages. Millennials are a lot more likely to tote their laptops with them and work from the road: while close to 60 percent of Boomers told the AARP they don't think it's important to stay connected to work while they're on vacation, close to 80 percent of Millennials say they bring work with them. I may be a sample size of one, but the number of vacations I've taken as an adult where I've totally disconnected and done no work is zero. I wrote significant sections of this book while on "vacation."

The technological age has also democratized information and made education more efficient (if not always higher-quality). The proliferation of online learning, pitched to people who may otherwise be excluded from the classroom—full-time workers, busy parents, those who can't afford traditional higher education—has opened a world of opportunity for anyone who can swing it. When the coronavirus pandemic put Americans across the country on lockdown, millions of schoolchildren and college students continued their learning via Zoom and other online platforms. While clearly no replacement for a classroom led by a trained educator—just ask any parent stuck suddenly homeschooling their kid, or any kid taught by inexperienced Mom and Dad—online learning tools can at least help to fill some educational gaps. And the ease with which tech innovations allow us to move through the world is stunning, from summoning a vehicle via your phone, to mapping the most efficient route to your destination, to finding the closest health care clinic with a few taps.

Boomers have taken advantage of technology, too, although their tech use looks different. That stereotype of the older person using both hands to hold their massive iPad aloft, shooting a photo with a loud click? Well, it's kinda true: while Millennials are much more likely to own smartphones and laptops, Boomers are the tablet generation.

The tech revolution has, in so many ways, been a bright one for Millennials, who have reaped disproportionate benefits from all of the new ways we work, travel, meet, date, and learn.

But oh boy, are there consequences.

Did the Internet Break Our Brains?

As Millennials entered adulthood, the social rules of engagement radically shifted as we went from IRL to online. While social media opened new and innovative opportunities for connection and conversation, our phones, and the social media apps that live in them, turned out to be fiercely and intentionally addictive—after all, the greatest minds of our generation designed them to be.

Facebook was honed to give users "a little dopamine hit every once in a while, because someone liked or commented on a photo or a post," the company's founding president, Sean Parker, told journalist Mike Allen of Axios. When building the platform the primary question was "How do we consume as much of your time and conscious attention as possible?" The company's designers, Parker said, were knowingly "exploiting a vulnerability in human psychology." Each like, retweet, or comment comes with a rush, and our more connected and publicly cultivated lives carry with them cruelty, envy, comparison, competition, resentment, and a lingering sense that everyone else is more successful, better traveled, richer, happier, and better looking than you. Social media connections are also shallower connections: knowing that a college friend now has two dark-haired children with rhyming names doesn't mean you know *her*. Being connected to someone via an app is not nearly the same as forging a real relationship with another person. No wonder researchers have found that social media use is correlated with anxiety, depression, low self-esteem, loneliness, and even suicidal ideation.

Some experts wonder whether these always available tools for comparison contribute to Millennial loneliness and low self-esteem. Forget about keeping up with the Joneses; young people today are trying to keep up with half of their high school classmates, coworkers, friends from college, and beautiful quasi-famous people relevant only for having seemingly unlimited resources. And it all comes to us via an ever-refreshing feed of photos of everyone's best moments and most flattering angles: enviable vacations, well-behaved children, sun-dappled outings, adorable pets, chiseled abs.

Of course, early adulthood has long been associated with loneliness. The loneliness of the early years of parenting; of long work hours with little time for social lives; of a world where there aren't ambient friendships past college or grad school. But technology has likely exacerbated even age-typical feelings of loneliness. There is first and most obviously the fact that social media use causes loneliness and depression, and reducing social

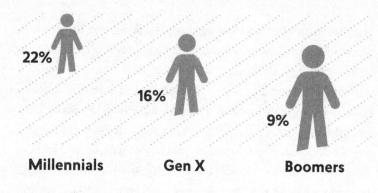

22% Millennials

16% Gen X

9% Boomers

Millennials are much more likely than Boomers or Gen Xers to say they have no friends: 22 percent of Millennials, but just 14 percent of Gen Xers and 9 percent of Boomers, listed the number of friends they have as zero.

media use has been shown to make people feel less lonely and less depressed. Millennials are the heaviest adult social media users (and those younger than us, who now say they prefer to text rather than talk in person, are even more addicted). We may also be the generation that sees the most significant divide between what we observe on social media and what we have access to. That is, as the brokest generation, with little chance of ever making a full recovery, it's particularly dispiriting to watch a steady stream of fortunate lives scroll by every time we pick up our phones.

Then there is the fact that Millennials may also be the adults most able to isolate ourselves because of technology. The Millennial shut-in posted up in his mother's basement and playing video games all day is an ugly and inaccurate stereotype, but when a full quarter of Millennials say that they don't have a single acquaintance beyond their family members or their partner—not even friends, *acquaintances*—you have to wonder what's going on.

Not even one in ten Boomers says the same. A majority of Boomers say they have at least twenty acquaintances, and 40 percent say they have fifty or more. By contrast, a majority of Millennials say they have fewer than ten acquaintances, which suggests a lot of us just aren't getting out much. Millennials are also much more likely than Boomers or Gen Xers to say that they have no friends: 22 percent of Millennials, but just 16 percent of Gen Xers and 9 percent of Boomers, listed the number of friends they have as zero.

Most Americans with no friends list shyness as the reason for their solitude. Introversion is not unique to Millennials, but it's now easier than ever to turn natural shyness into total isolation. Even in an office setting, communication tools like email, Slack, and text mean you don't actually have to talk to anyone. In-person service industry jobs—working the counter at a fast-casual restaurant, let's say—may include in-person interaction with coworkers, but also routinely come with tracking and surveillance. Friendly conversation decreases efficiency, which hurts the bottom line. Appearing to dawdle can lead to termination.

The gig economy jobs that are staffed by a lot of Millennials—shopping for Instacart, driving for Uber, running an Etsy shop—are nearly all done solo. Outside of work, our phones, tablets, and laptops bring a host of entertainment options—nearly unlimited television and movies, video games, pornography, food delivery—immediately and affordably into your home. This impulse to isolate can be exacerbated by chronic illness, physical or mental, something large numbers of Millennials experience and cannot afford to treat.

Those dating apps? Yes, they're great for finding a date, and a lot of people meet long-term partners on them. But they can also contribute to a sense that there is a bottomless pool of romantic and sexual partners. That makes app users less likely to invest significant time and effort into any given person. (One study by two network scientists found that close to half of messages on dating apps go unanswered.) And with so many possibilities out there, you may spend more time wondering, What if there's someone better out there? A plethora of choices, researchers have found, is what we think we want, but too many options overwhelm us and sink us into paralysis.

Take jam (really): one experiment conducted by Columbia University professor Sheena Iyengar found that while more supermarket shoppers gravitated toward a display with two dozen varieties of jam, just 3 percent of them actually purchased a jar. Among the customers who walked over to a smaller display of only six options, nearly a third bought one. People, obviously, are not jam. But when we look at their photos through a screen, along with carefully chosen clever descriptors, we do treat them quite like consumer products. Of course human beings were choosy before dating apps. But the ability to assess so many romantic partners, with so little effort, so rapidly, is unprecedented. And a lot of us find ourselves overwhelmed by the experience and, ultimately, we may give up.

The hustle culture that shapes Millennial work life is also a function of technology. Prita Piekara, who was choosing to keep up with work and networking through her maternity leave, can do so thanks to at-home Wi-Fi. Her husband, Evan, who dedicates significant spare time to networking and out-of-work career development, also relies on tech to keep up when he's not able to go out. "Now that Prita and I have a four-month-old, our focus has shifted slightly in the sense that we're not doing the evening things quite as much," Evan says. "But technology has enabled us to continue to hustle and continue to network." Even so-called social media isn't just for socializing; it's increasingly a reflection of your whole life, including your work—which, for many Millennials, partly defines our identities. "Technology has enabled us to be connected permanently," Prita says. "And our social media presence is starting to reflect our professions. Millennials are using platforms like Instagram and Twitter to build up their personal and professional brands—sharing their thoughts, defending their perspectives. It's not a separate platform for when I'm off duty. Our generation recognizes the blending of those two."

And all this networking and professionalized socializing and always-on working, notes Cassidy Theall, the New York barber, may mean we wind up with *fewer* friends, which may in turn fuel the Millennial loneliness epidemic. "I've been so focused on my job that all my friends are from the barber shop," Cassidy says. "How do you make new friends? Especially coming to a new city, all of my friends are my coworkers. Sometimes you go to parties with them and that's how you meet other people, but unless you're in a relationship with them or see them every day at work, what other time do you have to go out and meet people?" She recalls a recent conversation in which someone called New York "the city of isolation," and that resonated. Even back in her home town of Boulder, Colorado, she and her friends had drifted apart after high school; people had relationships and jobs, and eventually kids and marriages. They might like each other's photos on Instagram, but there was little depth to the relationships. "We were so busy with our own lives that we never had time to keep up a solid friendship," Cassidy says. That changed during the coronavirus shelter-in-place orders. "Now that everyone has time on their hands, I'm reconnecting with all of them. Even people I haven't talked to in like ten years. We're talking every day, we're sending pictures, we're FaceTiming. So it's really about time. Nobody has time to create friendships."

We also appear to be experiencing significant cognitive changes as a result of the technological innovations we now live with. As obviously world-changing as they may be, we have remarkably little idea of how all these technological shifts are affecting our brains and our bodies. We do know that many of Silicon Valley's tech masterminds have decided to raise their kids without screens, a choice that suggests they know something about their Frankenstein that we don't. ("I am convinced the devil lives in our phones and is wreaking havoc on our children," Athena Chavarria, a former assistant for Mark Zuckerberg who now works for his philanthropy, told the *New York Times*; Steve Jobs wouldn't let his kids use iPads.) What is fairly clear is that, due to our ever-present smartphones and computers, we are more easily distracted, more scatterbrained, and less able to focus our attention for sustained periods. (To anyone under forty reading this: Have you gotten through this whole chapter without checking your phone?) We know that some studies have found that media multi-tasking—like scrolling through your phone while you're also watching television—is correlated with attention deficits and sleep problems in young adults. We know that social media and skimming a million different things online trains our brains to scan for the top notes rather than learning to concentrate long enough to understand; we're less likely to retain important information, instead learning simply to remember where we can go find it again. Multiple studies have found that technology can increase or even create symptoms of ADHD in teenagers. UCLA researcher Patricia Greenfield has spent years examining the impact of technology, including social media, on young people. One of her studies found that social media drives narcissism: "Photos including the poster receive consistently more 'likes' than those that do not; thus the narcissism of constant self-presentation is audience-driven," Greenfield wrote. Nor is social media good for our social lives. Communicating via text or video is associated with poorer social well-being than in-person communication, and social media platforms create near ideal conditions for severe bullying. Moving through the world with our noses in our phones, Greenfield's research suggests, may even make us worse at reading human emotion, a finding that could have profound implications for basic human connection and empathy. What this all means long-term, we have no idea.

Moving through the world with our noses in our phones ... could have profound implications for basic human connection and empathy.

Millennials are remarkably self-aware when it comes to the drawbacks of technology. Globally, 64 percent of us say we would be physically healthier if we spent less time on social media, and 60 percent say we'd be happier. Just over half of us say social media does more harm than good. And yet most of us aren't willing (or able) to stop using it.

There's something else going on here, too: As Millennials grew up in the 1980s and '90s, we saw profound cultural shifts toward what researchers call "extrinsic goals"—things like money, status, and good looks—over intrinsic goals, like autonomy, meaning, and connection. Think 1987's Gordon Gekko, '90s-era Patrick Bateman, and the various Kardashians who have dominated reality TV culture for a decade. San Diego State University professor Jean Twenge, who has written about her research on generational differences in publications including the *Atlantic*, and her colleagues found that the steadily declining mental health of high school students from the 1950s to 2007 was largely the result of a culture increasingly oriented toward these kinds of external objectives. Twenge is also the author of a book about Millennials called *Generation Me: Why Today's Young Americans Are More Confident, Assertive, Entitled—and More Miserable Than Ever Before.* So she has a particular perspective on Millennial life. But, Twenge told me, "the name is not meant to be a knockdown. It is meant to convey the influence of increasing individualism in the culture." In their paper "Birth Cohort Increases in Psychopathology Among Young Americans, 1938–2007," Twenge and her fellow researchers put it bluntly: "As American culture shifted toward emphasizing individual achievement, money, and status rather than social relationships and community, psychopathology increased among young people."

The young people of the 2000s were, of course, Millennials. And that was before Instagram debuted and the lifestyles of the rich and famous were delivered directly to your phone; it was before the Kardashians and various other famous-for-being-famous celebrities became ubiquitous; it was just as America was tipping over from tabloid culture into a heavily filtered social media reality that glorifies "influencers" who both tout their love of various brands and are brands themselves. A 2011 study by psychology professors Yalda Uhls and Patricia Greenfield, published in the *Journal of Psychosocial Research on Cyberspace*, looked at the values portrayed in American tweens' favorite television shows from 1967 to 2007 and found some alarming changes over time. The values that declined the most over those fifty years were community, tradition, and benevolence. The ones that increased the most: fame (which was #15 in 1967 and #1 by

2007), achievement (#10 in 1967 and #2 in 2007), financial success (#12 in 1967 and #5 in 2007), and physical fitness (#16 in 1967 and #9 in 2007).

To be sure, Hollywood has always glamorized the rich and famous. The shift, it seems, has been prioritizing fame over other values, at the same time that technology has enabled many more people to be, and aspire to be, "celebrities" or micro-influencers themselves—Andy Warhol's idea of fifteen minutes of fame writ large. And we're all putting ourselves on display to be liked, shared, retweeted, pinned, and trolled.

There's an interesting twist, though. Twenge notes that Millennials became markedly less narcissistic after 2008. "The recession was a reality check," Twenge told me. "This kind of outsized optimism didn't work anymore." There were huge cultural changes, too, also spurred by the financial downturn. "That mid-2000s era was very much a new Gilded Age," Twenge says, from the Manolo Blahniks and conspicuous consumption of *Sex and the City* to the sneering rich-girl antics of Paris Hilton and Nicole Richie on *The Simple Life*. "There was all this emphasis on materialism and people seeking attention on reality TV, and then a lot of that changed. It became much less about revering people who are rich and materialistic, and much more about, we're going to protest them and call them the one percent." Those changes, she said, shifted us "more toward practicality and away from this overconfidence that characterizes narcissism."

Whether that practicality will continue in an age of social media is a different question.

"I thank my lucky stars every day that I did not grow up with social media," says Steph Larsen, the environmentalist and farmer in New York State. She wants to keep up with faraway friends and relatives but worries about putting her kids' faces on her social media accounts, a problem she tries to solve with careful privacy settings. She has a three-year-old and a one-year-old, and knows these questions are just going to get tougher as they grow up. But unlike questions about, say, how to get a baby to sleep or how to deal with an angsty teen, there's no one Steph can turn to when she's grappling with how to guide her children through the brave new world of technology. "My father is a computer science professor but I can't talk to him about this stuff," Steph says. "He got his PhD at a time when computer science was barely a thing. We've come so far since then. I can't look to any kinds of cultural norms about what I should do in any given situation. I have to just guess and experiment."

The largest number of American tech billionaires are Boomers, and many others are Gen Xers.

While Millennials, and increasingly Gen Zers, are participating in and manipulated by the new tech economy, who do you think is really running the companies that sustain it? Who do you think develops and produces the television shows that broadcast the values of fame, money, and beauty?

It's the same people who profit the most from the tech industry. That's not Millennials. The largest number of American tech billionaires are Boomers, and many others are Gen Xers.

Think Bill Gates (Microsoft), Jeff Bezos (Amazon), Paul Allen (Microsoft), and Steve Ballmer (former CEO of Microsoft). Larry Ellison of Oracle and Michael Dell of Dell each missed opposite ends of the Boomer cutoff by a year or two.

While Millennials may be more likely to be *employed by* tech companies, we are also the ones bearing the burden of an always connected workplace; we're the ones doing the low-paid and benefits-free grunt work of the gig economy. We are the ones who are going to be living out whatever dystopian future that mass surveillance tech companies develop. We are the ones who will pay even more dearly than we already have for the proliferation of fake news and the authoritarian campaigns to undermine journalistic legitimacy and suggest that facts are malleable. (Gen Z and our kids will pay, too.)

All of this crashes right into the spot where Millennial malaise meets Millennial do-gooderness. On the television show *Silicon Valley*, a parody of that eponymous tech hub, the tech pioneers declare that their products are going to "make the world a better place." The promise was that a more connected world would be a kinder, more empathetic world. Instead, it's a world where women are harassed as a rule, not an exception; young people are bullied into suicide; long-standing bigotries are nurtured and broadcast; and very few of us have any idea what our privacy rights might be, let alone how this is shaping our brains and our futures.

The optimism we were raised on has been dimmed by financial collapse, global conflict, and the very technology we were promised would be our salvation. Millennials, at least, know that we should be worried.

Only 20% of Millennials were married at age thirty. Boomers were twice as likely as Millennials to be married by that age.

For the first time ever, college-educated women are more likely to marry than women without college degrees.

Mothers today spend more time with their kids than moms did in 1965, when mothers were much more likely to be full-time parents.

The average Baby Boomer had eleven sexual partners. The average Millennial? Eight.

Millennials have made marriage as an institution its most stable in a half century, while Baby Boomers have the highest divorce rates of any generation in American history.

College-educated Millennials overwhelmingly get married before they have babies; by contrast, Millennials who didn't go to college are more likely to have a child without being married first.

FAMILY

The idealized image of the American family that flourished
when Boomers were being raised was a nuclear family in a stand-
alone house, Dad working full-time, Mom at home raising babies. Today, we think of this as traditional; in reality, the 1950s
Leave It to Beaver model was something of a historical blip. Rosie
the Riveter's wartime tiptoe toward feminism, with women entering the workforce in large numbers, built on decades of movement toward female independence. Birth rates had been going
steadily down for nearly 150 years. Couples were marrying later.
Women had been securing more rights and asserting greater
economic independence.

In the aftermath of World War II and at the beginning of the
Cold War, that was all quickly walked back. Rosie was out, replaced by über-homemaker June Cleaver. Birth rates went up for
the first time in more than a century. In 1890, the average man
was twenty-six when he got married, and the average woman
was twenty-two. By the 1950s, men were on average between
twenty-two and twenty-three, and women just twenty, when

they tied the knot. The teen birth rate hit its highest point since data on teen births was collected; American teenagers had more babies in the 1950s than at any other time in modern history (no, not even in the teen mom freak-out of the 1990s). But unlike in the 1990s, the teen moms of the 1950s typically got married before they became mothers—and those who didn't saw their babies whisked away.

Boomers reversed course from their parents, marrying later, having fewer babies, and essentially bringing the American family back on the course charted by their grandparents. Millennials have simply followed their lead.

That's not quite as exciting a story as the claim that Millennials are ruining marriage and engineering a baby bust, but it's a true one.

Millennials are staying single longer. But like so much else in our lives, sex, marriage, and child-rearing remain rife with inequality.

Both Boomers and Millennials reshaped dating, sex, marriage, and child-rearing in significant ways. To see the whole picture, though, we first have to shatter 1950s nostalgia and consider that when it comes to our sexual, romantic, and reproductive lives, Millennials are doing the best with what's been handed to us—and that the choices we're making suggest a clear way forward to something better.

Sexual Anarchy

In the 1950s, when most Baby Boomers were kids, the rules were pretty clear: sex was for marriage (or, okay, a little before marriage, so long as you planned on getting married), marriage was the first step to building a family, and the ultimate goal was to have children within the confines of marriage. "Beneath these notions was a deep fear of women's economic and sexual independence," wrote Elaine Tyler May, author of *Homeward Bound: American Families in the Cold War Era*, in a 1988 *Los Angeles Times* article. "The best way to contain their career aspirations was to professionalize homemaking; the best way to contain their sexual emancipation was to encourage early marriage and to sexualize the home. Female sexuality unleashed within marriage would strengthen the family; outside marriage, it was seen as a destructive force." Sexual satisfaction was important, but marriage was its proper container. Sexual profligacy was treacherous, and unmarried, sexually active women were a danger to themselves and others: in movies, the femme fatale was a devious Russian spy; in postwar propaganda, the allegedly disease-ridden "victory girls" could leave a nice young man returning from war with more than a fond memory; in real life, a woman who gave birth out of wedlock might very well find herself ostracized and socially isolated.

Then in 1960, just before the oldest Baby Boomers came of age, came the Pill. Maybe you know what happens next.

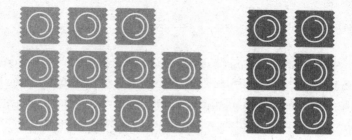

The average Baby Boomer had eleven sexual partners.
The average Millennial? Eight.

Baby Boomers were the first American generation to come into sexual maturity with available and extremely reliable birth control fully in women's hands. They were also the first American generation to see such a rapid transformation of gender roles and sexual life. The sexual revolution spurred on by the contraceptive pill and, later, legal abortion redefined the American relationship with sex, and relations between men and women. As Baby Boomers became adults, they did what every generation of Americans had done (outside of Baby Boomers' own parents): they got married later than their parents did, and they had fewer children.

Boomers also had more sex, and with more people. Which doesn't mean Americans were prudish before—researcher Jean Twenge found that folks in the Greatest Generation averaged three sexual partners apiece, so Grandma wasn't as prim as she might have seemed. But Boomers really went for it. The average

Boomer woman had ten sexual partners in her adult life. Boomer men? Twelve.

Some of these partners are likely from post-divorce dating (or during-marriage dating), but a whole lot of Boomers dated around before settling down, and sex was a part of that. While 83 percent of Silent Generation adults were married when they were between twenty-five and thirty-seven years old, just about 65 percent of Boomers were—a pretty significant dip. And Boomers who went to college were less likely to be married at that age than those with a high school degree or less.

This new sexual openness shocked older adults. A 1966 *U.S. News & World Report* story asked, "Is the Pill regarded as a license for promiscuity? Can its availability to all women of childbearing age lead to sexual anarchy?" Pearl S. Buck, the famous novelist who penned *The Good Earth*, wrote in *Reader's Digest* that the Pill's "potential effect upon our society may be even more devastating than the nuclear bomb."

The Pill did indeed allow women to have sex without quite as much fear of pregnancy. But whether it unleashed sexual anarchy is another question. Yes, older Boomers were the generation of "free love" and, a little later (with younger Boomers participating), swinging. But the cultural tides were already shifting in that direction pre-Pill. In the immediate hangover after the early 1950s, young women were staying single longer. They were going to school and working in increasing numbers. The cultural emphasis on virginity before marriage was in recession. Did the Pill come into being just as these changes were at a tipping point?

Yes. Did it add a little velocity to what was already accelerating? Sure. But the sexual revolution would likely have happened in some capacity or another even without the birth control pill. What the Pill did was drive down what could have been soaring rates of unintended pregnancy and, by extension, maternal mortality and unsafe (and until 1973 mostly illegal) abortions.

Single women had already been inching their way into cities, and while nearly all young women sixteen to twenty-one said they wanted to be married, most by twenty-two, that cultural corset was loosening. In 1962, Helen Gurley Brown's *Sex and the Single Girl* didn't so much invent a new category of person—the single, sexually active, financially independent woman—as cast a spotlight on a nascent force. By the mid-1960s, the United States was, as *Time* magazine put it in 1964, in "an era in which morals are widely held to be both private and relative, in which pleasure is increasingly considered an almost constitutional right rather than a privilege, in which self-denial is increasingly seen as foolishness rather than virtue." But the sixties sexual revolutionaries, the magazine was quick to point out, weren't quite the radicals they thought they were: "In the 1920s, to praise sexual freedom was still outrageous; today sex is simply no longer shocking . . . Adrift in a sea of permissiveness, they have little to rebel against."

The "they" here? Boomers.

In hindsight, sex in 1960s America doesn't exactly sound hedonistic. "'Nice girls don't' is undoubtedly still the majority view, but definitely weakening, as is 'No nice boy will respect you if you go to bed with him,'" *Time* wrote in that same 1964 article. A nice girl could still be nice and have sex with the man she planned to marry, or maybe even a guy she was going steady with, because "the loss of virginity, even resulting in pregnancy, is simply no longer considered an American Tragedy."

"This was a generation that was new to these kinds of issues," author, historian, and director of research and public education for the Council on Contemporary Families Stephanie Coontz told me. "This was a generation that wasn't completely new to sex but was certainly much more ambivalent about the role sex played in your life and when you did it. For women in particular, just because of biology in addition to the cultural pressures, you needed to be aware you could get pregnant, and it was safest to only have sex with someone you thought would marry you if you did get pregnant. All these things have changed for the next generation."

Over the next decade, sexual mores in America liberalized even further. Decoupling sex from pregnancy allowed American women to live more independent lives than ever before. The pop culture landscape reflected this profound shift. In 1961, Mary Tyler Moore made a splash as Dick Van Dyke's television wife, Laura Petrie, a stay-at-home mother who had met and married him at seventeen. By 1970, she was the lead character, Mary Richards, in *The Mary Tyler Moore Show*. With an iconic toss of her hat in the air, she became the joyful single career woman forging her own path.

In 1973, the Supreme Court decided *Roe v. Wade* and legalized abortion nationwide. That newfound right gave women veto power over pregnancies and with it the ability to delay marriage and motherhood until they felt ready. The relationship between the feminist movement and these legal and scientific advances (abortion rights, the Pill) was a mutually reinforcing one. It was feminists who pushed for the invention and then accessibility of the Pill; it was feminists who pushed for abortion rights. Reliable contraception and safe, legal abortion in turn enabled women to be increasingly independent and feminist-minded. Yes, women were already heading to college in larger numbers than in previous decades, but it's hard to imagine that quite so many would have been able to stay in school and in the workforce without this degree of control over their reproductive lives.

By the time Millennials entered adulthood, marriage was no longer a required stepping-stone to an acceptable adult life.

These shifts were revolutionary, but sexual freedom didn't mean that Boomers forewent marriage. They just married a little later than their parents. By 1975, the average newlyweds were twenty-three and a half (men) and twenty-one (women) on their wedding day; through the early 1980s, when the tail end of the boom babies were marrying in significant numbers, the average groom was twenty-five and the average bride was twenty-three.

But they were also divorcing.

When young marriage was practically required for social acceptance, a lot of young people settled into mediocre or even bad marriages. Maybe you were in a just-okay marriage with someone you didn't like all that much and to whom you weren't particularly attracted, but the relationship was a vehicle to an acceptable middle-class life; maybe you were married to someone who was intolerable, cruel, or even abusive. As the expectation of marriage as a social requirement waned, divorce rates initially surged. By the time Millennials entered adulthood, marriage was no longer a required stepping-stone to an acceptable adult life. We may marry less frequently, but so far, our marriages are more stable because of it.

Boomers can't say the same. If anything really sets Boomer marriages apart, it's divorce—they do a lot of it. Older Boomers brought the nation a glut of divorce in the 1970s and a national divorce rate that peaked in 1980. While younger generations of Americans divorce less often, Boomers just keep splitting up into middle and even old age. While dissolving these marriages might be for the best, divorce is financially hard on Boomer women in particular. The National Center for Family & Marriage Research at Bowling Green State University found that while divorced men over fifty have slightly better than a coin's toss chance of remarrying, only about a quarter of divorced women over fifty tie the knot again (perhaps by choice). Divorce is rarely financially lucrative, but women over fifty who experience these "gray divorces" see a much larger gap between their post-divorce assets and their husband's (and women who first divorce before age fifty and then divorce for a second time after fifty are left with the least). Susan Brown, a sociology professor at Bowling Green

FAMILY

229

and the center's co-director, told *Bloomberg News* that, according to the center's yet-to-be-published research, gray divorce halves women's wealth. Older women also experience more than twice the household income decline older men do when they divorce—and about twice the decline younger women experience (young divorced men see little impact on their household income). These same over-fifty women, Brown said, recover neither their pre-divorce wealth nor their previous standard of living. This is in part because Boomer women were more likely to work part-time or not at all—they were caring for the kids so their husbands could work full-time. But that depressed their earnings, leaving them much more financially vulnerable later in life. Brown and her fellow researchers found that 27 percent of women over the age of sixty-three who are either gray-divorced or never married live in poverty. For men in that same demographic, the poverty rate is just 11 percent.

Roughly one in three Boomers is unmarried. Widowhood and never marrying in the first place play a role, but declining Boomer marriage rates are mostly because of divorce. Boomers are the first generation that has increased its divorce rate as the cohort aged into their fifties and beyond, making Boomers—the same generation that came of age with the Moral Majority, founded in 1979—the generation with the least stable marriages in American history.

Sexual Squares

By comparison, Millennials are pretty square. According to psychology professor Jean Twenge's study on sexual behavior, we have fewer sexual partners (eight on average) than our Gen X predecessors (ten), and fewer than our Boomer parents (eleven). We have far fewer unintended pregnancies, births, abortions, and sexually transmitted infections than the generation before us, and as we reached adulthood, rates of unplanned pregnancies hit thirty-year lows. A lot of this is thanks to innovations in contraception: long-acting and enormously effective birth control methods like the IUD, faulty and even dangerous in the 1970s, are now common and safe. The internet means better information, so even though a lot of us were raised on Boomer-taught abstinence-only education and told we should wait until we were married to have sex—something very few Americans, and virtually no Boomers, have done in the last hundred or so years—we were still able to access basic health information when we needed it.

Plus, we're having less sex.

The numbers fly in the face of stereotypes about Millennials who grew up watching *Sex and the City*, embraced "hookup culture" in college, and moved to big cities where they lived, as one writer put it in the conservative *Washington Times*, in a "wasteland of sexual promiscuity" captured by Lena Dunham's *Girls*.

For Millennials, it's more like a wasteland of sex. Frequency of sex is down. The number of sexual partners is down. The last young people to be more celibate than we are were born in the

1920s. And while it's hard to gather reliable data on how often people are actually having sex, many researchers and sociologists agree that today's young people are less sexually active than teenagers and young adults of previous generations. When Jean Twenge and her team of researchers asked people in their twenties about their sex lives, today's younger Millennials—those born in the 1990s—were more than twice as likely to report no sex at all after the age of eighteen than Gen Xers were. Millennials were also more likely than Gen Xers to have had zero sexual partners in their adult lives. Curiously, compared to earlier generations, Millennials are also the most accepting of sex outside the bounds of marriage—we're just the least likely to be having it.

We're also more likely than our predecessors to identify as LGBTQ, and Gen Zers are even less likely to hew to heterosexuality. A 2017 study by GLAAD found that 20 percent of adults under thirty-four (overwhelmingly Millennials) identified as LGBTQ, while just 7 percent of Boomers did. And more than one in ten Millennials said they were transgender or gender-nonconforming. We're also more accepting of LBGTQ people than any generation before. So we may not be having as much sex as our parents, but we're a lot more open about who we are, and a lot less likely to reject normal human sexual diversity.

In a country where youth sex has been a national source of panic for the entirety of our existence, you'd think this Millennial sexual desert would be met with a shrug, or even applause. Instead, it's a whole new source of worry for the Kids Are Doing It Wrong brigade.

A 2017 study by GLAAD, an LGBTQ rights organization, found that 20 percent of adults under thirty-four (overwhelmingly Millennials) identified as LGBTQ, while just 7 percent of Boomers did.

Conservative *New York Times* columnist Ross Douthat fretted in 2018 that "like other forms of neoliberal deregulation the sexual revolution created new winners and losers, new hierarchies to replace the old ones, privileging the beautiful and rich and socially adept in new ways and relegating others to new forms of loneliness and frustration." The American sexual recession, he wrote, was one outcome of "sexual liberation and its discontents." *Bloomberg View* columnist Leonid Bershidsky warned in 2016 that "there could be an ugly side to this that could turn what looks like increased responsibility into a demographic threat." In 2018, the conservative *National Review* called it a "national bonkruptcy."

This is quite a turn from the early-aughts moral panic about Millennial hookup culture. Millennials were taught, when it comes to sex and drugs alike, to just say no. Southern Baptists created True Love Waits in 1993, just as the oldest Millennials were hitting their teen years; it pushed teenagers to pledge to abstain from sex, sexual thoughts, pornography, and masturbation, and now claims to have "educated" more than 2.4 million young people. The Silver Ring Thing, which encouraged virginity pledgers to wear silver purity rings and was for a time partly funded by the federal government, was founded in 1995. By 2002, one in eight teenagers—Millennials—had taken a virginity pledge (the purity pledges didn't work; most pledgers broke the promise and had premarital sex, and they were actually more likely to get pregnant unintentionally when they did).

As more Millennials hit their teens, the same sexual anxieties that brought abstinence-only education into our schools (with ample federal funding) only grew. In 2002, conservative writer and pediatrician Meg Meeker published the book *Epidemic: How Teen Sex Is Killing Our Kids* (those teens were Millennials, and, spoiler, in an age of HIV awareness, condoms, penicillin, contraception, and safe abortion, sex was not killing them). "Spicing up her statistics with obscene rap lyrics and lurid reports of teen orgies and the high school 'craze' for oral sex, she blames the usual suspects: post-60s permissiveness, the misguided equating of condoms with safety and sexualized media imagery in, for example, *Cosmopolitan* and *Ally McBeal*," wrote *Publishers Weekly*. "In opposition to a 'conspiracy' of sex-ed 'bureaucrats' to 'maintain sexual freedoms rather than prevent disease,' Meeker advocates teaching teens to 'postpone sex as long as possible' and, when they don't, to reflower themselves as 'secondary virgins.'" In 2007, former *Washington Post* reporter Laura Sessions Stepp published the best-selling *Unhooked: How Young Women Pursue Sex, Delay Love and Lose at Both*. The stories she told were shocking: middle school girls, as many as a dozen, performing oral sex on the same two or three boys; blow jobs replacing kissing in spin the bottle; college-age women "stripping in the student center in front of dozens of boys they didn't know, pantomiming sex onstage and later doing the real thing without saying much, if anything, to their partners." Television talk shows from *Oprah Winfrey* to *Montel Williams* warned parents about oral-sex-fueled "rainbow parties" and sex bracelets. The concerned adult consensus was that Millennials, and especially Millennial girls, were having too much sex and they were having it too young; the result was going to be a generation scarred by venereal disease, promiscuity, and romantic cynicism.

Suddenly, those Millennials who were having too much sex far too young hadn't had enough sex.

And yet when the numbers told a different story, the concern didn't end. It just flipped. By the mid-2010s, researchers, most notably Twenge, were finding that Millennials were in a sexual slump. The kids-these-days media hand-wringing reversed direction: suddenly, those Millennials who were having too much sex far too young hadn't had enough sex, and *that* spoke to some sort of fundamental generational problem and broader social decay.

Is it really so bad that Millennials are having a teeny tiny bit less sex than previous generations of young people? Yes and no. To the extent that we're less sexual because we're isolated and distracted, that's not great. And there's real concern there: we spend many, many more hours of our day socializing through screens—which, it turns out, isn't comparable to real-world socializing at all, and may actually make us feel worse about our lives rather than better. Maybe, as the children of helicopter parents and abstinence education, we are simply constitutionally risk-averse and avoid sex because we're scared of the consequences.

It's pretty hard to get laid consistently when you're living with Mom and Dad. Given that so many Millennials can't afford to live on their own, it makes sense that sex has gone down. Young adults living at home may not even try to date, feeling ashamed or embarrassed about their living situations. Perhaps they simply can't afford to take someone out to dinner. Even if they are going out, it's pretty awkward to invite a romantic interest over to tiptoe past your mother's room and into your twin bed.

Or maybe the sexless Millennial claims are overstated. How much less sex are Millennials actually having? According to Twenge's study, young adults who were eighteen to twenty-nine years old between 2010 and 2014 (Millennials all) had sex an average of 78.5 times a year. By comparison, that same age group in 1989 to 1994—Gen Xers and the youngest Boomers—had sex an average of 81.29 times a year. Do the math: that means Millennials enjoyed about two and a half fewer bonks a year—not exactly a "national bonkruptcy." It is true that sexual frequency went up for the Gen Xers and oldest Millennials who were eighteen to twenty-nine in the early 2000s. They got laid an average of 86.6 times a year. Still, that means Millennial sexual frequency only dropped by eight lays a year—not nothing, but also not national celibacy. And when Millennials ourselves talk about sex, we seem pretty satisfied. According to a 2010 study published in the *Journal of Sexual Medicine*, young people are experimenting with a wide variety of sexual behaviors, something that is associated with more satisfying sex and more female orgasms. A 2019 survey by *Cosmopolitan* found that Millennials value quality of sex a lot more than quantity. Maybe that's exactly what we're pursuing. And that's new: there's some indication that, for all the sex Boomers were having, that sex wasn't particularly great, especially for women. While the sexual revolution might have dovetailed with the feminist movement, men still held (and continue to hold) most of the social, and by extension sexual, power. When Erica Jong famously wrote about the "zipless fuck" in her 1973 feminist (and Boomer) classic *Fear of Flying*, it wasn't just the anonymity that her characters, and so many female readers, found so titillating. Rather, a sexual encounter with a man you didn't know and weren't tied to meant that "there is no power game. The man is not 'taking' and the woman is not 'giving.' No one is attempting to cuckold a husband or humiliate a wife. No one is trying to prove anything or get anything out of anyone." That kind of pleasure without a gendered power play, Jong wrote, "is rarer than the unicorn."

Reading with twenty-first century glasses, some of the sex Boomers were having sounds a lot closer to rape (and some of it inarguably was). Until the mid-1990s, men in certain US states could still legally rape their wives. Oregon was the first state to outlaw marital rape, and even they didn't get around to it until 1977. The assumption of female sexual availability within a marriage led to a lot of bad sex, and probably a lot of nonconsensual sex that today we would understand as criminal. In 1991, as Americans were coming off the hangover of the sexual revolution, one in ten American high schoolers said that they had had sex before the age of thirteen. Thirteen! For those not keyed into American law, these kids are too young to legally consent to sex in every state in the nation.

The preteens who were having sex in 1991 were Gen Xers, not Baby Boomers. The Youth Risk Behavior Survey that tracks these results wasn't in place before that year, so we don't know how many Boomers were having sex as preteens. But we do know that things like early sexual initiation tend to track with other markers, like unintended pregnancy rates, teen pregnancy rates, and abortion rates. The abortion rate hit an all-time high in 1980; the teen birth rate was its highest in 1957, then went down, only to tick back up (but not all the way up to that 1957 peak) in the late 80s. This all suggests that preteen sex was not a Gen X invention and was probably relatively common among Boomers, too—and much less likely to be recognized as exploitative.

The public reaction to notorious sex abuse cases show just how much these norms have changed. In 1977, when forty-four-year-old film director Roman Polanski was arrested for drugging, raping, and sodomizing a thirteen-year-old girl, there was widespread outcry—in his defense. Polanski absconded to Europe, where he continued making films, winning awards, and having sex with underage girls. Just two years after the (most famous) rape, he told Martin Amis, "I realize, if I have *killed* somebody, it wouldn't have had so much appeal to the press, you see? But . . . fucking, you see, and the young girls. Judges want to fuck young girls. Juries want to fuck young girls—*everyone* wants to fuck young girls!" When he won an Academy Award for *The Pianist* in 2003, the crowd gave him a standing ovation. Polanski, still a fugitive overseas, didn't attend.

By the time the youngest Millennials were thirteen, the age of Polanski's victim, the tides were changing. The #MeToo movement hadn't yet hit, but feminists had spent decades pushing back on the kind of misogynist sexual standards that enabled Polanski to rape a child, agree to a plea deal, flee before sentencing, and remain beloved in Hollywood. In 2009, the Los Angeles District Attorney's office tried to extradite Polanski from Switzerland, an effort that eventually failed. Hollywood, again, rallied to his defense. Natalie Portman, Tilda Swinton, Penélope Cruz, Harrison Ford, Martin Scorsese, Wes Anderson, and Emma Thompson were among the more than 100 celebrities who signed a 2009 petition calling for his release. That same year on *The View*, Baby Boomer Whoopi Goldberg noted that Polanski pleaded guilty to statutory rape, not "rape-rape." But this time, they faced a backlash. Emma Thompson asked for her name to be removed from the petition. In 2018, and in the wake of #MeToo, Portman apologized. When Polanski won the French equivalent of an Oscar in 2020, anti-Polanski demonstrators waved placards outside, and several prominent actresses walked out.

High schoolers in 2009—Millennials all—were less likely to have had sex before the age of thirteen, and high schoolers in 2013 (seniors that year were the tail end of the Millennial generation) were about half as likely as students in 1991 to report preteen sex. I think we can all agree it is good news when fewer kids under thirteen are sexually active (or, more likely, being sexually abused). It's also probably a contributor to Millennials' lower number of sexual partners.

Even outside of what we now understand as rape and abuse, Millennials are also much more progressive when it comes to sex, pleasure, and gender. The concept of "affirmative consent"— the idea that consent isn't just "she didn't say no," but "both parties are really excited and happy to be here"—was initially developed by Gen Xers, but it was also widely mocked. Millennials, though, have run with it, and it's increasingly our expectation. We don't just want sex; we want *good* sex, and that means sex that's good for everyone involved. For some Boomers who see sex as transactional and often something men "get" from women who have to be finessed into it, this concept is ludicrous. Close to half of Boomer-age women, for example, say they feel pressure to have sex with a date if he picks up the tab at a pricey restaurant; less than a quarter of younger Millennial women say the same. For a growing number of Millennials and Gen Zers, sex as something you get as long as no one says no or fights you off sounds pretty rapey.

The #MeToo movement, founded by Gen Xer Tarana Burke, has also been instrumental in both shaping and reflecting Millennial expectations of sex, work, and power. Baby Boomer Anita Hill brought the term "sexual harassment" into the national lexicon when she testified at the Senate confirmation hearing of Clarence Thomas, and inspired—and outraged—a generation of women with her bravery facing down all-male interrogators. When Thomas was confirmed, women struck back, electing a record number of women to the US House of Representatives (twenty-four) and the Senate (four). Two and a half decades later, Millennial women faced a similar reckoning when Christine Blasey Ford testified before the Senate Judiciary Committee against Brett Kavanaugh, yet another accused sexual predator now enjoying a lifetime appointment to the Supreme Court. Her testimony came amid an international conversation about consent, coercion, and men exploiting their power to sexually manipulate and abuse women. Donald Trump, credibly accused of harassing or assaulting dozens of women and caught on tape bragging about his penchant for grabbing women's genitals, had nonetheless been elected president. Journalists Jodi Kantor and Megan Twohey of the *New York Times* and Ronan Farrow of *The New Yorker* had exposed filmmaker Harvey Weinstein for using his vaunted position to extract various sexual acts from young women hoping to make it in Hollywood. Women spoke up and said "me too" about indignities large and small; it was about sex, yes, but it was more about power, and all of the ways in which men leveraged theirs at women's expense. For so long, women had lost opportunities and jobs, or seen themselves diminished, degraded, and flattened into sex objects, by powerful men who called the shots. Now, at least some of those men were losing, too. Roy Moore, accused of preying on teenage girls when he was in his thirties, lost his Senate race. Media icons including Charlie Rose and Matt Lauer lost their shows. Harvey Weinstein went to jail.

Of course there was a backlash. In 2018, Austrian filmmaker Michael Haneke said the movement created a "new, man-hating Puritanism." French actress Catherine Deneuve signed a letter published in *Le Monde* claiming that #MeToo's French counterpart "serves the interests of the enemies of sexual freedom." That's the heart of the matter: for many Baby Boomers (and those older than them), "sexual freedom" was pronounced with a silent "male," and meant men's bad behavior was overlooked or accepted; suggesting that women may not find groping, workplace harassment, or sexual coercion all that pleasurable was prudish. Millennials, along with our Gen X and Gen Z siblings, want a sexual freedom that doesn't cover for male predation. Maybe that means a little less sex, but it also means better sex—not to mention greater freedom for women generally.

Then there's the fact that young people are simply staying single longer. Couples who are married or cohabiting have more sex than single people, which makes sense—there's more opportunity for sex when your primary sexual partner is in bed next to you every night. The upside of this is that when we do get married, our marriages are better, happier, and more stable (more on that later in this chapter); we're also choosing to spend more of our young lives focused on education and early career opportunities.

Or maybe we're all watching too much porn.

Porn viewing has been on a steady rise across generations, and the internet has allowed it to skyrocket. Whatever your preference or fetish, you can find it in just a few clicks, in the privacy of your own home, usually for free. Millennials have taken particular advantage: Millennials, according to Pornhub, make up 60 percent of the site's viewing and clicking audience (Pornhub is the largest porn site on the internet). Three-quarters of these Millennial Pornhub users are men, most of whom are using their phones, and who stay on the site for an average of just over nine minutes. Porn use has always been cause for social alarm, even when "porn" was just a racy novel or a photograph with visible nipples. For centuries, people have been fascinated by images of naked people and of people having sex. So there's little cause for panic just because you can now pull those images up on your phone.

Porn viewing has been on a steady rise across generations, and the internet has allowed it to skyrocket.

But still, it *is* new that you can pull those images up on your phone. Porn is not just more readily available than ever, it's more diverse than ever, and there's more of it—*Popular Mechanics* calculated that it would take a person seven thousand years to watch all the porn on Pornhub alone.

Some people, most of them men, sure seem to be making a valiant effort. About 9 percent of straight men under forty say they view porn more than six times per week, and of those frequent users, a third say they both prefer porn to having sex with an actual woman and have related erectile issues. Some studies have found that watching porn decreases men's relationship satisfaction with real-life partners. But much of the research on porn is highly ideological. The evangelical Barna Group, for example, found that men who are frequent porn users are more likely to be Millennials, who report watching porn much more often than do Baby Boomers. Nearly 70 percent of Boomers in Barna's data say they never seek out pornography, but more than half say they occasionally come across it, which could suggest either that they indeed don't seek it out but do accidentally stumble upon it or that they are liars. It's probably the latter, given that there is a direct relationship between seeking out porn and coming across it (the more you look for porn, the more it pops up in the form of targeted advertising). In any event, about 10 percent of Millennials report seeking out porn daily, and another 20 percent or so say they seek it out weekly (older Millennials seek out porn slightly less; younger Millennials and Gen Zers, slightly more). However they encounter it, 40 percent of older Millennials are seeing porn at least once a week, at least according to the Barna data.

So even less-reliable data from right-wing organizations with a vested interest in fear-mongering about porn indicates that no, we are not a porn-addicted generation, even though a whole lot of us look at porn, and even as there's little question that porn has at least shifted sexual expectations. For a small minority of heavy users, modern technology has made it easier than ever to choose porn over real people. At the risk of sounding crass, though, I'm not sure that the self-isolation of the occasional porn addict is any big loss for the broader Millennial dating pool.

In other words, there's not one single reason why Millennial sex is down. Some of the possible reasons—addiction to our devices, loneliness, self-isolation, living with parents—are cause for concern. But others—maybe women are rejecting men who treat them badly, maybe a lot of folks just weren't all that into sex and romantic relationships in the first place, maybe we're choosing quality of sex over quantity—are actually pretty positive steps.

Marriage, Millennial Style

You might say the same thing about Millennials and marriage. Almost 40 percent of Baby Boomers were married by age thirty; only 20 percent of Millennials were married at thirty. Today, the average woman gets married for the first time at twenty-eight, and the average man at thirty. These numbers also vary quite a bit regionally. Young (and not so young) adults in large coastal cities like New York, San Francisco, and Washington, DC, marry even later.

For this you can mostly thank Boomers (and you can mean it). Marital ages have risen in part because of economic forces but largely because of cultural ones. Marriage, while still widely desired, is less of a social requirement than ever before, and it was Boomers who began to break down the link between marriage and assumptions of adulthood. Marriage for love is more than a century old, but marriage as optional is very much a Boomer gift to the rest of us. And the idea that marriage is not just for raising children and building a family but also a center of meaning, connection, and growth is also fairly new.

Millennials are the first generation in America to hit the average marital age with the right to marry a person of any gender.

Millennials have continued what Boomers started, and as a result, Millennials have made marriage more egalitarian and more stable. We are more open-minded and more likely to seek love across racial and religious lines. While fewer than 20 percent of marriages in 1960 were between people of different faiths, today closer to 40 percent are. Interracial marriages are more common, too. In 1967, when the Supreme Court decided *Loving v. Virginia*, the case that struck down anti-miscegenation laws, just 3 percent of American marriages were interracial. Among couples who wed in 2015, 17 percent were entering an interracial union. Americans with some college or a bachelor's degree are more likely than those who never attended college to marry across racial lines; so are whites who live in metropolitan areas; so are people who are marrying in their thirties.

Millennials are also the first generation in America to hit the average marital age with the right to marry a person of any gender. We still don't have the full picture of Millennials and same-sex marriage, and we won't for another decade or so. But early numbers indicate that LGBT Millennials are less likely to be married than straight Millennials. The embrace of LGBT rights, and the divorcing of strict gender roles from marriage, has helped to make Millennial marriages better more broadly.

"Growing up I was like, I would be so happy to be like Oprah—just have a man that I'll live with," says Faith Gingrich-Goetz, a twenty-five-year-old in Cincinnati. "Marriage was always kind of a maybe, maybe not. I never wanted my relationship to be my decision-maker. And then I met Tatum and it was all out the door."

The two women planned to get married in 2020, when both women would be in their midtwenties, which Faith characterizes as "outrageously young." They're both law grads; both do mission-driven work that isn't particularly well-compensated (Tatum is a public defender, Faith is a political organizer); and both have student debt. Their lives aren't exactly where they want them to be yet, but they feel like they're on their way—like they're adult enough to make this choice. And, well, marriage is supposed to be about love, isn't it? The two women have both profound mutual respect for each other and a deep love they feel is enduring. "We like the idea of marriage and the symbolism of it," Faith says. "But it was not all logical."

The only problem is that these great Millennial marriages are mostly on offer for the best-educated and most prosperous Millennials. A happy marriage, and often a marriage at all, is very much a class privilege.

Millennial divorce rates are startlingly low, and the later in life we marry for the first time, the less likely we are to split up. Even when Boomers were early in their first marriages, those with college degrees reported higher levels of marital happiness than those with a high school education or less. But married people with college degrees were a minority; there were many more people with only a high school education. For Millennials, college graduates are still a minority, but we're a much larger one. The marital happiness gap between college grads and high school dropouts is extreme, with a college degree making people about 10 percentage points more likely to say they are "very happy" in their marriages. And it's not just marriage: The college-educated report significantly higher levels of financial satisfaction as well; they are more likely to say that their lives are exciting and that they're very satisfied with their jobs. Those whose educational attainment is a high school degree or less are much more likely to say that life is routine or even dull. In other words, it may be less that marriage makes you happy, and more that the people who are doing pretty well and are generally satisfied with life are better positioned to get married and have happy, fulfilling marriages.

For many Millennials with college degrees, changing social norms around marriage have worked out well. We want a partner who fulfills not just an economic need but an emotional one. We want to be sexually well suited for each other. And we have a general sense that we should know ourselves well, and establish good lives, before we are ready for a lifelong romantic partnership. For many Millennials, that means years of living alone or with roommates in big, exciting cities. It means dating around, traveling, trying out new jobs, and figuring out what our adult lives look like before we find someone to share them with. We are much more likely to cohabitate today than in the past: in 2019, about 15 percent of young adults twenty-five to thirty-four (all Millennials) were living with an unmarried romantic partner, while about 40 percent were living with a spouse. Compare that to the same age group in 1980 (all Boomers): close to 70 percent were living with a spouse, while the percentage living with a partner was tiny (statistics on cohabitation before 1995 are imperfect, but in 1980, the proportion of cohabiting unmarried couples looks to be about 3 percent). And cohabitation is on the rise. For adults under twenty-four (a few Millennials but most Gen Zers), only about 7 percent are married, while close to one in ten lives with a partner. Some of these cohabiting couples will go on to marry; others will split up, move out, and move on. It's this second group that might have been the Boomer divorcés and divorcées two generations ago.

Perhaps the biggest Millennial marriage shift is in what we believe marriage means and what role it serves, something our Boomer parents passed on to us. While Boomers were raised to see marriage as a cornerstone of adult life—something that you did as one part of being an adult, and that could happen before total financial stability—Millennials largely see marriage as a capstone, the final recognition of the transition into adulthood. That is, we think we need to have the rest of our adult affairs set-

FAMILY

tled before we marry. We need to be financially secure and independent, even if we aren't financially prosperous. We need to have a handle on our debt, even if we haven't paid it all off yet. We need to have a job and be living independently (or at least with roommates instead of Mom) before we move in with a partner—another thing most of us do before we get married, even if we don't necessarily always see cohabiting as a step toward marriage. These premarital milestones weren't considered requirements for many Baby Boomers; they were also more broadly achievable, and they were achievable earlier. Millennials see stability as a prerequisite for marriage, and yet we came of age in painfully unstable times.

Which is why you see those of us who do have our arms around a stable life heading to the chapel (or, in our less religious times, City Hall), while those of us who have fewer of the traditional trappings of adulthood are forgoing marriage.

Kendra (a pseudonym to protect her privacy), thirty-four, lives in Tampa, Florida, with her boyfriend of eight years. She has a graduate degree and spent some of her adult life living in New York City and Peru. Two years after graduating, she still couldn't find a job in her field. That meant working in restaurants, babysitting, and doing odd jobs before eventually starting her own small business. When she was younger, Kendra says, "I would have wanted a big wedding. Now I just want a little courthouse wedding and a party." Her partner is unemployed, and she doesn't make much money. "There's always something in flux, which feels like not a good time to get married," she says. "I don't know if that's just the state of the world being in flux—if it's mirrored in our relationship."

Kids? She would consider, but it's a hard no right now. When Kendra got pregnant, the timing was just so off, even though she loved her partner and saw a future with him. "I don't have health insurance," she says, and she was also afraid that having a child before she was ready would derail her career goals. "I have a friend who had a baby and she is struggling so much," Kendra says. "They're so expensive. And it's hard to do what you really want to do. And I want to save the world."

Kendra ended her mistimed pregnancy, but marriage and kids aren't totally off the table. "I'm not opposed to kids," she says. "But I want to do it right."

This is the first time in American history that women with college degrees are more likely to be married than women without. While college-educated Boomer women in their late thirties and early forties were told (falsely) that they were more likely to be killed by a terrorist than married, women who have graduated from college are now more likely to marry than women who haven't, and they're generally marrying partners who are also college-educated. Overwhelmingly, these couples are creating two-earner families, putting them on much more stable financial footing than their noncollege peers. Millennials in this camp often grew up with lopsided privilege to begin with: they're disproportionately white and disproportionately affluent; they're the same people who are more likely than the general population to have a parent who can help them to buy a house, who paid for their college educations, or who will pass on an inheritance. These two-degree families are much more prosperous than the general Millennial population, and that baseline of financial security means less stress and less marital strife, which means happier and longer-lasting marriages.

Many Boomer families had these stable foundations, too, and yet their divorce rates are high. Why? It's perhaps in part because Boomers came of age at a time of great social upheaval around gender roles. With the ascendancy of feminism, a lot of women changed their ambitions and expectations very quickly. A lot of men did not. Beliefs were shifting, especially around the roles and obligations of women, and what women wanted for themselves. Expectations for men shifted less quickly and less radically, which caused—and continues to cause—significant strife at home. Women joined the workplace, augmenting family income, but often came home to husbands who were not even picking up their own socks, let alone taking significant responsibility for running a household and caring for children. And it's not that men were the universal bad guys: even while women were changing their own views of their roles, they weren't necessarily shifting the expectation that men be the primary breadwinners.

"I can still remember how entrenched that expectation of male breadwinning was," says Stephanie Coontz, the researcher, marriage expert, and historian. "Even as someone who was very independently motivated, I remember at one point in my life, early in college, fantasizing about marrying a guy who would build me a separate wing of the house where I could do my research. It never occurred to me that I could build myself a wing of the house, far less buy my own home. So here I am, ambivalent about marriage, and yet thinking that's the only way I could afford to live."

Millennials have not solved sexism—not even close—but many of us at least say we want egalitarian family structures. Whether those egalitarian structures actually remain in place after we have kids is a different question (many report they don't), but at the very least the intentions are there. And those of us who are more likely to marry are also more likely to have these egalitarian values. For our Boomer parents, that was far less likely to be the case. "There's a huge change in terms of what people expect from marriage," Coontz says.

Millennial divorce rates are startlingly low, and the later in life we marry for the first time, the less likely we are to split up.

"My generation, even the feminists, those who entered marriage thought they'd have to struggle. They just understood that it was a thing where men were going to support women and women would have to struggle to find a place that would allow them the independence they needed."

Millennial women don't expect marriage to be a struggle; we expect it to be a partnership.

But that cuts both ways. Because Millennial women largely don't need, or don't choose, to be married for either financial or social solidity, we can analyze whether marriage is a value-add or a potential loss. "Nowadays it's not just a choice for women to go to work and for men and women to share things, it's a necessity," Coontz says. "Women in particular are aware that there's a real new calculus to marriage. If you yourself are emotionally mature enough and educationally set enough to take this kind of risk and you can pull your own weight and you're sure your partner can and will pull his own weight, marriage has all sorts of attractions."

But if you aren't sure of that—and given bottoming-out wages, people without college degrees may correctly doubt that a partner can pull his own weight—the calculation doesn't look as positive. Women invest a lot of time, energy, and money into their marriages; if a woman isn't sure a partner will give back, she might decide that energy is best dedicated to improving her situation on her own. Marriage today, Coontz says, has the potential "to set you back more than it would have in the nineteen-sixties, because in the sixties women didn't have that many opportunities to pursue their own education and income and earnings and savings. The compromises people make in marriage, both men and women but still more women, mean that if the marriage doesn't work, you're likely to be worse off than if you had invested in your own earnings power, your own education, and your own emotional growth." Men who don't have college degrees, or who struggle to find work because of incarceration or addiction, are not often seen as great marital partners; women assess that the time and energy they'll put into marriages with these men, including the work they'll have to do outside of the home to support them, won't be met in kind.

And unlike the marriages of the 1950s, where one (male) partner working full-time meant the other (female) partner was taking on nearly all of the child-rearing and housekeeping, when the gender roles are reversed and it's women doing the bulk of the breadwinning, men do not typically pick up the slack at home and with the kids. Women are the larger wage earners in 30 percent of heterosexual marriages, but the majority of these families say they don't consider the wife the breadwinner: they don't imbue women's financial contributions with the same power and authority they give men's. And while the more financially dependent a woman is on her husband, the more housework she does, the same does not apply when the roles are reversed. And regardless of who is making more money, the husband's job is routinely seen as valuable and necessary while the wife's is seen as optional—even if she's the one paying most or all of the bills. If your potential husband is also a relatively high earner, this may be tolerable. If he's not, or if his employment prospects look dim and you are self-sufficient, you may not be eager to sign on to the partnership if he doesn't pull his own weight financially, emotionally, or in the household.

For Baby Boomer women, the calculation was different: neither the benefits of an average marriage nor the drawbacks of a below-average one were as high—at least compared to the other available options. Millennials in dual-earner marriages see significant benefits to both spouses; these are the highest-earning households, and the "marriage premium" these couples enjoy is larger than the one seen by dual-earner Boomer couples (the marriage premium is a financial benefit that accrues from being married). When both spouses in a heterosexual Millennial marriage work, both gain a marriage premium, although men benefit more than women. The same was not true for Boomers: only men reaped a financial reward from marriage, and they got it whether their wives worked or not. Basically, whatever Baby Boomer women did—whether they worked or didn't work, whether they were the primary breadwinner or not—marriage didn't bring them a financial benefit. On the other hand, whatever Baby Boomer men did—whether they married working women or were the breadwinners—they benefited solely from the status of being married.

For Millennials, the biggest benefits accrue to couples who both work. While both male and female Millennial breadwinners see some financial benefits to marriage, people in relationships wherein one spouse works for pay and the other stays home tend to be poorer, less educated, and less financially secure. For these disproportionately working-class couples, the financial benefits derived from marriage are lower.

Men who are unemployed, under-employed, or financially unstable often suffer from crises of self-esteem and worth. In 2017, seven in ten Americans, men and women alike, told Pew that a man's ability to financially support a family was very important for him to be a good husband or partner (just 25 percent of men and 39 percent of women placed the same level of importance on a woman's ability to provide). When masculinity and male purpose are tied up in earning ability, what happens to a man who doesn't earn? Many men who can't adequately provide also don't pull their own weight around the house: housework is feminized, and if your sense of masculinity has already taken a significant hit, you want to assert your manliness elsewhere, not reinforce your feelings of emasculation by picking up a vacuum. A lot of young men who struggle to find consistent living-wage work also don't see themselves as ready to wed; others walk down the paths of despair that wind through addiction, alcohol abuse, and suicide by middle age. If men need to be gainfully employed and capable of supporting a family before they get married, then a lot of men who are reliant on (or hopeful for) good working-class jobs in traditionally male fields may never get there.

Even supposedly progressive Millennial men hew to masculine stereotypes over financial stability. Upper-class couples can afford to outsource some of the traditionally female labor that men won't take on by hiring nannies and housekeepers; even then, women across class lines take on a second shift of childcare and housekeeping after their paid work is done. Working-class women, who are already struggling and are more likely than college-educated women to have children in their twenties, might be understandably skeptical about getting too involved with men who are unemployed or underemployed and still won't do their fair share at home—and who are possibly depressed, angry, or despairing.

This isn't just a man problem. Lots of women ascribe to this same vision of masculinity, too, and reject men who don't fit it.

"I don't subscribe to that 'a man should be a breadwinner' model," says Ray, the Texas man who now has trouble finding steady work because of his criminal record. "But there are Millennial women who take the old-school approach, 'I need a man to take care of me and I'll be at home to clean and cook.' And then there are women who are independent, like, 'I make eighty thousand dollars a year, I don't need no man, if you can't help me build an empire you are useless to me.' So you get it on both ends: your worth as a man is established on financial credentials and status."

But of course, Ray notes, it's a bigger problem than just masculine stereotypes; it's also about the waning importance of family as a social value, something he himself feels. "I don't have that strong of a family desire," Ray says. "I would have to find somebody that I enjoy their company first, and then we can decide if we want to have children after we've enjoyed each other's company long enough. But it's hard to find that these days. Everybody is pickier now because everybody has options, myself included."

Millennials, in other words, are making rational marital decisions in response to our circumstances. Boomers did this, too: their circumstances emphasized marriage as a necessary social marker across class lines, and their life prospects were far less tied to a college degree. Opportunity across class lines, if not racial and gender ones, was more equal; wealth inequality existed but had not yet broken open into a chasm. And so there weren't significant differences in marital prospects for poor Boomers and rich ones, for college-educated Boomers and those who hadn't completed high school. Most people got married.

Millennials live in an entirely different context. For those whose circumstances are pretty good, marriage looks pretty great—and in practice, well-educated and well-off Millennials enjoy marriages that may be the best in American history. But for too many Millennials, the circumstances suck.

What to Expect When We're Not Expecting

You've probably heard two things about Millennials and parenthood. The first is that we aren't having babies. The second is that those of us who *are* having babies are much more likely than previous generations to do so out of wedlock.

Both of those things are indeed true. But neither is necessarily bad.

Yes, Millennial women (and men!) are having fewer children. A lot has been written about the reasons for this baby bust—in this book, we've touched on some of them in the chapter on climate change. Many on the political and religious right see the baby bust as a cultural problem resulting from later marriage, the separation of marriage from childbearing, and a turn toward prioritizing individual happiness over continuity, obligation, and traditional social roles. Many on the political and secular left argue that it's a policy, economic, and political problem; they maintain that American women might be more eager to have children if the US had paid parental leave and universal childcare, and if Millennials weren't saddled with student loan debt, the looming threat of climate disaster, extreme overwork, and a precarious financial future.

Everyone is a little bit right. And everyone is a little bit wrong.

First, the facts: Women are indeed having fewer children. The American fertility rate has now hit a thirty-year low. The average American woman of childbearing age is estimated to have 1.73 children in her lifetime, which is about half of what it was at the height of the baby boom, and a bit lower than when those Boomer babies were giving birth to Millennials.

But the drop in birth rates can be attributed in part to the fact that women are not having children as early as they once did. The youngest Millennials are just creeping into their midtwenties, in a nation where the average age of first birth is twenty-six (and even older in big cities: it's thirty-one in New York City and closer to thirty-two in San Francisco). Millennials will not have as many babies as the Greatest Generation did during the baby boom. In 1976, 40 percent of women in their early forties had four or more children; by 2012, just 14 percent did. But it was postwar parents, not Millennials, who were anomalous in their childbearing. We're on track to have about as many babies as Gen Xers had, and about as many as our Boomer parents had—we're just doing it later.

As with marriage, there are major class and educational gaps here. The average woman with a college degree gives birth after her thirtieth birthday; the average woman without a college degree has her first baby at twenty-four. More than nine in ten women with college degrees are married by the time they give birth, according to sociologist Victor Tan Chen. The opposite is true for women with high school degrees only, of whom six in ten are unmarried when they have their first baby.

Fertility Chicken Littles point out that women are having fewer children than they say they want, arguing that just 6 percent of Americans between the ages of eighteen and forty say they don't have kids and don't want them, and yet way more than six percent of us are childless. Women, the argument goes, say they want between two and three children, and instead they're having between one and two. This is taken as evidence that women aren't having the families they desire.

But that's not quite the whole story. The decision not to have kids often shifts with age, and what someone wants when she's graduating high school at eighteen can look a lot different than what she wants as a happy and successful thirty-five-year-old. It's also not the case that women say they want an average of two-point-five children. What women (and men) say is that *the ideal family* has about two and a half children. But that doesn't necessarily mean *my* ideal family. The question—"What is the ideal number of children for a family to have?"—is asked on what's called the General Social Survey, a questionnaire that has allowed researchers to collect data on American demographics, behaviors, and attitudes since 1972. The ideal family query is asked of people between the ages of fifteen and fifty, so a lot of young women are answering well before they know what their

FAMILY

adult lives will look like, and a lot of older women are answering in purely theoretical terms. In other words, it doesn't tell us a lot about what women and men actually desire in their own lives.

As women finish high school and go to work or college, move out of their childhood homes, and develop into independent adults, we know that most of them use contraception and take concerted steps to plan their families. That isn't just about pragmatism; especially for women having kids later in life, it's also about finding purpose outside of child-rearing and seeing a life of possibility unfold. It's telling that the younger people are, the higher their average "ideal" number of children. As women exit adolescence and enter adulthood, their desires change. Perhaps the disconnect between ideal family size and actual family size is less a case of women not getting what they want, and more one of women getting more than they had hoped for in all other areas of their lives, including education, work, romance, adventure, and ambition. Perhaps the desire for a certain number of children changes as women encounter possibilities they hadn't considered before and enjoy opportunities they hadn't previously imagined.

Amanda Gomez, a young Millennial at twenty-four, is living the question of how to reconcile the life she imagined as a girl with her adult reality. She was raised in McAllen, Texas, in a community where young marriage and childbearing are the norm, and as an unmarried young woman, "I feel almost like a spinster," she says. Amanda grew up in a lower-income household, and when she graduated as valedictorian of her high school and won a full scholarship that paid for her degree at Texas A&M, she was the first in her family to go to college. Her parents, she says, "attributed their difficulties to not having pursued higher education. That was really ingrained in me, that if I wanted any sort of social mobility, I needed a degree, and that degree would get me in the door."

When Amanda looks around, though, she doesn't feel like she's in the door.

She lives with her public school teacher boyfriend and their dog in North Carolina, where she's a doctoral student in a maternal and child health program at UNC. She would like to get married and have a family in her late twenties, but she also loves her work and feels strongly about the career she's building. Plus, she and her boyfriend feel constantly broke and stretched thin. To Amanda, a happy life isn't extravagant: it includes meaningful work, a stable income, and a happy, healthy family, including children. But right now, that seems beyond the realm of possibility. "I'm spending all this time in school, and I'm working, and I'm a TA, and I research, and I'm a leader of a student organization," she says. "I'm putting in a lot of work every day. I think about my mom, who for a portion of my childhood stayed home. I feel like I can barely take care of our dog." Balance, for Amanda, "might mean I have to delay getting married or delay having my own children."

Like everything else in life, adults make choices that fall in line with their values and circumstances. Maybe you want three children, but you also want to marry someone you're head over heels for, and that person doesn't come along until you're thirty-five—something you don't know when you're twenty-six and deciding not to start procreating alone. Maybe you thought you would have two children, but postpartum depression is a real bitch and you're not willing to risk going through it again. Maybe you didn't give kids much thought and then find yourself in your thirties, happy with your job, loving a life that lets you travel at will and eat out and sleep in, and you think, absent some great desire for children, why have them?

There is some evidence that most Millennials are actually *not* having fewer children than they want. A poll conducted by the *New York Times* and Morning Consult found that only about a quarter of young women said they had, or planned to have, fewer kids than their ideal.

That's not exactly a crisis of Millennial women forgoing their childbearing dreams. Instead, it suggests that three-quarters of young women are meeting their family planning goals. And yet it's worth looking at that smaller number, and asking why a quarter of young women aren't building the families they want.

Overwhelmingly, women say the answer is two things: time and money.

Of the one-quarter of women who have less than their ideal family size, 64 percent cited expensive childcare as a reason. More than half said they wanted more time with the kids they already have. The grind of working, networking, freelancing, and side-hustling doesn't leave many hours in the day to spend quality time with your children. Millennial women who delay or reduce their childbearing are worried about the economy; they say that they can't afford more children, and that they have waited to have kids because of financial instability. When center-based care for an infant costs more than $1,200 a month, according to a 2018 analysis by the Center for American Progress—about as much as the average rent for a one-bedroom apartment—it should come as no surprise that parents or would-be parents hesitate before having a child, or having a second.

This is what happened to Prita and Evan Piekara, the hustle-hard couple. They waited two years to have a child, struggling toward financial stability. And then, Evan says, "things hit really quick. We closed on our house in November, moved in in December, and found out we were having our daughter in January. Once things fell into place, we have the house, it gave us a sense of security. Prita was starting a new job that offered good maternity leave and a substantial salary increase, so that factored into, 'we can now do this and make this work.'"

Whether they have a second is an equally daunting question. Prita had only been at her company for six months when she took leave to care for her newborn daughter, and she worries about what it will do to her career if in a year or two she takes more time off for a second child. But she knows there's a finite number of years to decide. "I'm thirty-six," Prita says. "If I was younger I would be able to take a few more years and space it out, but I'm not." And then there's the cost of childcare, which affects everything—sometimes even before the child has been born. "Our due date was supposed to be September 27, but she

FAMILY

265

was late and came October 2," Prita says. "When we were picking a date to induce, we were like, do we induce earlier because the school cutoff is September thirtieth? Do we do that and save on this really expensive curriculum? I'm in this mom group and at least five of the twelve moms in there chose to induce because of the school date."

Millennials were raised to be financially and personally responsible, personally conservative, if you will—even if not politically so. The average cost of raising a child to the age of eighteen in the US is more than $233,000 and doesn't take college into account. When you couple that generational sense of responsibility with an economic crash, a housing crisis, unconscionable levels of student debt, a bleak financial future, and now another economic crisis, what you get is a significant minority of young people who decide it doesn't make sense to add another child to their families.

Boomers didn't make this calculus. By one estimate in a Bank of America report on finances and parenting, about three-quarters of parents today said that they took money into account when deciding whether to have children and how many to have, something just a third of parents considered in 1970.

And then there's the reality of parenting today, which has a unique intensity. Millennials were intensively parented, too—thanks, Boomers—and we've carried that on. But consider this: working mothers today spend as much time with their children as stay-at-home mothers did in the 1970s, when the oldest Boomers were having babies and the youngest were kids themselves. The average woman in 1965 spent eight hours a week doing paid

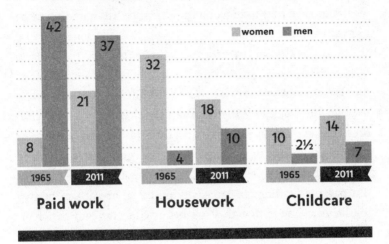

Average hours per week spent on . . .

women   men

	Paid work	Housework	Childcare
1965	women 8, men 42	women 32, men 4	women 10, men 2½
2011	women 21, men 37	women 18, men 10	women 14, men 7

work, thirty-two hours a week on housework, and ten hours a week on childcare. By 2011, her paid work had nearly tripled, housekeeping time was cut in half, and hours spent on childcare increased by 40 percent, to fourteen hours per week.

Men still only spend about half as much time on housework and childcare as women, and they still spend more time than women working for pay. But they've changed, too, picking up more at home and doing less for pay. In 1965, the average man spent forty-two hours a week at work, four on housework (compared to his wife's thirty-two!) and just two and a half hours on childcare in a week (about twenty-one minutes a day). By 2011, men were working thirty-seven paid hours per week and spending ten hours on housework and seven hours per week with their kids.

Parents of both sexes are spending much more time with their kids than they used to, but mothers are still spending twice as much as fathers.

And the kind of time Millennial parents—and particularly Millennial mothers—dedicate to their children is fundamentally different than it was in the seventies. While 1970s mothers may have spent about as many hours in the presence of their children, today's mothers spend that time interacting with their kids: reading, crafting, doing homework, going to lessons and events, attending sports games. Is this by choice? Technically. But parents (and again, especially mothers) are driven by two big factors. One is that they are better educated and better informed than ever before; Millennials are a generation of women who grew up with more opportunities than ever, and who did better in school than male peers. Part of being a "good girl," for Millennials, was achieving highly. Predictably the same women who worked hard in school and kill it at work bring that same ethos to parenting. The other factor is the instability of Millennial life. We are seeing, for the first time, a future that is not as bright for ourselves as it was for our parents. Once we start raising children, that anxiety gets ratcheted up even further, and we busy ourselves with worrying about how we can give them a leg up in a world that feels both more competitive and less socially mobile than ever before.

Nor is intensive parenting the sole province of the highly educated and well-to-do. New parenting norms have taken hold nationwide, and while wealthier parents may have more time and resources to funnel into their kids, high expectations for parenting are everywhere. Washington University in St. Louis sociologist Patrick Ishizuka examined the parenting practices of more than 3,600 parents of elementary school–aged children and found that "parents of different social classes express remarkably similar support for intensive mothering and fathering across a range of situations," whether the child was male or female, and whether the parent was college educated or not. "These findings," Ishizuka wrote in his 2019 study, "suggest that cultural norms of child-centered, time-intensive mothering and fathering are now pervasive." The stereotype of the intensive "helicopter" parent as an upper-middle-class phenomenon is simply not true for today's young parents. Many Millennials who grew up in more challenging circumstances are committed to giving their kids more opportunities than they had—not just financially but in terms of time and care.

"I look at the environment I came out of, and my parents did the best they could, but I do want to give my kids more than I had, and there's a financial cost," Justin Pinn, the Teach For America director in Miami, says. "I know there's no perfect number to have a family, but I want to make sure I'm not in survival mode all the time when I invite another blessing into my life and prepare that blessing for the opportunities that he or she should be afforded."

And it's not just him. Justin looks around at his peers and sees that they're all struggling with similar questions as they look toward tenuous futures. "I don't think there's been a full accounting of what our country has put Millennials through," he says. "We haven't asked, How do you break generational poverty? How do you break that tie in a generation of people of color who are living lives that their parents didn't have the opportunity to? Where I can position my kids to not go through the same types of challenges? We are holding off on having kids because we've overcome so much and we don't want to put our kids through that. But there's a biological time clock."

This emphasis on being a good parent applies whether you're married or not, and, as with much of the rest of Millennial life, there are huge class and race divides. For Millennials with college degrees, marriage is broadly considered a prerequisite to parenthood, and that makes sense: The kinds of demanding jobs college graduates often enter require more working hours than they used to and are concentrated in cities that are more expensive than ever. A two-parent and two-income household often feels like the only way to make child-rearing work. And there are all kinds of positive outcomes for kids raised in married two-parent homes, including better behavior and academic performance. They're more likely to go to college. They're more financially successful as adults. Their own marriages tend to be more stable.

But it's not the case that marriage offers some magical benefit. When Kimberly Howard and Richard V. Reeves at the Brookings Institution's Center on Children and Families reviewed the research and literature on childhood outcomes, they found that it was less the marriage itself that benefited kids, and more two big factors: money and engaged parenting. People who are already better educated, wealthier, happier, and more stable are more likely to get married before they have kids, and likely to bring in two incomes as they raise their kids.

"Comparisons between the outcomes of children of married and unmarried parents are then, at least to some extent, comparisons between the outcomes of children from well-off families and children from poorer families," Howard and Reeves wrote. People who possess the skills that enable them to be good parents—commitment, sensitivity, and patience are three the researchers listed—may also be more likely to marry. And two parents simply have more time for the kind of engaged parenting that helps kids to thrive. When Howard and Reeves looked at the outcome for kids in continuously married two-parent households versus the outcome for kids of single or discontinuously married mothers *and* controlled for both income and engaged parenting, the marriage benefit was small. Parenting skills and income levels mattered much, much more than marriage itself.

The issue, then, isn't marriage itself—in some European countries where co-parenting by unmarried couples is prevalent and where there are high rates of cohabitation, children do just fine. For a lot of American women for whom a stable marriage to a guy who pulls his own weight seems unlikely, it also makes a lot of sense to have kids young. Young motherhood means you're healthier and less likely to suffer serious health complications during or after pregnancy, something that is acutely important for women who are already less likely to have good health insurance and reliable health care. Young Millennial first-time mothers are more likely to be black or Hispanic and without a college degree; they are also more likely to be unmarried than older Millennial first-time mothers.

But even young Millennial mothers aren't as young as young mothers used to be. Rates of teen births have radically declined. Today's "young moms" are in their early twenties, which was for most of modern history an entirely normal time to begin childbearing. For college-educated women today, one's twenties (and even one's thirties) are seen as a time to get a foothold on a career; delaying childbirth has tangible financial benefits. For women without college degrees living in low-income communities, comparable incentives don't exist. Your wages are unlikely to go up substantially if you don't have kids until you're thirty. You're not going to get more time off if you delay childbearing. Instead, your own parents will be older and possibly less able to help out.

Then there is the less quantifiable question of purpose. Women have long found purpose, status, and respect through motherhood. Now, for some lucky women who have reached the top, purpose, status, and respect can come in forms traditionally reserved for men: work, achievement, money, a full life lived outside of the home. When I look around at the women I know who are in their thirties and have chosen to delay or forgo children, nearly all have careers they have spent the last decade developing. They mostly say their work feels purposeful and intellectually stimulating, like they're doing more than just collecting a paycheck, and their identity is partly tied up in what they do. They want a partnership, not just a co-parent. They have rich friendships and packed social calendars. Life feels meaningful and often exciting.

This is also why, contrary to the claims of many progressives, more family-friendly policies are not the singular solution to increasing the birth rate. Generous paid parental leave, and family allowances and universal childcare, are still the right things to do, and should be on offer in any society that can afford it (and ours can). But the drop-off in Millennial births is a global phenomenon, including in the Scandinavian nations that have the most lavish family benefits in the world.

Family policies that help parents to take a reasonable amount of time off work when they have children do bring some benefits and may incentivize women to have children earlier in their lives, and possibly even have more babies. But the policies themselves matter. Too much parental leave can backfire for women who leave their field for a year or more; lack of a comprehensive childcare plan means people don't have as many babies. And the effect of these policies in America remains an outstanding question, given that studies on parental leave often focus on European countries with lower fertility rates than the US.

I suspect that people who have the privilege of work that feels purposeful beyond a paycheck, whose professional lives bring with them the status markers of adulthood, and who live in places where being child-free or an older parent is relatively normal are also more likely to choose not to have children at all, or to have just one, for reasons that are not purely financial. And on the flip side, if working a job isn't necessarily a signifier of adulthood or a conduit to respect; if employment is unpredictable; if a job is primarily a way to keep the lights on and not much more; if being a mother is the way women obtain positive attention and respect or, importantly, fulfillment; and if young and single parenthood is normal in your community, you're a lot more likely to decide it makes sense to become a mother sooner rather than later. And you're a lot more likely to decide to do it whether you're married or not.

It has long been the case that women with lower levels of education and lower incomes have higher rates of unintended pregnancies and births than better-educated, more affluent women; low-income women are less likely to use contraception and less likely to end unintended pregnancies if they do become pregnant. Contraception is now more affordable than ever because of the Affordable Care Act, which requires most insurance plans to cover the cost of a variety of birth control methods. But that's only been the case for a few short years. Getting contraceptives still requires a doctor's visit and pharmacy refills, which can be challenging for women with unpredictable work schedules, or for those whom the volatility of poverty forces to move more frequently. Despite broadly decreasing rates of unintended pregnancy, low-income single women remain more likely than wealthier women to get pregnant without meaning to.

Wealth doesn't protect women from unintended pregnancy,

but wealthier women are much more likely than poorer ones to end a pregnancy if they feel they're too young or otherwise not ready for a child. (Still, the majority of women who experience unintended pregnancies give birth.) Abortion also costs money, and in many states it isn't covered by Medicaid or private insurance; legal attacks on abortion clinics have also shuttered many of them, rendering abortion inaccessible for a great many resource-constrained American women. There are many women who would have had abortions but weren't able to for reasons of finance or geography—the closest abortion clinic may simply be too far away. After giving birth, these women wind up poorer than women in similar circumstances who were able to have abortions, and they are less likely to have left an abusive partner. Overall, low-income single women have an unintended birth rate that is five times higher than women with greater resources.

Many of these women are Millennials: our childbearing years have coincided with a rise in single motherhood. That's not in and of itself a bad thing. What *is* bad is our broader lack of social mobility and the tattered safety net that leaves too many Millennial mothers struggling unnecessarily.

It's important to note here that "unmarried" doesn't necessarily mean "single," and that having a child without being married doesn't necessarily translate into instability. When you look at countries with generous social welfare policies and feminist politics, including Sweden, for example, you see higher rates of unmarried motherhood than we have in the United States. But these "single mothers" often aren't single at all. They're stably partnered and raising children in a committed two-parent household; they just haven't wed. And their children thrive. By comparison, American children raised in single-parent households don't do as well.

This is very much a political choice. The United States could offer the kinds of generous social welfare benefits that enable Swedish families to stay intact whether Mom and Dad are married or not, but we don't; instead, we leave families to figure it out alone. Today, according to the Pew Research Center, a quarter of American parents living with their child are unmarried. But statistics about "single parenthood" often obscure the reality that many of these "single parents" are *unmarried*, but not actually "single." Among unmarried parents, most of them—53 percent—are indeed solo mothers (mothers who are parenting without a live-in romantic partner or co-parent, who we often think of when we imagine a single mother). But even solo mothers are often not alone—22 percent of them live with one or both of *their* parents in a multigenerational household (solo fathers are even more likely to be living with Mom or Dad: 31 percent of them do). And 35 percent of "single parents," including 18 percent of "single mothers," are actually raising their children with a live-in partner. This is a significant shift from when Boomers were having their first babies. In 1968, 88 percent of unmarried parents were mothers parenting alone; that dropped to 68 percent by 1996, but the entirety of the shift has been toward cohabitation. The percentage of dads who are parenting solo—12 percent—has not changed since 1968, even though back then there were just 4 million unmarried parents, and today there are more than sixteen and a half million. Unmarried fathers today are not any more likely to take on the role of solo parent than they were in the late 1960s or mid-1990s. But significant increases in cohabitation, at least, mean that millions more fathers live with their children, even if they aren't married to those children's mothers, than did fifty and even twenty years ago.

These cohabitating couples tend to be younger and less well educated than both married couples and solo parents. But that also tell us something interesting: Millennial fathers seem more likely to stick with their child's mother than were fathers of previous generations, who were more likely to just bounce and leave Mom on her own. This is probably a turn for the better.

The way Millennials form families may be different from generations before, but in what is by now a familiar refrain in this book, different is not bad. The problem is a lack of support and a lack of political recognition of what our families look like now. Policy-wise, we still act like the norm is a two-parent heterosexual family, with Dad working and Mom at home. That assumption has been a disaster for all but the most affluent families. And unless there's a big change, we will continue to see young families—and, disproportionately, young mothers—struggle.

Boomers are more likely to watch Fox News than just about any other network, and close to half of them say they got their news from Fox in the previous week.

People over sixty-five are the most likely to spread fake news via Facebook.

By the time the average Boomer was sixteen, he had watched more than 12,000 hours, or more than 500 days, of television. Today, Baby Boomers watch more than six hours of television every day.

Twenty years after the radical sixties, 64% of Baby Boomers said they had become more conservative.

CULTURE

To hear journalists, critics, and cultural commentators tell it, they're a generation of self-involved, self-indulgent narcissists. They want hookups without consequence, delayed marriage, and the occasional "polymorphous perversity"—group sex, inviting a third into a couple's bed, copulating outside the bounds of monogamy—and are hung up on their sexual identities. "Most people, historically, have not lived their lives as if thinking, 'I have only one life to live,'" one writer put it. "Instead they have lived as if they are living their ancestors' lives and their offspring's lives and perhaps their neighbors' lives as well."

This generation lives only for themselves, according to a new set of rules. Some of them have created "extended families" to replace the nuclear option, while others cohabit. They live in a kind of perpetual adolescence, marrying later, having fewer children, fetishizing fame and celebrity, and doing whatever they can to put off the responsibilities of adulthood. Technology makes them feel ever surveilled, but they are also preoccupied with capturing their lives in photographs. They troll each other mercilessly and cruelly and yet still come back for more, putting themselves out there again and again because, even in the face of sustained harassment, they loved it as long as it was about them: according to one writer, "No matter how dreary the soap opera, the star was *Me*." To a one, and with a nearly religious fervor, they believed they were individually special.

Millennial snowflakes, am I right?

Nope. Baby Boomers.

The "Me" Generation

In a series of books, essays, and criticisms throughout the 1960s, '70s and '80s, writer after writer eviscerated Baby Boomers as a generation of self-absorbed navel gazers, infatuated with self-discovery and, primarily, themselves. The most famous may be "The 'Me' Decade," Tom Wolfe's August 1976 cover essay in *New York* magazine. Christopher Lasch's *The Culture of Narcissism: American Life in an Age of Diminishing Expectations* (1979), which won a National Book Award in 1980, plays on similar themes, and similarly condemned Baby Boomers. The parallels to Millennial stereotypes, clear enough to anyone today who has spent five minutes watching Fox News or listening to a Boomer complain about Millennials, come into particular focus if you look at a 2013 *Time* magazine cover story playing on Wolfe's, "THE ME ME ME GENERATION: Millennials Are Lazy, Entitled Narcissists

Who Still Live with Their Parents," by Joel Stein. (At least "they'll save us all," added *Time*.)

To be fair, the picture of Baby Boomers that Wolfe painted isn't one that's entirely replicated by flattened Millennial stereotypes. There was one big difference: young adult Boomers, in Wolfe's estimation, were also newly, notably spiritual: they were drawn to Eastern mysticism and hippie-Jesus charismatic Christianity; they used therapy and self-analysis as religion itself. "This curious development has breathed new life into the existing fundamentalists, theosophists, and older salvation seekers of all sorts," Wolfe wrote. "Ten years ago, if anyone of wealth, power, or renown had publicly 'announced for Christ,' people would have looked at him as if his nose had been eaten away by weevils. Today it happens regularly." Wolfe called Boomer neo-religiosity the "Third Great Awakening," and he's right that it opened a new era in American life and politics. But he focused on EST and religious mysticism to the exclusion of the real story: the rise of evangelical Christianity and the Moral Majority, which ferried Ronald Reagan to office in the 1980s and continue to wield enormous power on the American Right.

Lasch, a historian and academic, took it a step further. The generation he defined as narcissism maximized was one of preening men selling an image of themselves, more interested in the now than in either the past or the future. But his depiction of Baby Boomers in adulthood will sound familiar to anyone even moderately fluent in the genre of Millennial-bashing: "Having no hope of improving their lives in any of the ways that matter, people have convinced themselves that what matters is psychic self-improvement: getting in touch with their feelings, eating health food, taking lessons in ballet or belly-dancing, immersing themselves in the wisdom of the East, jogging, learning how to 'relate,' overcoming the 'fear of pleasure,'" Lasch wrote. "Harmless in themselves, these pursuits, elevated to a program and wrapped in the rhetoric of authenticity and awareness, signify a retreat from politics and a repudiation of the recent past."

Cynical that the future even exists, self-involved, wellness-obsessed . . . Boomers?

Lasch further worried that "a society that fears it has no future is not likely to give much attention to the needs of the next generation, and the ever-present sense of historical discontinuity—the blight of our society—falls with particularly devastating effect on the family." Reading Lasch is telling: the less generous among us may agree that Boomers really didn't think too much about their future, and as a result, ours have suffered. It's also difficult to ignore the similarities between his indictment of Boomers and contemporary conservative critics' complaints about Millennials. Indeed, Lasch sounds a lot like the right-wing writers who wring their hands at Millennial women slowing down childbearing, and project out from that a series of dire conclusions about American culture, future fear, and self-indulgence over self-sacrifice. Take the *Times*'s Ross Douthat, in 2012: "The retreat from child rearing is, at some level, a symptom of late-modern exhaustion—a decadence that first arose in the West but now haunts rich societies around the globe. It's a spirit that privileges the present over the future, chooses stagnation over innovation, prefers what already exists over what might be. It embraces the comforts and pleasures of modernity, while shrugging off the basic sacrifices that built our civilization in the first place."

While today we worry about technology and the psychological devastation of comparing your life to heavily curated images online while also being constantly surveilled, Boomers, Lasch argued, were the original image-obsessives. "Another such influence is the mechanical reproduction of culture, the proliferation of visual and audial images in the 'society of the spectacle,'" he wrote. "We live in a swirl of images and echoes that arrest experience and play it back in slow motion. Cameras and recording machines not only transcribe experience but alter its quality, giving to much of modern life the character of an enormous echo chamber, a hall of mirrors ... Modern life is so thoroughly mediated by electronic images that we cannot help responding to others as if their actions—and our own—were being recorded and simultaneously transmitted to an unseen audience or stored up for close scrutiny at some later time."

These young adult Boomers wanted to be envied, not respected. They wanted to be admired, not esteemed. They wanted praise for their attributes, not their achievements. They wanted the glory that comes from attention, and "those who win the attention of the public worry incessantly about losing it."

Boomers: they're just like us!

I present this extended fretting about then-young Boomers not to paint the generation with a broad brush but to say that

By the time the average Boomer was sixteen, he or she had watched more than 12,000 hours, or more than 500 days, of television.

perceptions of change are remarkably cyclical. Every generation looks at the young and chafes at the idea that they are doing things differently; every generation seems to have a particular kind of amnesia and forgets that they, too, were once the kids-doing-it-wrong. When they were young, Boomers were branded narcissists; now they're accused of ruining the country and are even, according to a 2017 book, "A Generation of Sociopaths." In turn, Boomers tell Millennials that *we're* the truly narcissistic and needy ones, and that we are, per the title of another book, "The Dumbest Generation."

I suppose you could draw a few conclusions here. One is that both Boomers and Millennials have been unfairly maligned, all of our stories told in half truth, our very human struggles pathologized by pop critics long on antipathy and short on history. The other is that a "me" generation of narcissistic sociopaths predictably raised an even larger generation of uber-narcissists who have only magnified Boomers' own pathologies, character flaws, and vanities.

The truth is far closer to the former than the latter. And with the benefit of hindsight, we can see that some of the changes Boomers made were really good. For starters, they began to break down restrictive gender roles, challenged racial hierarchy, and asserted that individual feelings and experiences do matter. Other changes—the continuation and exaggeration of postwar consumerism, the political shifts to the right and the destruction of the social safety net, the stubborn refusal to plan for society's future instead of just hoarding resources for one's own—were significantly less good.

Distilling down an entire generation's experience to a single definition of that cohort's "culture" is impossible work. But there are certain aspects of Boomer life that make Boomers different from generations before. One is that they were the first generation raised with screens, although theirs were televisions, not computers or phones. By the time the average Boomer was sixteen, he or she had watched between *12,000 and 15,000 hours* of television. This kind of TV-centric lifestyle persists among Boomers today: Nielsen found that Baby Boomers watch more than six hours of television *every day,* and folks over sixty-five watch close to seven and a half hours; by contrast, people who were eighteen to thirty-four in 2018 watched closer to two hours of TV a day.

And what Boomers watched as kids and into adulthood matters. Television in the 1950s and 1960s very much reinforced the values of that era: that meant traditional hierarchies of race and gender, female subservience, white Christian cultural dominance. Shows that pushed more progressive values came later and were exceptions to the conservative rule.

Boomers were also the first generation brought up in a developing consumer culture. Born into a postwar boom, America of the 1950s was defined by the material goods that set us apart from our ideological enemy, the Soviet Union. According to the American narrative, we had single-family homes, electric vacuum cleaners, Marlboro cigarettes, cake you could make from a box, Levi's jeans; they had bread lines, clothing castoffs, and Potemkin villages. Our material goods were tied up in our freedom. Capitalism meant all the stuff money could buy; socialism was deprivation and repression. This materialism went hand in hand with regressive gender roles: part of the character of America was its feminine women happy at home, who were often contrasted with their allegedly masculine and unattractive Soviet counterparts. And part of the appeal of capitalism and technology came from the ease both promised to bring homemakers, who no longer needed to bake cakes from scratch or wash clothing by hand (not that these innovations actually saved women much time).

This love of stuff didn't decline as the Cold War waned; instead, Boomers' relative financial stability allows them to fuel consumer culture—indefinitely, due to their long lives. Today's

Baby Boomer men are the twenty-first century's most common car buyers. Boomers spend more on tech than young people do. Americans over fifty—some 117 million people—wield a spending power of more than $8 trillion every year, of which $3 trillion is spent on consumer goods. And, frankly, they're increasingly spending like Millennials: while Boomers used to spend a lot more on things like clothes, today they're dedicating more of their resources to education and to experiences like travel. They're also helping their adult children, with 71 percent saying that they helped pay for their kids' education or let their kids live at home rent-free.

Myrna Blyth, senior vice president and editorial director of AARP Media, wasn't wrong in 2019 when she told Axios, "OK, Millennials. But we're the people that actually have the money."

Yes, we know. And that's one reason there's a generation war brewing.

Okay, but What About Feminism, Civil Rights, and the Antiwar Movement?

If you're a Baby Boomer reading this, you might be pretty annoyed at this point. I can practically hear your objections: You Millennials think you invented open-mindedness, activism, and political liberalism? We brought you civil rights! We brought you the women's movement! We were out in the streets protesting against Vietnam when you were barely an egg clinging to a follicle!

Boomer, you're right—kind of.

Despite pop memory (or hagiography), the civil rights, feminist, and antiwar movements were not particularly popular in their time. They were incredibly influential and powerful, yet huge swaths of the American public weren't on board.

It's also not true that Baby Boomers either led or made up significant majorities of all of these movements.

As Pulitzer Prize–winning historian and professor Louis Menand put it in a 2019 *New Yorker* piece, "There are many canards about that generation, but the most persistent is that the boomers were central to the social and cultural events of the nineteen-sixties. Apart from being alive, baby boomers had almost nothing to do with the nineteen-sixties."

Let's start with civil rights. The civil rights leaders we now learn about in school—among them Rosa Parks and Martin Luther King Jr.—were much older than Baby Boomers, and the movement itself hit many of its most famous milestones while Boomers were still being born. Parks was forty-two in 1955, when she performed her most famous of many acts of civil disobedience and refused to get up from her seat in the white section of a Montgomery, Alabama, bus. That day, the very oldest Baby Boomers were nine years old. Martin Luther King Jr. gave his famous speech at the March on Washington in 1963, near the tail end of the baby boom; any Baby Boomers who came were either high school students or toted along by their parents. When the

Little Rock Nine risked their lives to integrate Little Rock Central High School, it was 1957, and so they, too, were too old to be Boomers. The very oldest Baby Boomers were just turning eighteen in 1964, the year of the Freedom Summer, when activists fought racial discrimination and intimidation to register black voters in Mississippi, only to be repeatedly attacked—more than a thousand were arrested, eighty were beaten, four were critically wounded, and four were killed.

The Civil Rights Act of 1964 and the Voting Rights Act of 1965 were both signed before the overwhelming majority of Boomers had graduated high school, and as the youngest ones were still in infancy. Even later pieces of important civil rights legislation, such as the Fair Housing Act, were advocated for, drafted, and signed without Boomer influence.

The civil rights leaders we now learn about in school were much older than Baby Boomers, and the movement itself hit many of its most famous milestones while Boomers were still being born.

And these movements were not particularly popular: Through the early 1960s, large majorities of Americans said civil rights protests hurt the cause. Sixty percent of Americans in a 1963 Gallup poll held unfavorable views of King's March on Washington. And while in 1964 a majority of Americans supported the Civil Rights Act, about 30 percent opposed it. A majority also said they only wanted it "moderately" enforced— vigorous enforcement was unpopular. By May of 1965, 45 percent of Americans told Gallup pollsters that racial integration efforts were moving too fast; just 14 percent said integration was not moving fast enough.

That doesn't mean that Boomers get no credit for civil rights activism, which called upon a vast network of activists, many of whom were much younger than the most visible leaders. Some Boomers do deserve significant and unrestrained praise here, including the college students who in the mid-1960s were the rank-and-file members of the Student Non-violent Coordinating Committee (SNCC), the primary student organizing arm of the civil rights movement. They put their lives on the line for the right to vote. Among them were activists like Ruby Sales, who marched from Selma to Montgomery as a teenager, registered voters with the SNCC, and spent seven months mute from trauma after her fellow marcher, Jonathan Daniels, was assassinated by a bullet aimed at her (the killer, who showed no remorse, was acquitted by an all-white all-male jury).

There are also the Baby Boomers who were exceptionally brave as very small children. Ruby Bridges was just six years old when she put on her little white ankle socks and patent-leather shoes and walked, accompanied by US marshals, past a raging white mob, becoming the first black child to integrate a white southern elementary school. It was an act of nearly unimaginable courage from both Bridges and her family, a moment of such valor and such vulnerability that the iconic photo (and even more iconic Normal Rockwell painting that Barack Obama hung in the Oval Office) of tiny Bridges flanked by adult legs can still make a viewer's heart seize and tug.

In no way do I wish to minimize Boomer contributions to civil rights, nor the ways in which the civil rights movement determined so much of the political narrative for Boomers as they entered adulthood. But let's also be honest: they don't get to take all or even most of the credit for it. Per Menand: "it is almost impossible to name a single person born after 1945 who played any kind of role in the civil-rights movement, Students for a Democratic Society (SDS), the New Left, the antiwar movement, or the Black Panthers during the nineteen-sixties. Those movements were all started by older, usually much older, people." (To whit: two co-founders of the Black Panthers, Bobby Seale and Huey Newton, were born in 1936 and 1942, respectively; Students for a Democratic Society leader Tom Hayden was born in 1939.)

But this is worth emphasizing: while Baby Boomers were not the leaders of the civil rights movement, black Baby Boomers still *lived* the civil rights movement.

"I was born one year after the Montgomery bus boycott," ACLU lawyer Jeff Robinson told me. "And even though it was illegal to make us ride in the back of the bus after 1955, I rode in the back of the bus until I was ten or eleven years old." Jeff met his childhood best friend, Opie, on the playground of an all-white Catholic school, the summer before he was the first black child to enter the second grade there. When they were teenagers going to see the 1970 film *Patton* in theaters, they had to sit up in the balcony—Jeff wasn't allowed in the main area. So you have to understand, Jeff says, where his generation was coming from. Between 1877 and 1950, the Equal Justice Initiative found records of 3,959 lynchings in a dozen southern states. That's at least one black person lynched *every week* for seventy-three years. "So when all of a sudden the law says you can ride at the front of the bus, when all of a sudden my brother and I are going to a white Catholic school and some years later we integrate a white neighborhood, those things seemed at the time to be earth-shattering," Jeff says. "It's easy to say that riding in the front of the bus is a superficial accomplishment. It's easy to say that unless you couldn't."

It was Jeff's parents who, like nearly everyone else they knew in Memphis, were active in the civil rights movement; Jeff was just a kid. But that didn't make him absent, or a mere spectator. "The week before King was assassinated, there was a march in support for striking sanitation workers that broke into violence," Jeff remembers. "My dad took my older brother and I down to that march and we saw it degenerating and we ran." It was after that march, watching the court appearances of protesters who had been arrested, that Jeff decided he would be a lawyer.

The antiwar movement follows a similar trajectory, although here, Boomers do get to claim more credit, in large part because protests against the war began more than a decade after the start of the civil rights movement. The leaders of the antiwar movement were largely older, while a lot of the movement's foot soldiers (and, in the case of the war itself, actual soldiers) were Baby Boomers. Indeed, though they came in the second wave of the conflict, as the war and the death toll scaled up, Boomer men accounted for the majority of the casualties in the last half of the war. As for the conflict back home, students were shutting down university campuses to protest the war as early as 1965, meaning that the very oldest Boomers were taking part in sit-ins and protests from their earliest adult days. And some didn't wait until college; plenty of high-school-age Boomers joined the antiwar effort, too. The youngest Boomers may have been infants, but when hundreds of thousands of marchers took to the streets of New York City and 70,000–100,000 marched on Washington in 1967, the high school and college students among them (and many of the kids they brought along) were Baby Boomers. And it was college students and campus activists who powered the antiwar movement, staging sit-ins and marches and recruitment protests. When four unarmed students were shot and killed at Kent State in 1970, they were Baby Boomers to a one.

Second-wave feminism began to swell a little later than both the civil rights and the antiwar movements, but most of its early and most notable leaders weren't Boomers. Gloria Steinem (b. 1934), Florynce Kennedy (1916), Dorothy Pitman Hughes (1938), Betty Friedan (1921), Alice Walker (1944), Germaine Greer (1939), Audre Lorde (1934), Robin Morgan (1941), Susan Brownmiller (1935), Kate Millett (1934)—all not-so-silent members of the Silent Generation. Shirley Chisholm, the first woman to run for the Democratic Party's presidential nomination, was born in 1924. The Equal Pay Act was signed in 1963, when the oldest Boomers were teenagers and the youngest weren't even yet zygotes—which means that Boomers benefited but didn't lobby. Sarah Weddington, the young lawyer who argued *Roe v. Wade* before the Supreme Court, was born just before the baby boom; her co-counsel, Linda Coffee, was born in 1942. Only Norma Mc-Corvey, the woman known pseudonymously as Jane Roe, was a Boomer; she also transitioned from abortion rights activist to anti-abortion crusader as she entered middle age. The famous protest at the Miss America pageant, where feminists allegedly burned their bras (they actually just threw a bunch of undergarments into "freedom trash cans"), was in 1968. Were Boomer women there? They definitely attended, but the oldest would have been twenty-two. The woman who organized the protest, Carol Hanisch, was twenty-five or twenty-six at the time—not a Boomer.

Of course the feminist movement, like the civil rights and antiwar movements, was more than just its leaders, and a great many Boomer women spent their young adult years fighting for feminist causes, even if their names weren't the ones in the newspapers. And whether or not any given Boomer took to the streets, these movements cleared important paths for Boomers and fundamentally shaped their adult lives. Baby Boomer women walked through the doors older feminists opened for them, via, for example, Title IX of the Education Amendments Act of 1972, which barred sex discrimination in any educational program or institution receiving federal funds. Boomer women flooded into institutions of higher education and into the workplace, continuing a rise in women's workforce participation that began after World War II. Boomer women pushed for expanded rights for women, including protections from workplace harassment. But when we think of the famous feminists of the 1960s—the women who featured heavily in 2020's *Mrs. America*, for instance—they're all too old to be Boomers.

It is the LGBT rights movement, which they do not as often claim as their own, for which Boomers can most clearly take credit. The Stonewall rebellion was in 1969, and a lot of the participants were young. They included Sylvia Rivera and Yvonne "Butch" Ritter (yes, both Boomers). Yes, others were older, including Stormé DeLarverie and Marsha P. Johnson, who, along with Rivera, are recognized as having started the uprising. But Boomers made up a significant portion of the protesters standing up for themselves and against police abuses over those summer nights at the Stonewall Inn.

As the gay rights movement mounted in the 1970s and then, driven by the deadly bigotry that enabled the AIDS crisis to devastate LGBT communities, hit full tilt in the 1980s, Boomers did indeed emerge as leaders. While many of the names we most closely associate with gay rights in this era, from Harvey Milk to Larry Kramer, weren't Boomers at all, LGBT Boomers saw their communities and loved ones ravaged by the government's refusal to do much of anything about HIV/AIDS. Deaths from HIV-related causes scaled up rapidly in the 1980s and peaked in the mid-1990s, making HIV the third leading cause of death for men twenty-five to forty-four by 1988. Those men were nearly all Baby Boomers. So were their friends, partners, families, and loved ones who hit the streets with groups like ACT UP to demand change.

"I agree with any Millennial who is criticizing the Baby Boomers for claiming credit for the civil rights movement," Jeff says. "My view is, I was born a year after the Montgomery bus boycott. I didn't have shit to do with that. I was eleven during the strike when King was assassinated. I may have gone to march, but I didn't have anything to do with that—those were my parents making those gains." But, he says, "I think Millennials have no concept of how dark it was. If you were born in 1980, your experience of the world and the bend toward recognizing racism is completely different than the experiences of my generation. We were coming into basic human dignity. And if basic human dignity is a major step up, that tells you about where we were coming from. So the one thing I would say to Millennials is: Recognize. Before you critique so hard, recognize where this prior generation came from."

A great many Baby Boomers worked tirelessly to push the gains of the civil rights, feminist, and LGBT rights movements forward, but the list of their names might surprise you. They aren't who we think of as the founding mothers of second-wave feminism, or the pathbreakers of the civil rights movement, or even those on the cutting edge of LGBT rights. Instead, they're women and men who are today's critics, artists, lawyers, activists, thinkers, leaders, creators, and writers: Social critic, philosopher, and activist Cornell West (1953). *Vagina Monologues* playwright Eve Ensler (1953). Drag performer and television personality RuPaul Charles (1960). Politician, commentator, and civil rights activist Al Sharpton (1954). Philosopher and gender theorist Judith Butler (1956). Feminist writers Katha Pollitt (1949), Rebecca Solnit (1961), Susan Faludi (1959), and bell hooks (1952). Actress turned talk show host Ellen DeGeneres (1958). Reproductive justice advocate Loretta Ross (1953). Lawyer and social justice activist Dorothy Roberts (1956). Sex columnist Dan Savage (1964). American legal scholars and critical race theorists Patricia J. Williams (1951) and Kimberlé Williams Crenshaw (1959) (the latter developed the theory of intersectionality). James Obergefell (1966), the plaintiff in the Supreme Court case that finally legalized same-sex marriage. Former president of Planned Parenthood Cecile Richards (1957). Lawyer and social justice activist Bryan Stevenson (1959). Hillary Clinton (1947). Barack Obama (1961). And radical feminists Catharine MacKinnon (a pioneer of feminist legal theory) and Andrea Dworkin (a writer and philosopher), as well as lesbian feminist socialist Barbara Smith, who were all born in 1946, the first year of the baby boom.

So, thank you, Boomers. You may not get credit for beginning or leading all of these movements, but you are leading and contributing to many of them now. For that, Millennials are profoundly in your debt.

We're also justifiably angry.

Baby Boomers are also largely responsible for the political and cultural backlash to all of these movements. And that's why, Jeff Robinson says, "I would say to my generation, If you can't take the critique of Millennials, if you feel unfairly put-upon, then take a look around at the way things are, and ask yourself: Are you going to say to Millennials, 'This is what we did and this is what we're leaving you with'? I feel I owe an apology. Because we didn't do enough."

Joy Ladin, the poet, puts it in harsher, starker terms: "I feel the world will be better off when our carcasses drop in the wilderness."

The Boomer-era backlash to social progress was real and it was swift. And some of it started when most Boomers were kids. As the civil rights movement made significant gains desegregating schools in the South, whites took notice and fled to the suburbs. Conservative politicians sought to exploit that flight. Though the GOP's "Southern strategy"—to draw the votes of racist whites opposed to civil rights—was not a Boomer invention, it was Boomers who helped to hone it. Political consultant Lee Atwater (Boomer born in 1951) asked not to be quoted in a now-infamous 1981 interview with Alexander Lamis, a Case Western professor and the author of *The Two-Party South*, before explaining:

You start out in 1954 by saying, "Nigger, nigger, nigger." By 1968 you can't say "nigger"—that hurts you. Backfires. So you say stuff like forced busing, states' rights and all that stuff. You're getting so abstract now [that] you're talking about cutting taxes, and all these things you're talking about are totally economic things and a byproduct of them is [that] blacks get hurt worse than whites. And subconsciously maybe that is part of it. I'm not saying that. But I'm saying that if it is getting that abstract, and that coded, that we are doing away with the

OK BOOMER, LET'S TALK

298

racial problem one way or the other. You follow me—because obviously sitting around saying "We want to cut this" is much more abstract than even the busing thing, and a hell of a lot more abstract than "Nigger, nigger."

In the same interview, Atwater had the gall to tell Lamis that "My generation"—Boomers—"will be the first generation of Southerners that won't be prejudiced."

By 1986, 64 percent of Baby Boomers said that they had become more conservative since the 1960s. About twice as many said they were conservative as said they were liberal. And while Boomers were happy to nod at the accomplishments of movements for equality, they were less likely to support contemporary movements for racial and gender parity. Two-thirds of white American adults in 1996, for example, opposed using busing to racially integrate schools, the exact kind of racially coded issue Lee Atwater described. And the number of Americans who identified "big government" as a threat steadily ticked up from 1967 on, as "states' rights" became code for "the right to discriminate" and "big government" tied to the enforcement of civil rights legislation.

> **The Boomer-era backlash to social progress was real and it was swift.**

"Let's face it: no one understands the baby boomers," Ronald Brownstein wrote in the *Los Angeles Times* in 1987. "Their parents didn't know how to reach them when they were growing up, and since they've reached voting age, politicians have had the same problem—a big problem." Boomers were set to make up half the electorate by 1988, but neither party had totally figured out how to activate them. They were more conservative than previously believed, but Democrats still tried to draw on the Boomer idealism that, Brownstein wrote, "marched its way through the 1960s. Their target was the tanned, toned yuppie who stopped hating capitalism somewhere around the time his income hit six figures, but who still harbored hopes of making the world a better place. Baby boomers were said to be conservative on economic issues and liberal on social ones, just waiting for an inspiring leader to reawaken social consciences."

That Democratic effort to appeal to Boomers' sense of social justice wasn't working. Ronald Reagan's appeal to Boomers' pocketbooks won him elections in 1980 and 1984, in part because "there is no evidence that a majority of the '60s generation felt part of anything but adolescence at the time," Brownstein wrote paraphrasing Democratic pollster Stanley B. Greenberg. "Many younger voters, worrying about making ends meet in their own families, even resent the appeal to idealism; it implies they have the time to worry about someone else's family."

The backlash to feminism also came into full effect as Boomers hit adulthood and began taking control of the levers of politics and culture. There's enough here for a whole book, and indeed, Boomer Susan Faludi wrote one, called *Backlash*. (Read it!) But in short: one significant culmination of the feminist movement was the Equal Rights Amendment (ERA), which slowly but steadily won support in state after state, until a right-wing counterforce led by Phyllis Schlafly took it on swiftly and efficiently, sidelining it for decades (it still hasn't been ratified). Around the same time, anti-feminism was creeping into movies, television, satire, and media. In 1986, a *Newsweek* cover story warned readers about a terrifying new study:

> The dire statistics confirmed what everybody suspected all along: that many women who seem to have it all—good looks and good jobs, advanced degrees and high salaries—will never have mates. According to the report, white, college-educated women born in the mid-'50s who are still single at 30 have only a 20 percent chance of marrying. By the age of 35 the odds drop to 5 percent. Forty-year-olds are more likely to be killed by a terrorist.

"You're more likely to be killed by a terrorist than get married after forty" became conventional late-eighties wisdom, so much so that it made its way into a scene in Nora Ephron's 1993 film *Sleepless in Seattle*. When reporter Annie Reed (played by Boomer Meg Ryan) argues that the stat isn't true, her friend and editor Becky (Boomer Rosie O'Donnell) tells her she's right—"but it feels true," Becky says.

Annie was right: it wasn't actually true that white college-educated women were more likely to be killed by a terrorist than marry after forty, but the debunking came too late for a generation of women who spent years being terrorized out of their feminist inclinations. The *Newsweek* cover hit in the era of *Fatal*

Attraction, a 1987 film in which a psychotic man-hungry career woman attacks a nice stay-at-home mom, threatening her family and boiling their pet bunny. The anti-abortion movement, which partly spun out of the earlier segregationist movement, was broadening its influence and diversifying its tactics; it began a multipronged and decades-long attack on women's rights, seeking to legally curtail the access to abortion and contraception that had enabled so many women to progress so quickly. Extremist members of that same anti-abortion movement expanded their protests at abortion clinics and engaged in violent attacks, which at times culminated in the murder of abortion providers, clinic staff, and patients.

The Boomer-fueled New Right, Jerry Falwell Sr.'s Moral Majority, and the Reagan administration leveraged racism and sexism to make scapegoats of white women who worked outside the home (cold careerists, feminist witches, and child neglecters) and black women who didn't ("welfare queens" who lived large on the government dime). Demands on mothers scaled up: the "latchkey kids" of the 1970s gave way to the helicopter parents of the 1980s and 90s, which meant a whole lot of mothers were working double duty, taking on full- or part-time paid work while being expected to intensively parent their children as if it were their only job. "Satanic panic" investigations and trials riveted the country, as day care workers across the US and Canada were falsely accused of satanic ritual abuse of children; many had their lives ruined, and some are still in jail. That national moral panic is now best understood as a devastating response to changing gender roles and women working outside the home.

There's another under-discussed aspect of Boomer cultural life: fear.

Boomers were born and raised during the Cold War, practicing nuclear alarm drills in school and brought up against a backdrop of potential annihilation. That would screw anyone up. Then add to it getting sucked into a pointless war, a wave of political assassinations of momentous public figures, tremendous social upheaval, and political malfeasance that killed off an earlier era of general trust in government, and you have a generation raised on anxiety.

From this fear came isolation. Racist white families who decamped to the suburbs in the face of integrated schools—people whose views we might today minimize as "racially anxious"— were fearful. Boomer parents in the 1980s and 1990s watched and worried over very real increases in crime rates while the media suddenly paid closer attention to abduction, molestation, and other crimes against children. This was a necessary corrective to decades of shrugging off child abuse, neglect, and endangerment, but one that often tipped overboard into hysteria. "Stranger danger" was driven partly by real crimes but also by the paranoia-fueled white flight and the social isolation and fear of outsiders that the single-family suburban life cultivated. The individual solution was buckling down with the nuclear family, giving in to a suspicion of strangers, and shifting away from broader community ties. The political solution was to win votes by scaring the shit out of people, and promising to crack down on violent criminals and social deviants (you can probably guess what color they were). "A majority of boomers now believe the loosening in attitudes toward sexual conduct that occurred in the 1960 [was] for the worse," wrote Brownstein in the *Los Angeles Times*. "[A]nd a majority now support criminal penalties for possession of even small amounts of marijuana." That majority got its way.

It was into this mess that Millennials were born and raised.

Bringing up Snowflakes

Millennials were, as a general rule, enthusiastically parented by people who systematically consolidated whatever resources they had into their own families while sweeping politicians into power who yanked the safety net out from under everyone else (this was especially, although neither universally nor exclusively, true of white Millennials). And then we spent our young lives hearing about how spoiled, entitled, and rotten we are.

Here's what is true about Millennials: We are more liberal and more accepting than Baby Boomers. We are less nationalistic, less patriotic, and less religious. We are a much more racially diverse generation than Boomers. Boomers were born into overwhelming racial homogeneity: According to the Pew Research Center, fewer than 20 percent of six- to twenty-one-year-olds in

Millennials are just over 50 percent white, and our kids are the least-white generation in American history.

1968—young Baby Boomers, who were even more diverse than their older counterparts—were racial or ethnic minorities; 82 percent were white, while 13 percent were black and just 4 percent were Hispanic. Baby Boomers have grown more diverse over time, largely due to immigration. The American Hispanic population went from 9.1 million in 1970 to 53 million by 2012. According to the 2000 Census, Hispanic Boomers made up 10 percent of a still mostly white generation. Millennials, on the other hand, are just over 50 percent white, and our kids are the least white generation in American history.

We are also a generation that grew up in an era of increasingly personalized media. While Boomers were raised on television, programming was limited, and so everyone more or less watched the same things. There was, for most of a Boomer childhood, a monoculture. Consider how radical it was for Fred Rogers to dip his toes into a plastic kiddie pool with his African American friend on an episode of *Mr. Rogers' Neighborhood* in 1969, a time when many pools remained segregated: it was unusual to see interracial *friendships* on television, let alone black-driven programming.

That began to change as black, brown, Native, and Asian creators gained greater visibility (although white cultural artifacts still dominate American popular culture). African American life began to appear more often on network television: *Soul Train, Good Times, The Jeffersons, Diff'rent Strokes, Sanford and Son*. By the late 1980s, the Huxtables were America's darlings, with Bill Cosby, later exposed as a serial sexual predator, in the role of a lovable gynecologist. Cable television, which Millennials spent our childhoods watching, meant a rapid expansion of content, and increasingly targeted shows and networks. BET launched in 1980, just as the Millennial generation was poised to enter the world. A year later, MTV burst on the scene—a defining moment for the youth of Gen X, for sure, but also a harbinger of the kind of identity-sorted programming Millennials grew to expect. The proliferation of personal technology only amplified this dynamic. Family television time, the programming ostensibly chosen by one of the adults, ceded to individualized decision-making: I can watch a sitcom on my laptop while my sister watches a reality show on her tablet while my parents watch the news in the living room. Now, with sophisticated algorithms tracking and predicting our preferences, this kind of individualism is on steroids. Netflix predicts what I want to watch, and I click. Instagram shows me what I want to see, and tracks how long I look at a particular image so it can suggest what I want to buy. Monoculture is a thing of the past.

The fact that popular culture has splintered into a nearly uncountable array of microcultures makes it harder to generalize about Millennial culture than Boomer culture (and nearly impossible to define Gen Z by their cultural preferences).

So how do you define Millennial culture? Well, according to a 2010 Pew Research Center study of the differences between generations, Millennials themselves say that our generation is unique in its use of technology, in our music, in our liberalism and tolerance, and in our intelligence. Boomers, on the other hand, define themselves by their work ethic, their sense of respect, their values and morals, and their large numbers (they also say, as do other generations, that they're uniquely smart). And many of the Boomers I talked to pointed to their generation's music as uniquely excellent. When I interviewed Jeff Robinson, the first words out of his mouth were: "There is no other generation whose music is better. That is just an objective fact. There are some things to which every head must bow and every tongue must confess, and that is one of them." Then he quoted lyrics from Pink Floyd and the Clash.

For Millennials, markers of aesthetic individuality— Millennials are two and a half times as likely to have a tattoo as Boomers, and twenty-three times as likely to have a piercing

Millennials are twice as likely to have a tattoo as Boomers, and twenty-three times as likely to have a piercing somewhere other than in their ear.

---

somewhere other than in their ear—pair with a political sensibility that places a premium on open-mindedness, diversity, and community. We are more likely to say society is better-off with more racial and ethnic diversity, with same-sex marriage rights, with interracial marriage, and with more women running for political office. We are significantly less likely than Boomers to own guns, and more likely than Boomers to say that adult children should open up their homes to their elderly parents.

But we're also alienated from traditional politics, even as we're active in social movements. The GenForward Survey, a University of Chicago project that collects and analyzes data on Americans aged eighteen to thirty-four, found that about 70 percent of young people across racial groups believe politicians care little about them. And in the 2020 Democratic primary, youth turnout was disappointing.

Nor are Millennials' more progressive views on race reflective of our whole cohort. Rather, Millennials as a whole appear to be less racist in polling data because we're more racially diverse. White Millennials do have more progressive politics than older generations when it comes to race, and researcher Candis Watts Smith of the University of Pennsylvania found that a majority believe racism is a major problem in America—but don't connect racial inequity to the systemic advantages they enjoy. When you separate out white Millennials and look at their views compared to those of previous generations, as Scott Clement, the polling director at the *Washington Post*, did in 2015, this cohort doesn't look all that

We are more likely to say society is better-off with more racial and ethnic diversity, with same-sex marriage rights, with interracial marriage, and with more women running for political office.

different from their Boomer parents. Clement found that, when it comes to markers of racial bias, white Millennials are only marginally less racist than Boomers and Gen Xers. Our gender politics aren't much better.

So, no, white Millennials are not as woke as we get credit for (or are accused of). But nor are Millennials as a whole as resentful of Boomers as one might think. A great many Boomers raised their Millennial kids with mutual respect, making the parent-as-friend a new familial innovation. When Boomers and Millennials know each other intimately, we tend to like each other. Overwhelming majorities of Millennials say our parents are a positive influence, and more than three-quarters of us regularly turn to them for advice. One 2012 study found that more than half of

Millennials communicate with their parents by text, email, or phone almost every day.

We essentially have a "not my Boomer"/"not my Millennial" view of generational relations: Boomers think that most Millennials suck—except their own kids, who are phenomenal. And Millennials are quick to deride Boomers as selfish right-wingers, except our own parents, who are super-generous and bighearted.

This is perhaps because there are indeed two different groups of Boomers: those who continue to agitate for equality and progressive politics, and those who fuel the backlash against them. Boomers have long been a deeply divided generation. Our current political polarization is highly racialized, with white people, and white men in particular, leaning heavily Republican and most of the rest of us generally voting for Democrats. But our polarization also reflects the fact that Boomers are politically split in half in a way Millennials and Gen Zers are not. When it comes to issues—gay rights, immigration, the environment, the role of government—the Pew Research Center has found that Boomers have generally grown more liberal as they age. But when it comes to partisan identification, conservative Boomers are more dug in. While Boomers are divided evenly between Republican and Democrat support, many more Boomers identify as conservative Republicans than identify as liberal Democrats. Gallup found even more extreme results: in 2015, more than twice as many Boomers (44 percent) said they were conservative as said they were liberal (17 percent). Millennials, by contrast, are much more likely than older generations to identify as Democrats generally, and as liberal Democrats in particular.

It's these political divisions—between Boomers themselves and between Boomers and Millennials—that spawned the now ubiquitous genre of "how to survive the holidays" articles advising readers on how to endure dinner with a relative whose politics you detest, and the anguished letters to advice columnists wondering how to deal with a Trump-voting uncle or socialist niece over Thanksgiving. And the cleavages are real. Amber Bearden, a young Millennial at twenty-five and an active-duty member of the military, says she is "very leftist," while her family is very conservative. "I have now gotten to the point where when I go home, I try and make it as minimal as possible," she says. "Like for Christmas, I was there for three days and I left. It's not that I don't love them; I do, and they've done so much for me. But two years ago, I went home for Christmas and my family started talking about building the wall, and I was like, oh my god, and I started an argument. And all six of them over the Christmas dinner table started yelling at me."

For Amber, like many Millennials, liberalism grew with adulthood. Just 9 percent of Millennials in 2004 held views that Pew researchers qualified as "consistently liberal." By 2017, 25 percent of them did. Amber, a self-identified Republican in her teenage years, was one of them. "My underlying values? Empathy," she says. "That's really what drives me. Other people that are struggling aren't my enemy. If they want to immigrate to America, we shouldn't be keeping them out. If people want abortions, that's on them, that's their life, I don't have any say in whether or not they should have a child or carry a fetus to term. Empathy drives all of my political ideas." For her family? "Money," she says. "They think we shouldn't let immigrants in because they're going to take their jobs and we shouldn't have universal health care because they'll be paying more taxes. And I'm like, 'You're middle class, half of this doesn't affect you.'"

Millennials are also a generation raised on fear and catapulted into adulthood by trauma. The young among us saw relatively peaceful childhoods punctured by the terrorist attacks of September 11, 2001, while older Millennials experienced 9/11 as a defining moment of our first years as legal adults. Two economic crashes dampened our job prospects, and we know that we may be screwed for the rest of our lives. The internet and the advent of the smartphone made us more connected than ever but brought with them a totally new way of interacting with other human beings, the consequences of which are still not well understood.

And yet we're an optimistic generation, too. While we worry there's no future for us, we still create art, write books, make movies, play music, have babies. We're civic-minded: We made our first big mark on politics when we turned out to vote in huge numbers for Barack Obama in 2008. We powered a whole series of movements for social justice, including the resurgence of feminism, the #MeToo movement, and the increased push for transgender rights and equality. Millennials organized with Black Lives Matter and Occupy Wall Street; we were a huge part of the surge in Democratic Socialists of America memberships, as young people expressed their disenchantment with unfettered American capitalism and its discontents. We have marched against war, climate change, and police violence; we've surrounded airports to oppose bigoted immigration laws. We were key organizers of the Women's March, and on January 21, 2017, Millennials joined a massive multigenerational coalition at the largest public protest in US history. A little more than three years later, we spent weeks in the streets agitating against police brutality and a racist, punitive system of law enforcement. We are the most activist-minded generation since the 1960s.

We see the water rising around us, but we think we can right this ship.

Contrary to what you hear on cranky Fox News segments, so do some Boomers. Joy Ladin spends much of her time these days speaking about issues of gender diversity and equity, often to college students, and often drawing on her own experiences as a trans woman. When it comes to Boomers, she wonders "whether we can do enough to push past the place where we've gotten, post Jim Crow but nowhere near past white supremacy. Can we do that work? I don't know. Can we do the work to renegotiate our understanding of gender, not just for trans people but for women?" Joy doesn't know. She can imagine it, she says, "but I don't know that I've lived to see that kind of change. I've lived to see the backlash. We've gotten close enough for folks, particularly in my generation, to get scared out of our

We are the most activist-minded generation since the 1960s.

wits and run in the other direction. But I haven't seen us make it the whole way." And yet she's optimistic. "As a teacher of your generation, the light that I see in the faces of my students, that is a light that I believe in," Joy says. "I don't know that I'm going to live to see that change. But I do believe that you can do it."

Having surveyed and spoken with hundreds of Millennials, and having delved into the research on generation differences, here is what I would say: Millennials put a high premium on individuality without political individualism. We are personally invested in our own identities and how those identities shape us and our opportunities, while being politically more communitarian than Boomers, and more concerned with the well-being of others. We do think each person is unique and worthy in his or her own right. You could call that a precious snowflake. You might just see it as a human being deserving of dignity and respect.

We are motivated by a desire to improve the world around us. Sometimes that manifests as direct support of a policy proposal like Medicare for All; sometimes it takes the form of forgoing plastic straws and toting canvas bags to the grocery store; sometimes it means talking about our own relative privilege or pressing others to use more sensitive language. Does that sometimes make us insufferable and self-righteous? You bet. But is it really so bad that we're a generation of people who fundamentally strive to be kind, to cheer each other on, and to support one another in living lives that feel authentic and meaningful?

Baby Boomers grew up in a white-dominated postwar culture that was a bit like a snowplow, flattening everything in its sights into a monolith and crushing anything that stuck out. To their credit, many Boomers set about trying to change that, and through a variety of political movements and artistic endeavors, and often in the face of great personal risk, many of them succeeded. Others, their voices getting louder as their generation ages, seem increasingly agitated that the cultural machine of their youth is sputtering out.

Conclusion

Millennials have played our part in maintaining intergenerational strife, too. Dismissing anyone over forty with "OK Boomer" is not exactly conducive to discussion. What's striking, though, is how little power we actually have. Boomers may feel hurt by "OK Boomer," but there's not much Millennials can do to cause them harm in a country where they maintain near-total control over politics, entertainment, and the economy. And Boomers simply lived a materially different reality than Millennials. As a result, both groups have different priorities, desires, and perspectives. But Boomers' dominance means they can enforce their will. And Millennials can do little more than mock them.

As Gen Zers come of age, we see these gaps between the young and the aging grow. Take the 2020 Democratic primary: Joe Biden cleaned up among voters over forty, while those under forty backed Bernie Sanders and, to a lesser but still significant extent, Elizabeth Warren. Older folks hang tight to a Republican Party the young have largely fled. These stark political differences don't reflect the "identity politics" young people are often accused of having—all three of these politicians are older and white, and two of the three are male—but rather a profound shift in what each generation sees as the challenges ahead of us. For Boomers, familiarity and stability seem to be driving forces. As they came of age, one only had to look at the nightly news reports about the Soviet Union to see how much better we had it in America. America's longstanding ethos of individualism took even deeper root among Baby Boomers, many of whom had tremendous assistance and yet still hit middle age convinced they had done it all for themselves. Many of those Boomers rode into the middle class on the backs of the same programs they later defunded; government investment is often invisible, and its benefits are easily confused with bootstraps.

Millennials, by contrast, grew up with the twin forces of technological innovation and deep trauma shaping our lives. The most pressing existential threat to our existence isn't a cunning evil empire but rather climate change, a monster of our own making. Our parents were promised that hard work would pay off, and for a lot of them it did. But Millennials were promised that, too, and yet here we are, constantly hustling while our circumstances don't seem to materially improve. Thanks to the internet, we can look across borders and see that young people in other prosperous nations may suffer from their own generational malaise and may also get hit by economic forces beyond their control. But they aren't going bankrupt paying for health care; they aren't *wishing* they could declare bankruptcy to wipe out their crushing student loan debt; they aren't deciding between having a job they love or having children.

We can see that there's a better way to do things. And since our lives haven't felt stable, the prospect of significant upheaval—making big, substantive, systemic changes to the American health care and education systems, to our environmental policy, and to our economy—doesn't appear quite as daunting as it does to our Boomer elders.

Boomers look at what they might lose if things change. Millennials look at what we *will* lose if things don't.

There's a lot more room for growth and understanding on both sides here. In so many ways, Millennials are Boomers' cultural heirs, carrying forward a commitment to individuality, pleasure, and purpose. Many Boomers were the foot soldiers in the movements that demanded America to be a better version of itself. And like us, Boomers spent their young adulthood being derided and chided for being different, and therefore narcissistic and wrong. Yes, Millennials could do more to foster intergenerational understanding, and to be less reactive and more nuanced in how we approach our Baby Boomers elders.

But: Boomers, we really need you to do your part. And that means we need you to consider what the world looks like to us, and what kind of world you want to leave us with.

Life at thirty for your average Millennial looks close to nothing like life at thirty did for you. We are deeply in debt. We feel burned-out and behind. And for most of our adult lives, we've been doubting ourselves—it's only very recently that we have collectively looked around, seen so many in our same boat, and started to conclude, *Maybe it's not just me.* Yes, we know that in the grand scope of world history, we are phenomenally lucky. But we also don't think it's unreasonable to hope that, in the most prosperous nation in the history of the world, we have control over our own lives and a reasonable shot at a good future.

For that, we need you to make decisions with everyone's interests in mind, not just your own. We need you to realize that we are rational adults with a different perspective, not indulged children who need reprimanding. We need you to vote with all of our futures in mind. We need you to lean into optimism for what could be. We need you to see that we will make this country, and this world, better if you'll let us. Mostly, we need you to hand over, or at least share, the reins of power.

Give us a hand, Boomer—okay?